STOKE CITY
101 Golden Greats

Stoke City: 101 Golden Greats	1-874287-46-5
Stoke City: The Modern Era – A Complete Record	1-874287-39-2
Ipswich Town: The Modern Era – A Complete Record	1-874287-43-0
Bristol City: The Modern Era – A Complete Record	1-874287-28-7
Colchester Utd: Graham to Whitton – A Complete Record	1-874287-27-9
Halifax Town: From Ball to Lillis – A Complete Record	1-874287-26-0
Portsmouth: From Tindall to Ball – A Complete Record	1-874287-25-2
Portsmouth: Champions of England – 1948-49 & 1949-50	1-874287-38-4
Coventry City: The Elite Era – A Complete Record	1-874287-51-1
Coventry City: An Illustrated History	1-874287-36-8
Luton Town: The Modern Era – A Complete Record	1-874287-05-8
Luton Town: An Illustrated History	1-874287-37-6
Hereford United: The League Era – A Complete Record	1-874287-18-X
Cambridge United: The League Era – A Complete Record	1-874287-32-5
Peterborough United: The Modern Era – A Complete Record	1-874287-33-3
Peterborough United: A Who's Who	1-874287-48-1
Plymouth Argyle: 101 Golden Greats	1-874287-47-3
West Ham: From Greenwood to Redknapp	1-874287-19-8
West Ham: The Elite Era – A Complete Record	1-874287-31-7
Wimbledon: From Southern League to Premiership	1-874287-09-0
Wimbledon: From Wembley to Selhurst	1-874287-20-1
Wimbledon: The Premiership Years	1-874287-40-6
Aberdeen: The European Era – A Complete Record	1-874287-11-2
The Story of the Rangers 1873-1923	1-874287-16-3
The Story of the Celtic 1888-1938	1-874287-15-5
History of the Everton Football Club 1878-1928	1-874287-14-7
The Romance of the Wednesday 1867-1926	1-874287-17-1
Red Dragons in Europe – A Complete Record	1-874287-01-5
The Book of Football: A History to 1905-06	1-874287-13-9
England: The Quest for the World Cup – A Complete Record	1-897850-40-9
Scotland: The Quest for the World Cup – A Complete Record	1-897850-50-6
Ireland: The Quest for the World Cup – A Complete Record	1-897850-80-8

STOKE CITY

101 GOLDEN GREATS

Series Editor: Clive Leatherdale

Simon Lowe

Desert Island Books

First Published in 2001

DESERT ISLAND BOOKS LIMITED
89 Park Street, Westcliff-on-Sea, Essex SS0 7PD
United Kingdom
www.desertislandbooks.com

British Library Cataloguing-in-Publication Data
A catalogue record for this book is available from the British Library

ISBN   1-874287-46-5

Printed in Great Britain
by
Bookcraft, Midsomer Norton

Photographs in this book are reproduced by kind permission of:
Andy Peck, Anthony Brown, Julian Boodell

~ *Contents* ~

~ *Preface* ~

I would like to thank those who subscribed to this excellent book for voting me as their favourite Stoke City player. It is a great honour and reflects the fantastic times we had at Stoke during my seven years at the club. My career would not have been such a success had it not been for the incredible support I received from you – the supporters. It always made such a difference to me and helped me produce the best football of my career.

I hold many great memories from my time at Stoke. Who can ever forget the FA Cup semi-finals, however disappointing the results turned out to be? How can any Stoke fan forget Peter Dobing lifting the League Cup at Wembley in 1972? And the amazing reception the following day from massed supporters as we returned through the city on an open-topped bus from Barlaston to the middle of Stoke. The scenes were incredible.

Parading my first cup as captain, albeit the Watney Cup at the Victoria Ground, and the 3-2 defeat of Leeds, which halted their quest for the longest unbeaten run from the beginning of the season in the old First Division, are two personal highlights which I will always treasure, as I know many Stoke fans do. These memories are what this book is all about. Wonderful times – and the men who made them, not only of my era, but of many others.

Thank you for all your support and loyalty for myself and Stoke City. I pray that the successes of the past soon return to the present team, bringing the good times back to the Britannia Stadium.

JIMMY GREENHOFF

~ *Author's Note* ~

It's the great pub debate. Who was the best player you've ever seen. It is, of course, unanswerable. However, I decided to detail the careers of Stoke City's 101 greatest players as chosen by the public of Stoke-on-Trent on radio debates and in straw polls. But I soon came across a problem. The same 30 or 40 names kept cropping up. How then was I to choose the remainder – in fact, the bulk – of the players for the book. I used the criteria of appearances, goals, and trophies to assemble a crude list of 120. Fine-tuning took place using two factors. First, the level at which the player performed for Stoke, and second, whether their Stoke career could be called 'great'. Not whether they were great players in themselves. No one can doubt the eminence of goalkeepers Peter Shilton, Bruce Grobbelaar and Neville Southall. Although all three played for Stoke, none can be called a great Stoke City player. Shilton, in fact, played in a relegated team and lost his England place whilst at the club. Other notable omissions include Harry Ware, Lee Dixon. Lee Chapman, Roy Vernon, Alf Smith, Charlie Parker, Johnny Malkin, Geoff Hurst and Wayne Biggins. All can consider themselves unfortunate not to be included, but I found reasons why each should not be one of the chosen 101.

In recent years I have interviewed over half the 101 golden greats named in this book, although several of them are no longer with us. For each 'Great' I have attempted to provide background, character portraits and amusing anecdotes, as well as strictly footballing information (accurate up to October 2001). To all those former players who have helped me, thank you. There are few higher pleasures than whiling away the hours chatting about Stoke City.

Not that an amusing story in itself guarantees a player's inclusion. I have been forced to omit the Rev EJ 'Churchy' Wilson, an 1870s vicar who played in carpet slippers which, he maintained, gave him a better feel of the ball. Also Jim Westland, who chose a career with Stoke City rather than as a professional ballroom dancer, and Charlie Burgess, who signed for Stoke whilst sitting on a haystack on his father's farm!

I would like to thank my publisher, Clive Leatherdale, for proposing this book to me. My thanks also to Terry Conroy, without whose help you would not be reading this, Julian Boodell, Norman Croucher, Andy Peck, Les Scott, Martin Smith, Martin Spinks, Tony Tams, David Marks, Brian Calvert, and my girlfriend Kath.

SIMON LOWE

Chapter One

~ *Stoking the Fires* ~

No 1. **TOM SLANEY**

Thomas Charles Slaney was the man responsible for turning a collection of 'sons of business men, manufacturers and county gentlemen', into a club recognisable as Stoke FC. Born in Stoke-on-Trent in 1852, Slaney was a pupil and protégé at Stoke St Peter's School of John William Thomas, the first Honorary Secretary of the formative Stoke Ramblers team. Thomas was well-known in local sporting circles, holding simultaneously the secretarial positions of the Football, Cricket and Athletic clubs. Thus the young Slaney, who showed much promise, acquired an early interest in local sport.

From 1874, after training at Saltley College, Birmingham, Slaney taught at St John's School, Hanley, rising to headmaster within ten years. He joined the Stoke football club and was elected captain. Stoke's President, local MP Colin Minton-Campbell, influenced by the now retired Thomas, appointed Slaney honorary secretary in August 1874. Although the committee – chairman, vice-chairman, four ordinary members and captain – still picked the team, Slaney effectively organised it, arranging away travel and ensuring his colleagues knew kick-off times. His status ensured he played in the glamorous centre-forward role, but he was described as 'a fine dashing player'. His style was typical of the time, dribbling alone or in a huddle with other forwards. Slaney took corners and free-kicks and was described as 'judicious and energetic'.

The tall, slim Slaney wore long sideboards down jaundiced cheeks. He was renowned as a model captain, expecting his men to behave with gentlemanly decorum. Press reports refer to 'a man of great geniality with a great sense of humour'. Indeed, Stoke were noted for their post-match hospitality during his time in charge, which counted for much in those amateur days. Under Slaney, Stoke defeated Nottingham Forest, Aston Villa and Blackburn Rovers at home, but travelled poorly, setting a precedent which would haunt the club for decades to come.

During Slaney's tenure the club played at Sweeting's Field – a meadow owned by Alderman Sweeting. Writing in the *Sentinel* in 1916, columnist AJB recalled seeing Stoke play Wolstanton in the autumn of 1875: '... the ball being kicked, not thrown in from the side. It was common for the Stoke club's match advertisements to be left blank for their opponents to be filled in on the day. Admission charge for crowds (as many as 200) cost 2d, Ladies free.'

On 23 March 1878, in its inaugural season, Stoke lifted the Staffordshire Cup, defeating Talke Rangers 1-0 with a goal by W Boddington. Though ten minutes remained, the crowd of over 2,000 surged onto the pitch to chair the scorer. Slaney implored them to 'clear the pitch' to permit the game to finish. The following season he lifted the trophy a second time, after Stoke overcame Cobridge 2-1. In fact, having been instrumental in the formation of the Staffs FA in 1877, along with Stoke's Harry Allen, Slaney became its first secretary-chairman – which meant he twice had to find someone else to present the Staffs Cup to himself!

Despite his high profile, it is hard to find reference to Slaney actually scoring goals, with one notable exception. He notched a club record *nine* in the Stoke's 26-0 Staffordshire Cup thrashing of Mow Cop in 1882-83. In his 30s he became the club's 'umpire'. Although neutral referees officiated in all games, the umpires (later called linesmen, and then assistant referees) were provided by the competing clubs. By 1880 Slaney had lost his place in the team to Teddy Johnson, destined to become Stoke's first England international. From October 1881 Slaney operated almost exclusively as an umpire, only playing during an injury crisis or in the reserves.

After retiring as captain in 1882, Slaney changed Stoke's colours from black and light blue hoops to red and white stripes, which were aired for the first time against Notts County in 1883. The previous year the club's first badge was added to the shirt – a large S with small FC. In 1883, along with Minton-Campbell, Slaney masterminded the club's merger with the Stoke Victoria Athletics Club, and the subsequent move a few hundred yards from Sweeting's Field to the Victoria Ground. In May 1883, with the club poised to abandon 'shamateur' principles for much-derided professionalism, Slaney resigned, being eventually succeeded by Harry Lockett.

Slaney's influence lingered at the Victoria Ground long after his departure. Lockett, a friend and former playing colleague, oversaw Stoke's entry into the embryonic Football League and became the League's first secretary, in offices at 8 Parkers Terrace, Stoke. Slaney's assistant schoolmaster at St John's School, Horace 'Denny' Austerberry, became one of his successors as secretary-manager of Stoke from 1897-1908. Tom Slaney died in 1935.

Magic Moment: *Leading the singing, along with winning goalscorer Boddington, at the celebratory dinner to mark the historic occasion of the first Staffordshire Cup final.*

Worst Nightmare: *At Nottingham Forest in February 1873, Slaney's Stoke were 'ripped apart' in losing 1-3 when, to cope with a frozen pitch, Forest players put nails in their boots!*

No 2. **TOMMY CLARE**
Debut: v Crewe, 31 October 1885
Farewell: v Sheffield United, 15 April 1897

Thomas Clare was Stoke's captain on the first day of the Football League – 8 September 1888 – and followed Slaney as the next great club skipper. Born in Congleton in March 1865, Clare joined Stoke in 1884 from Burslem Port Vale. When Stoke turned professional in 1885, under the chairmanship of Abraham Fielding, Clare was joined by goalkeeper Philip Birch, fellow back Edgar Montford, half-backs Ted Smith and George Shutt, and forwards Alf Edge and Bernard Rhodes, as the club's first professional footballers. After the farce of the preceding years, when amateur footballers received 'shamateur' payments, despite the FA's ban on professionalism, Clare received a 'broken-time payment' of half a crown (12.5p) per match. As a result of a strike later in the season, on account of a team-mate earning five shillings, Clare's money was doubled.

Standing over 6ft tall and weighing 12st 10lbs, Clare was a fine header of the ball at a time when the convention was to dribble. He towered over opposing forwards and was not averse to using his frame to out-muscle them. Despite his bulk, he was described as 'quick and resolute' with 'capital style', characterised by his appearance, smart, with a neatly trimmed moustache. Although full-backs were solely defensive players, in an FA Cup-tie v Caernarvon Wanderers in October 1886 Clare scored twice in a 10-1 win. Among his representative honours was a seventeen-game run of appearances for the Staffordshire FA XI.

Clare earned one Football League call-up and four full England caps, the first alongside Stoke keeper Billy Rowley against Ireland in March 1889 in a 6-1 win. The fact that Stoke in that inaugural season propped up the twelve-team division makes the duo's selection remarkable. Three years later Clare teamed up with Rowley and Stoke left-back Alf Underwood to represent England against Ireland in Belfast, and later against the Scottish League.

At League level Stoke's defensive trio belied the club's second successive wooden spoon, which resulted in Sunderland's election to the League in Stoke's place. Reports bemoaned the inability of the forwards, labelling them 'lackadaisical' and once claiming that 'a child could have stopped any of the shots the custodians had to negotiate'. Stoke scored only 26 goals that season, although their defensive record befitted a mid-table side. Football League referee Tom Bryan opined: 'the backs and the goalkeeper are superior to any three men playing with one club.' Frustrated, Clare often tried to dribble the whole length of the field, only to find that his forwards simply stood and watched, leaving him no one to pass to.

Clare often committed 'wild and dangerous tackles'. Opponents protested about his fairness and opposing supporters dubbed the team 'Dirty Stoke'. These lapses were commonplace among defenders of the era, but in Clare's case they also resulted in self-inflicted injuries. Yet opinion held that a lame Clare was better than any replacement. In 1889-90 Stoke lost 1-6 to Aston Villa, 0-8 to Blackburn, and 0-5 to Bolton, with Clare absent on each occasion.

Clare was ever present in 1890-91 as Stoke won the Football Alliance championship and immediate re-election to the expanded Football League. From Christmas 1894 to the end of 1896-97 he played 82 consecutive League games – then a club record – and remains one of only four Stoke players to complete three full seasons of League football. His consistency earned him two more caps – against Wales in 1893 and a final game for England in a 2-2 draw in Scotland in April 1894. He scored his first League goal – in a goalmouth melée at Bolton – on his 110th League outing. Clare was the first man to pass 200 League and Cup appearances for Stoke, and his record was not surpassed for over a decade.

In 1897, aged 32, he played a trial for Manchester City before becoming captain at Burslem Port Vale and assuming the mantle of player-coach. He retired from playing in 1899, after struggling to recover from a broken leg, although he was briefly called into action a year later during an injury crisis. He became Vale's manager in 1905-06, but soon emigrated to Canada. Clare died in Ladysmith, Vancouver, on 27 December 1929, aged 64.

Magic Moment: *Clare took over when keeper Rowley was hurt in a Football Alliance match v Birmingham St George's on 18 October 1890. Clare 'fisted out a close one' from Devey. Stoke lost 2-5.*

Worst Nightmare: *Clare was bamboozled by Nottingham Forest's winger McInnes, who beat him three times in five minutes to set up two and score a third as Stoke lost 0-3 in October 1894.*

STOKE RECORD	Appearances	Goals
Football League	199	4
FA Cup	22	–
Football Alliance	22	–

No 3. **WILLIAM ROWLEY**
Debut: v Caernarvon Wanderers, 30 October 1886
Farewell: v Aston Villa, 31 October 1896

William 'Billy' Spencer Rowley courted controversy throughout his career. Born in Hanley in 1865, Rowley joined Stoke initially from

Hanley Orient in 1883, along with future first-teamers Teddy Bennett and George Lawton. Rowley failed to displace Philip Birch as Stoke's first-choice goalkeeper and, after playing in the reserve side, 'The Swifts', he joined Burslem Port Vale in April 1884.

Whilst playing for Vale in the 1885 Burslem Challenge Cup final Rowley became so bored in goal that he joined his forwards who were having all the fun in a 12-0 win over Ironbridge – even scoring himself. He made several official appearances as centre-forward, but in 1886 his goalkeeping would earn him a call-up as first reserve to Preston's William Rose for England v Ireland.

In a competitive 'friendly' between Stoke and Vale in May 1886, Rowley was kicked and mauled to 'an insensible condition' by Stoke's forwards, causing two broken ribs. He was taken to the nearby Copeland Arms for treatment, consisting mostly of a tot of whisky, and was unable to work for four months

Stoke's next tactic to avoid facing Rowley was to sign him – oddly he agreed. Amidst much controversy, he and Vale centre-half George Bateman signed for Stoke despite being registered with Vale. That November the Valiants took the matter to the Burslem County Court and their grievance was upheld. Stoke were forced to pay £20 to charity and return the players. At the end of the season Rowley signed officially for Stoke, Bateman staying with Vale.

Small for a keeper at 5ft 9in, Rowley was stockily built, weighing 12st 3lbs, and was Stoke's joker in the pack – he seems to have a twinkle in his eye in every photograph in which he appears. He cemented his reputation for ebullience after becoming landlord of the Cock Inn in Stoke, where locals would gather to talk football. Described as 'regally marvellous' on the field by the press, Rowley was thought 'second to none in Great Britain' in 1888 – although this was possibly because he had such a porous half-back line in front of him! He was fearless in the face of oncoming attackers, whom he would tackle with his feet, and he would also rush out to fist away crosses. This was an era when any keeper holding onto the ball was fair game for forwards to kick, and when soccer fatalities from injuries sustained in such melées were not infrequent.

Against Nottingham Forest in October 1890 Rowley received 'a nasty charge against the goalpost and a kick on the cheekbone, opening the flesh'. Press reports described the injury as 'an unfortunate accident'. Two weeks later, against Birmingham St George's, he was knocked senseless by opposing forward Davies and carried from the ground. Serious chest injuries forced him to miss the rest of the season. This bravery endeared him to crowds across the country, and often earned 'a most enthusiastic applause'. Everton captain Ross commented after a brilliant display at Anfield in 1888 that he had 'never seen such an exhibition of goalkeeping'.

Rowley's weakness, however, was distribution. He often cleared badly, when kicking or throwing, putting his team in difficulties.

Rowley kept goal in Stoke's first League game in 1888 and just three games later the *Sentinel* declared 'may he [Rowley] always be able to play for Stoke, for if not, his loss to the team would be irreparable'. Rowley missed only one fixture in each of the League's first two seasons. He was selected for Staffordshire on numerous occasions, sharing with Tommy Clare a joint record run of seventeen successive matches.

For some time, however, it seemed that Rowley would be denied an England cap. For the international against Wales at the Victoria Ground on 23 February 1889, he was controversially omitted in favour of W Moon of Old Westminsters. He finally won his first cap in a 6-1 win over Ireland later that year. In 1892 he was again selected against Ireland, alongside club colleagues Tommy Clare and Underwood. Despite keeping a clean sheet in a 2-0 win, Rowley lost his place to George Toone of Notts County and never figured again. He did, however, represent the Football League against the Scottish League in a 4-2 win in Glasgow in April 1893.

Following an injury to Tommy Clare in 1889-90, Rowley became Stoke captain and performed proudly as the team romped to the Football Alliance Championship. Ever present in 1892-93, when Stoke finished in the top half of the Division One table for the first time, a recurrence of a knee injury at Burnley in September 1893 reduced his appearances thereafter. In 1894-95 Rowley lost his place to George Clawley, although he remained registered as an amateur, understudying occasionally.

In 1895, when Stoke became a limited liability company, Rowley became secretary-manager. His first season in charge saw Stoke finish sixth in the First Division, their best finish thus far, as the players responded to his charismatic persona. A wheeler-dealer in the transfer market, Rowley engineered one of the club's most bizarre deals. In 1896 Stoke signed centre-forward Allan Maxwell from Darwen. The fee was a new set of wrought-iron gates for the Lancashire club's ground! On more than one occasion Rowley paid transfer fees from his own pocket.

The lack of funds symptomised Stoke's plight. In 1892 debts exceeded £600 and the League requested other teams play benefit matches against the club. One of Rowley's proposed schemes that summer would have seen Stoke purchase the County Cricket Ground, where the team had played when the Victoria Ground was flooded by the River Trent, but the deal failed to materialise.

JT Fenton became club chairman in 1897 and Horace 'Denny' Austerberry secretary-manager. Rowley remained as Austerberry's assistant, but in August 1898 he again created a storm of newspaper headlines after cheekily transferring himself to Leicester Fosse, who paid him a signing-on fee, thus negating his amateur status. A Leicester director resigned in protest. Rowley played just once for the Foxes before the FA refused his registration. He and Leicester secretary William Clark were suspended for twelve months. Resigned to life outside football, Rowley became a postman in the Potteries before emigrating to the USA, where he died circa 1939.

Magic Moment: *Versus Burnley (FA Cup, January 1892) Rowley was 'kicked, charged and almost smothered by his opponents for fully half a minute as he succeeded in saving his charge', as Stoke inflicted the year's first home defeat on the Clarets.*

Worst Nightmare: *In Stoke's first ever League match, under pressure from three West Brom forwards, Rowley threw the ball directly to winger Wilson, who fired back the first League goal against Stoke.*

STOKE RECORD	Appearances	Goals
Football League	118	–
FA Cup	11	–
Football Alliance	6	–

No 4. **ALF UNDERWOOD**
Debut: v Port Vale, 5 October 1887
Farewell: v Wolves, 4 February 1895

Alfred Underwood formed the left side of the Stoke and England defensive trio (with Rowley and Clare) that faced Ireland in March 1892. Born in Hanley in 1869, Underwood joined Stoke in the summer of 1887 – having, like Rowley, played in the local Church League for Hanley Tabernacle and then Etruria.

Underwood (6ft tall and 13st 4lbs) and Clare formed an imposing barricade. They were often spoken of as a pair, rather than as individuals. Underwood's balding pate and sunken eyes lent him a demonic appearance. His principal assets were ferocious tackling and the range of his sometimes wild but long clearances. Elements of the press believed him to be impetuous and rash, endangering opponents. Occasionally he miskicked in clearing, putting his side in trouble. Indeed, in September 1888 a misdirected Underwood hoof allowed Accrington an easy third goal, causing one commentator to declare that Underwood had 'a fancy for breaking windows'.

He played at left-back in Stoke's first Football League game and missed only one match in the ensuing three seasons (at Walsall in the Football Alliance in March 1891) although that was to enable him to win an England cap. Having trialled for the North v South in January 1891, Underwood played for England against Ireland in a 6-1 win at Molineux. With the selectors seeking replacements for the amateur Walters brothers of Old Carthusians, they rotated full-back pairings over the next year until Underwood appeared again.

Underwood's bludgeoning style inspired the first verifiable Stoke terrace chant – 'Play Up Stoke' – first heard in 1891.

Stoke, Stoke, Play up Stoke / Show them how to play at football
Stoke, Stoke, all the folk / Will come to see you play at football
Bang down the field boys / And shove the other side away
For it's now time to play up / And win another game today

The Stoke crowd were earning a reputation as vocal and hostile. When, on 23 December 1889, inside-right Bob McCormick had his leg broken by a visiting Burnley player, the final whistle sparked a pitch invasion. Having sprinted for the dressing rooms, Burnley complained about 'intimidation', and Stoke, who had won 2-1, had to replay the game. Burnley won the second match 4-3.

Underwood injured a knee against Sunderland in March 1893. Water gathered under his kneecap and in May he was forced to retire. He was only 24. He became a potter, but suffered years of ill health. By 1908 he was too ill to work and became almost destitute. A fund was set up to assist, helped by Stoke secretary-manager Denny Austerberry. Underwood died in Stoke on 8 October 1928.

Magic Moment: *From one of his prodigious free-kicks, Underwood found the head of Wilmot Turner, who nodded the winning goal in Stoke's 4-3 defeat of Nottingham Forest in September 1892.*

Worst Nightmare: *With Stoke 0-1 down v Accrington in April 1889, needing a point to avoid a second successive wooden spoon, Underwood and left-half Bob Ramsey comically collided in trying to clear, allowing a clinching second goal to Accrington's Barbour.*

STOKE RECORD	Appearances	Goals
Football League	94	–
FA Cup	12	–
Football Alliance	21	–

No 5. **JACK ECCLES**
Debut: v West Brom, 15 March 1890
Farewell: v Small Heath, 16 February 1901

As long-term replacement for Underwood at left-back, Jack Eccles carried on the international's reputation as a fearsome tackler.

Born in Stoke on 31 March 1869, Eccles, at just 5ft 7½in and 11st 6lbs, bordered on skinny. Appearances proved deceptive. Despite the *Sentinel* believing that 'with a little more weight he would make one of the finest backs in the country', Eccles was as tough as old boots, often earning descriptions as 'redoubtable' or 'tackling stoutly and sturdily'. In team photos his vacant stare reminds the modern fan of a psyched-up Stuart Pearce.

In March 1890, whilst playing for local non-league London Road, Eccles was spotted by William Heath (manager of Stoke's reserves, Stoke Swifts) waiting at Stoke Station for a train to Leek, where he was due to play. With the Swifts a man short, Heath convinced Eccles to turn out for them instead, at half-back, and he showed enough promise to be offered terms. From then on Eccles built his reputation as a redoubtable kicker, once scoring from the halfway line against Stockport County reserves.

Being sufficiently two-footed to play on either flank, Eccles understudied the England pair, Clare and Underwood, for his first few seasons. He made his first-team debut as a replacement for the injured Clare, but took over from the prematurely retired Underwood late in 1893-94. Boasting the hardest shot in the team, Eccles was entrusted with free-kicks, although he would often forget himself and shoot directly into the net when a touch from a colleague was required! In fact, he was only credited with one goal for Stoke, in a 2-3 defeat by Bolton in September 1896.

Eccles' robust, no-nonsense style induced him to concede more than his share of free-kicks and penalties. Early in his career he reacted badly to decisions given against him and was noted for 'being too unconcerned when once beaten so far as recovering lost ground'. His tantrums and moods earned him a reputation for dourness, though obviously not with his wife. He is believed to have fathered fourteen children, one of whom, Joseph, later played for West Ham, Aston Villa and Coventry.

Called up by the Football League in April 1899 to play in a 4-1 win over the Scottish League, Eccles' selection at inside-left, alongside team-mate Joe Turner, reflected the esteem in which he was held as a footballer, but hardly gave him an opportunity to impress. The international selectors kept faith with Aston Villa's James Crabtree at left-back and Eccles did not feature again.

In 1897-98 eight defeats in nine games rooted Stoke to the floor of the First Division. Eccles was instrumental in the recovery, although Stoke finished on 24 points along with four other clubs and were dragged into the Test match system, which in those days decided promotion and relegation. Eventually Stoke were left facing Burnley in a game which became known as 'the Match with No Shots'. Knowing that a 0-0 draw would ensure survival for both clubs, neither side mustered a single attempt on goal. Indeed, on one of the few occasions that the ball went out of play, the crowd seized it and played amongst themselves for four minutes before the local constabulary intervened. Even then Stoke trainer Billy Potts tried to prevent the return of the ball by kicking the policeman holding it. The episode convinced the League to abandon play-offs, in favour of a two-up two-down promotion and relegation system, until their later re-emergence in 1986.

Eccles' partnership with the equally rugged but more skilful Tom Robertson was a major factor in Stoke's progression to the last four of the FA Cup in 1898-99. In the semi-final, Eccles was blamed for the clinching third Derby goal in a 1-3 defeat, allowing John Goodall to beat him and cross for Steve Bloomer to complete his hat-trick. Although found wanting at the highest level, Eccles' sterling service earned him a benefit against Billy Meredith's Manchester City in September 1898. As the club's elder statesman he also captained Stoke in 1899-1900, succeeding George Clawley.

Eccles kept his place until the beginning of 1900-01, when he lost it to Peter Durber. He spent 1901-02 with Burslem Port Vale's reserves, but returned to Stoke the following summer, becoming trainer in succession to William Allen. When the Stoke club folded at the end of 1907-08, Eccles joined Birmingham as trainer. He died in Small Heath, Birmingham, on 2 February 1932.

Magic Moment: *Eccles nearly scored the only goal at home to Notts County in March 1900. He 'relieved Notts pressure with a hearty kick, which sent the ball to Suter [Notts' keeper], who fell over in trying to get it away.' With the ball going in, Joe Turner tapped home.*

Worst Nightmare: *On 7 October 1889, the train returning Stoke's reserves from Wolverhampton ran into another at Stafford Station. The collision wrecked both trains and threw Eccles through a door onto the track. His injuries kept him out of the team for a month.*

STOKE RECORD	Appearances	Goals
Football League	165	1
FA Cup	21	–
Football Alliance	1	–

No 6. **GEORGE CLAWLEY**
Debut: v Liverpool, 10 November 1894
Final Farewell: v Bury, 22 April 1899

Stoke's search for a replacement for England international keeper Billy Rowley ended in August 1894 with the signing of George W

Clawley. Born in nearby Scholar Green on 10 April 1875, Clawley joined Crewe in 1893, as the Alex completed their first season in the newly formed Football League Second Division. He made just three first-team appearances for Crewe – enough to impress Stoke secretary-manager Arthur Reeves – who got his man for £10.

Although a hulking 6ft, Clawley's trademark cloth cap adorned a youthful, innocent-looking face. He made his mark with some commanding displays, becoming an instant favourite with Stoke's often fickle fans, proving that his burly 12st 7lbs frame could be nimbly thrown around the goal area. Shot-stopping was his forte. Press reports refer to 'brilliant saves' or that he would 'spring sideways to pick up well'. Clawley also became an early exponent of the quick recovery from an initial save to block a follow-up. Renowned for his ability to come out for crosses and corners, or clear through-balls from the feet of onrushing attackers – at a time when goalkeepers usually left such duties to their defenders – Clawley settled into a defensive trio, behind skipper Jack Eccles and Tommy Clare.

Clawley missed only four games in two seasons before, in 1896, he signed for newly established Southampton St Mary's of the Southern League, along with fellow Stoke players Joe Turner, Jack Farrell, Peter Durber and trainer Billy Dawson. All were attracted by the wages offered by Southern League clubs desperately seeking to compete with those in the Football League. Heated debate arose regarding the high wages that drove up the expense of football. One 1896 report bedevilled the South as 'the bugbear of both English and Scottish Leagues as, had they not become a power, the Leagues could have dictated terms by which players would be paid'. The same report bemoaned 'the agents and players who have everything all their own way'. The players helped Saints win successive Southern League titles, the second, in 1898, with Clawley as skipper. To cap it all, Saints also reached the semi-final of that season's FA Cup, losing to eventual winners Nottingham Forest.

Clawley, Farrell and Turner all re-signed for Stoke in May 1898, Clawley assuming the captaincy from Joe Schofield and leading the team to its first ever FA Cup semi-final in March 1899. The run included a famous 4-1 win over Tottenham in the quarter-final in which Clawley had his best game for the club. In the semi-final against Derby, with Stoke 1-0 up, Clawley conceded an equaliser through Steve Bloomer's close-range header, after right-back Robertson miscued a clearance up into the air, and Clawley could neither keep out Bloomer's next effort, which crept inside the far post, nor his third, which sealed a 3-1 win for Derby.

In the summer of 1899 Clawley signed for Tottenham, but broke his leg at Spurs' new White Hart Lane ground, missing much of their Southern League Championship season. He returned to win the FA Cup in 1901 as Tottenham defeated Sheffield United 3-1. Clawley returned to Southampton in July 1903, captaining Saints to another Southern League championship. After retiring in 1907, he ran the Wareham Arms Hotel in Southampton until his premature death in July 1920. He is buried in Kidsgrove, Staffordshire.

Magic Moment: *Within a minute of conceding the equaliser in the 1899 FA Cup semi-final, Clawley kept Stoke in the game with a diving one-handed save from Steve Bloomer's rapier-like shot.*

Worst Nightmare: *In the 1898-99 FA Cup first round, Clawley allowed a shot from an indirect free-kick to enter his net without realising that two Sheffield Wednesday players had touched the ball. The goal stood, putting Stoke 1-2 down.*

STOKE RECORD	Appearances	Goals
Football League	84	–
FA Cup	12	–

No 7. **JOE SCHOFIELD**
Debut: v Burnley, 10 October 1891
Farewell: v Wolves, 1 April 1899

Joseph Alfred Schofield was a gentleman amongst Victorian footballers. Born in Hanley on 1 January 1871, the son of an alderman, he was one of many who emerged through the church leagues that abounded in Methodist North Staffordshire in the late nineteenth century. Despite hailing from a strict religious background, he possessed individuality and flair and a fine left foot which ensured a quick promotion to Stoke's first team. He made his initial appearances at centre-forward, scoring in each of his first three games, totalling nine in sixteen games to finish as top scorer in Stoke's first season back in the Football League.

Schofield debuted in black and amber hoops. Each team in the Football League had to have a distinct kit and Sunderland registered their red and white stripes first. He sported a bushy moustache and behaved with gentlemanly decorum on and off the field – more the mark of an amateur than the professional he was.

By the start of 1892-93 Schofield had graduated to outside-left, in place of Billy Dunn, where he used his lithe, 9½st frame to sway from side to side to confuse opponents. He loved to entertain and press reports refer to his 'crowd-pleasing trickery' or that 'the crowd cheered for some neat tricks'. In his early seasons he was known for finishing his dribbles with a 'grand' scoring shot from distance. In a Staffs Cup first-round tie against Port Vale in 1896, following a dazzling left-wing run, Schofield bent the ball into the net from an acute angle, leaving Vale keeper Baddeley agog.

A feature of Schofield's goalscoring was his ability to draw the goalie as he bore down on goal from the left and then slip the ball past him. In later years keepers became wise to this manoeuvre and began to rush out to meet the oncoming winger, although in January 1899 Sheffield United's legendary 20st custodian, William 'Fatty' Foulke, was tricked twice by Schofield in this manner, during a 4-1 thrashing of the defending champions. Foulke showed his displeasure by going into a huff.

Schofield's classy play brought him to the attention of the selectors and he made his England debut at inside-left in March 1892 against Wales at Wrexham in a 2-0 win. A year later he won a second cap in a 6-0 mauling of Wales at the Victoria Ground. Schofield, supported by team-mate Jim Turner at left-half, made two goals and scored one. He was twice selected for the Football League – in 1893 against the Scottish League, and in 1897 against the Irish League. On three occasions Schofield finished as Stoke's top scorer, although this exposes the team's problems in finding a goalscoring centre-forward. He scored the 88th-minute goal which knocked Everton out of the FA Cup in a famous 1-0 win in 1894, and a third cap was earned in March 1895. Playing in his favoured left-wing position, he helped England thrash Ireland 9-0 at Derby. Oddly, he was never capped again, being passed over in favour of Sheffield Wednesday's Frederick Spiksley.

If 1893-94 was Schofield's best season – with fifteen League goals plus one in the FA Cup – then 1895-96 saw Stoke accomplish their then best League finish, sixth in Division One. Schofield and his inside-left partner, former Scots guardsman Tommy Hyslop, scored 26 League goals between them, with Schofield bagging a hat-trick against Small Heath (Birmingham City). When Scottish international Hyslop joined Glasgow Rangers in the summer, he deprived Schofield of an ideal wing partner.

After being made captain in 1897, Schofield took an interest in the political side of football. Writing in a national newspaper he complained: 'Something must be done. It is becoming more and more difficult to get a fairly even distribution of talent. We want to see the survival not of the wealthiest clubs, but of the most meritorious. The proposal, therefore, to pool gates and divide the income evenly between the competing clubs is of paramount importance.' This principle became enshrined in the rules of the Football League and was only abolished in 1983. The emergence of an elite, funded by vast gate receipts, had worried Schofield 80 years earlier.

Schofield suffered ill-health towards the end of his career and by 1898-99 he had lost his place to Joe Turner and the captaincy to

George Clawley. Despite scoring on his final appearance, Schofield retired, after earning a club benefit, becoming a schoolmaster at Broom Street School in Hanley. His final tally of 84 League goals set a club record that stood for nearly 30 years. He was only the second player to exceed 200 appearances for Stoke, and the first to pass that mark in the Football League.

When Stoke folded under dire financial circumstances in 1908, Schofield was one of twelve burghers who stepped in to become directors of a new club, rescuing Potteries football from the flames. During World War I he took on the secretary's duties and in 1918 Schofield moved to Port Vale as secretary-manager, overseeing Vale's re-entry into the Football League in place of Leeds City in 1919. Schofield died on 29 September 1929 with Vale top of the formative Third Division North table – which they went on to win.

Magic Moment: *In January 1892 Schofield scored a 'beauty' in his first season to level the FA Cup-tie with Burnley at 1-1. Stoke went on to become the first team to win at Burnley that season.*

Worst Nightmare: *In February 1899, in a match played in a blizzard at Liverpool, Schofield departed unnoticed, to reappear a little later with a change of boots. He then fell over, missing an open goal, to loud and ironic cheers from the Liverpool fans. Stoke lost 0-1.*

STOKE RECORD	Appearances	Goals
Football League	204	84
FA Cup	22	8

No 8. **WILLIE MAXWELL**
Debut: v Bolton, 2 September 1895
Farewell: v Notts Co, 13 April 1901

If Joe Schofield was the creative force behind Stoke teams of the 1890s, then William Sturrock Maxwell was the predatory goalscorer who revelled in the service from the wings.

Born in Arbroath on 21 September 1876, Maxwell began his career as an amateur. Whilst working as a solicitor's clerk he turned out for Hearts Strollers, Arbroath, Dundee and Heart of Midlothian. Maxwell did not turn professional until persuaded to sign for Stoke as an 18-year-old in 1895 by secretary-manager Billy Rowley. His upper-middle class background bequeathed him a liking for suits and a gentleman's stick, which earned him a reputation amongst the Stoke professionals as the quintessential dandy.

Although the young Maxwell scored on his debut, a prolific forward line featuring fellow Scots Tommy Hyslop and Billy Dickson forced him to bide his time. But with the emergence of right-winger Fred Johnson, the departure of Hyslop and retirement of Dickson, the naturally left-footed Maxwell became a first choice. Strangely, Maxwell fitted in where needed: the front line was not built around his natural inside-left berth. In each of his six seasons at Stoke, he appeared in every forward position bar left-wing, where Schofield was virtually ever present.

Hardly a typical inside-forward at 5ft 10½in, Maxwell's stocky 12st 7lbs frame and broad shoulders allowed him to shrug off challenges. His combination of physical presence and pace allowed him to develop into a fine goalscorer. His greatest asset was an ability to control the ball at full pelt, allowing him to race clear of opponents and into one-to-one confrontations with the goalkeeper. He notched double figures in five successive seasons from 1896-97, finishing as leading scorer on each occasion. In his best seasons, 1898-99 and 1900-01, he totalled sixteen League goals, while three FA Cup goals made his highest seasonal tally nineteen in 1898-99.

Maxwell loved to shoot on sight, often taking goalkeepers by surprise, although his penchant for long-range shooting often resulted in the *Sentinel*'s scribe, Nimrod, describing the ball 'going beyond the goal-line by some distance' or that Maxwell 'kicked it strongly towards yonder houses!'

A proud Scot, Maxwell's placidity did not extend to respecting authority. In October 1897 he disappeared home to Scotland without permission, earning a club suspension. That summer, presumably *with* permission, Maxwell had played cricket for Arbroath, where, the *Sentinel* reports, he 'ran up a very respectable average'.

Maxwell's scoring record won him a trial for the Anglo-Scots, and on 2 April 1898 he turned out for Scotland against the Auld Enemy. By contemporary accounts, Maxwell was one of only two Scotland players to perform creditably in a 1-3 home defeat. He remains the last Stoke player to receive a full Scottish Cap.

1898-99 saw three Stoke players suspended for drinking champagne during pre-season training. Poor form left Stoke languishing near the foot of Division One. Press criticism of players' lack of 'willingness to play the football that all know they can' targeted Stoke's spluttering attack. Centre-forwards Fred Molyneux and Jack Farrell failed to gel, leaving Maxwell as the only consistent scorer. Assistance came from the wet winter, as heavy conditions bogged down pitches. Maxwell's pace and bulk perfectly suited Stoke's long-ball game, described as 'no nonsense play with their mission the goal-net'. Stoke's revival saw them hammer eventual champions Aston Villa at a boggy Victoria Ground 3-0 on New Year's Eve. In the FA Cup quarter-final win over Spurs, Maxwell back-heeled the ball to the unmarked Joe Turner who put Stoke 3-0 ahead. The move, heralded as 'something to remember' in the press, killed off the Southern League side and sent Stoke through to face Derby. Maxwell's opener in the semi-final 'caused players to heartily shake hands in a memorable display of enthusiasm.' Despite their 1-3 defeat, Stoke's FA Cup exploits earned the players a £5 bonus.

Maxwell often received special attention from opposing defenders. Regularly crocked during games, he often finished by limping out onto the wing. Although respected as a gentleman, in October 1899 his temper snapped and he traded blows with A Jones of West Brom. He and his sparring partner were ordered off 'amid hoots, hisses and yells.' The *Sentinel* noted: 'Maxwell is not a great fighter and I have never seen the slightest tendency towards pugilism on his part.' Despite his previous exemplary disciplinary record, Maxwell received a fortnight's suspension, during which he turned out in a benefit match for Sheffield United's Arthur Watson, twisting his knee so badly it put him out for a further ten weeks. 'I wish I'd never seen a friendly match,' he sighed.

Maxwell was never quite the same again, losing his explosive burst of pace. In the summer of 1901 Stoke sold him to Third Lanark in Scotland. Maxwell's 86 goals left him second in Stoke's career goalscoring charts behind Joe Schofield. Aged just 25, the sale of the club's one prolific scorer seems, with a century's hindsight, senseless, but with finances in turmoil the directors jumped at the £250 on offer. His departure sparked the decline that would finally result in Stoke's demise in 1908.

Maxwell moved on to Sunderland, Millwall Athletic and finally, in 1905, to Bristol City, where he won a Second Division championship medal, bagging 27 League goals. The next season his eighteen goals helped make City runners-up in the top flight. In 1909 Maxwell retired from playing, moving to Belgium to coach Leopold FC. In 1920 he became national coach to the formative Belgian FA. He died in 1940, aged 64.

Magic Moment: *Maxwell put Stoke ahead in the 1899 FA Cup semi-final against Derby with one of his finest finishes, nodding down a Joe Turner cross to himself and volleying home.*

Worst Nightmare: *Against Small Heath in November 1899, Maxwell and Farrell bore down on keeper Clutterbuck but left the ball to each other. Clutterbuck's clearance fell to Wharton, who put Heath 2-1 up. The 'bungling' forwards earned the 'crowd's invective'.*

STOKE RECORD	Appearances	Goals
Football League	156	76
FA Cup	17	10

No 9. **JIMMY BRADLEY**
Debut: v Aston Villa, 3 September 1898
Final Farewell: v Swansea Town, 24 April 1915

James Edwin Bradley was born in Goldenhill, Staffordshire in May 1881 and signed for Stoke from non-league Goldenhill Wanderers as a 16-year-old in February 1898. Weighing 11½st, Bradley stood a lithe 5ft 9½in and oozed class. The *Sentinel* described him as having 'an old head on young shoulders' with 'a fine turn of speed' who 'tackles with excellent judgment'.

As a consequence of the transfer to Liverpool of centre-half Alex Raisbeck, Bradley found himself part of a youthful, hard-tackling, half-back line, featuring 23-year-old centre-half Alf Wood and fellow teenager Teddy Parsons at right-half. Stoke became a difficult team to score against, conceding just over one goal a game for the remainder of the season. The trio were noted for 'tackling like terriers' and they 'fed their forwards well', allowing the powerful front line to keep opposing defences under pressure.

Bradley's role was to disrupt the opposition's creative players, but he was no simple destroyer. A precise passer of the ball, his clever promptings from midfield set his forwards moving. When Stoke attacked, Bradley would hang back alongside Wood, while Parsons supported the strikers. Contemporary reports compare the trio's style to the backbone of the Sheffield United championship winning team of 1897-98 – the half-back line of Morren, Howell, and Needham. In Bradley and Parsons' first season as pros, Stoke reached a first ever FA Cup semi-final.

Following the departures of Wood and Parsons in 1900-01, 23-year-old Bradley found himself the elder statesman of the Potters' midfield. Now partnered by the older but less experienced Tom Holford and George Baddeley, a new half-back line helped keep Stoke in Division One for five more years. The press described Bradley as 'a model of consistency', although he proved he could play a bit too. He developed a trick whereby he would swing hard at the ball with his right foot and dummy the player facing him by kicking the ball with the outside of his left.

Despite the quality of their midfield, year after year Stoke clung onto First Division status by the skin of their teeth. The covering of the Butler Street side of the ground, built in 1903 at a cost of £2,000 to accommodate 12,000 spectators, swallowed the club's sparse cash reserves and led to the unloading of Stoke's prize assets – the players. In the summer of 1905 the board announced Bradley's sale to Southern League Plymouth. But Bradley refused, and signed instead for Liverpool for £420. He won a championship medal in his first season at Anfield and in total played 170 times for Liverpool, scoring five goals. In 1911 he moved on to Reading, who released him in the summer of 1913. An irate Bradley tossed the entire first-team playing kit into the Elm Park baths. He rejoined Stoke on a free transfer. Aged 33, his experience played a sizeable role in the Southern League Division Two championship team, but on clinching the title in April 1915 he announced his retirement.

Bradley worked for the Stoke-on-Trent Highways Department, and for a short time did part-time coaching for Stoke's reserves. Jimmy died in Blackpool on 12 March 1954.

Magic Moment: *In the 1898-99 FA Cup semi-final against Derby, Bradley set up Maxwell's opening goal by robbing England international John Goodall and playing a perfect pass forward to Turner.*

Worst Nightmare: *In a friendly at Port Vale on 24 April 1899 Bradley was chased by a runaway dog which relieved Vale's Lucien Boullemier of the ball and then threatened to bite Bradley's legs!*

STOKE RECORD	Appearances	Goals
Football League	199	4
FA Cup	27	–
Southern League	30	2

No 10. **TOMMY HOLFORD**
Debut: v Sheffield United, 17 September 1898
Farewell: v Fulham, 18 April 1908

During his ten seasons at Stoke, Thomas Holford filled every position in the team other than goalkeeper. Born in Hanley on 28 January 1878, Holford joined Stoke in May 1898 for a basic wage of 7s 6d per week – having played for Granville's Night School in Cobridge – initially turning out for Stoke's reserves at left-half.

Holford made his first-team debut at centre-half as Stoke struggled to make an impact in 1898-99. Although the *Sentinel* claimed he 'did not put a foot wrong', it took three seasons before he held down a regular first-team spot. When Alf Wood departed for Aston Villa in March 1901, Holford grasped the nettle to become the cornerstone of Stoke's team, stationed between Jimmy Bradley and George Baddeley in the half-back line. Holford became a hit with the Stoke crowd, setting a tradition of rugged, whole-hearted defenders, and can now be seen as the first of a line that directly links Turner, Mountford, Smith and Overson.

At just 5ft 5in and a puny 9st, Holford appeared scrawny. His appearance belied the reality of a mini-firebrand who steamed into tackles. Though often described as 'pugnacious', he was never sent off, although that era exercised greater tolerance. Even so, Holford soon earned himself the nickname 'Dirty' Tom. Smaller by four or five inches in team photographs than the rest of the Stoke side, Holford sported a moustache when almost all his team-mates were clean-shaven. He stands proudly and jauntily in relaxed fashion, while other players seem stiff and much more 'Edwardian'.

There were, however, those who felt he might be better suited to a different position. In a letter to the *Sentinel* in 1907, Mr W Chiswick aired his view that 'while not wishing to detract from the well-known abilities of the present centre-half, I feel I am not alone in considering that the position should be held by one above, rather than below, average size and weight'. At the time, Stoke had just been hammered 0-3 by a hefty, long-ball Clapton Orient. Holford's views are not known: never one to over-dramatise a situation, he was known as 'being a careful man in his habits' who rarely made public pronouncements.

Stoke became known as the 'Houdini' of the First Division as late runs averted relegation in 1900-01 and again the following season, when Tom starred as an emergency centre-forward, notching three goals in successive key games. Holford relished the challenge of each new position, filling in at full-back in 1905-06 and on the right wing in 1907-08. His abilities earned him an England cap against Ireland in February 1903, when he became possibly the smallest centre-half ever to be so honoured. Despite a 4-0 win, Holford lost his place as the selectors tried out various centre-halves before settling on Bristol City's Billy Wedlock.

Holford became Stoke captain, in succession to George Baddeley, from 1904-05 and led by example. He also became the team's penalty taker. His consistency was legendary. From March 1902 Holford missed just one game until March 1906. During that run he became the first man to play 100 consecutive League games for Stoke, achieving the feat on New Year's Day 1906. His unbroken run eventually totalled 105 games.

With debts mounting, the departures of numerous colleagues left Holford as Stoke's only class act. The perennial relegation battle ended in grief in 1906-07, when the Potters propped up Division One. However, when the club immediately struggled in Division Two, a group of Stoke fans chose Holford as the target for 'remarks which would try the patience of Job. There is no doubt that the influence this barracking has had upon the player this season has been considerable.' The sneers finally drove Holford to seek a transfer. Chelsea, Blackburn and Bradford City lost out in the race for his signature to Manchester City, who stumped up £350. The *Sentinel* lambasted 'the ungentlemanly sneers of that section who have caused the termination of an honourable service'.

Holford's departure effectively signalled the demise of the club. The apathy of supporters – only 1,500 turned up for the final home game of 1907-08 – meant that Stoke lost over £1,100 that season. The board decided enough was enough. The Stoke public no longer deserved to boast a professional football club if they supported it so poorly. Stoke's resignation was handed to the League.

Holford gave Manchester City equally sterling service until he joined Port Vale as player-manager in 1914. Vale wags nicknamed the vertically challenged Holford 'Big' Tom! He remained a regular until 1922. In April 1924, aged 46, Holford, now Vale's trainer, came out of retirement to play twice as emergency right-half against Derby, becoming the then oldest player to appear in the Football League. Holford loved being back in the limelight: 'I had some bonny tussles with Jackie Whitehouse, the Derby inside left. We spent most of the afternoon pasting each other. Nothing vicious mind you, but plenty of good old-fashioned shoulder-to-shoulder biffing. I'd always revelled at getting "stuck in".'

Holford continued to serve Port Vale as a scout until his 70s. He retired in 1950 and died in Blurton, Stoke-on-Trent, on 6 April 1964.

Magic Moment: *In October 1907, when asked to play as an emergency centre-forward against Gainsborough, Holford handed the captaincy to Ernie Mullineux, to allow himself to concentrate on his new position. Holford scored twice as Stoke won 5-0.*

Worst Nightmare: *Now a Valeite, in September 1917 Holford missed an open goal in a Potteries derby. The* Sentinel's *reporter pondered 'How Holford missed equalising from the goal-line is a mystery, because he was almost under the bar!'*

STOKE RECORD	Appearances	Goals
Football League	248	30
FA Cup	21	3

No 11. **GEORGE BADDELEY**
Debut: v Bury, 2 September 1901
Farewell: v Leicester Fosse, 27 April 1908

George Baddeley was the third and final member of Stoke's half-back triumvirate of the early twentieth century.

The Baddeley family hailed from the Fegg Hayes area of Stoke-on-Trent, to the north of the city, near Biddulph. George, born on 8 May 1874, began his career in the local leagues with Pittshill FC and signed for Stoke in 1900 from Biddulph.

George suffered from the family trait of possessing large, jug-like ears and distinctive thick, dark hair. He established himself in the Stoke side as a consistent and reliable wing-half, strong in the tackle and with sharp distribution. Awarded the captaincy in his first full season of 1901-02, alongside Tommy Holford and Jimmy Bradley, George completed a powerful midfield which effectively averted relegation throughout the early 1900s. Although occasionally criticised for 'marring a clever display by trying to do too much with the ball', George's consistency allowed him to play 99 consecutive games for Stoke from February 1902.

Despite home crowds averaging 8,600 in 1905-06, the directors bought badly and Stoke imploded. Amid the clear-out as Stoke folded at the end of 1907-08, George signed for West Brom for £250, along with centre-forward Freddie Brown.

Baddeley remained at the Hawthorns for six seasons until war broke out, winning a Second Division championship medal in 1910-11 and a runners-up medal in the 1912 FA Cup final at the remarkable age of nearly 38. He was 39 years and 345 days old when taking the field for the final time, against Sheffield Wednesday in April 1914, and remains the oldest player ever to appear for the Baggies. He retired to keep a pub and later became coach at the Hawthorns. He died in West Bromwich on 18 July 1952.

The Baddeley dynasty dominated early twentieth century football in Stoke. George's younger brother Amos was a speedy left-winger. Further family members included cousin Sam, a right-half who signed for Stoke in 1907 after Burslem Port Vale, for whom he made 30 League appearances, went bust. The final member of the clan was Sam's brother Thomas, a goalkeeper. As a prominent Wolves player at the turn of the century, Tom won five England caps. In 1909-10 he was the third of three Baddeleys, alongside Sam and Amos, to appear together for Stoke – a record.

Magic Moment: *Deputising in goal after Dickie Roose injured his hand against Wolves in September 1907, George kept a clean sheet, even surviving being catapulted into the net by a Wolves forward.*

Worst Nightmare: *On Boxing Day 1905, on the brink of becoming the first player to complete 100 consecutive League appearances for Stoke, George twisted his knee against Liverpool late in his 99th game, thus allowing Tommy Holford to reach that milestone first.*

STOKE RECORD	Appearances	Goals
Football League	208	14
FA Cup	17	5

Stoke's Staffordshire Cup winners of 1878, captained by Tom Slaney (middle left)

The Stoke side relegated from Division One in 1906-07

W. A. COWLISHAW, T. HOLFORD, C. BURGESS, L. R. ROOSE, A. COOK, S. LAKE, ESQ.
CHAIRMAN   CAPTAIN
H. CROXTON, R. FIELDING, F. W. ROUSE, G. BADDELEY, A. STURGESS, J. CHALMERS, G. GALLIMORE, J. MILLER

Edwardian superstar Tom Brittleton

The rebellious Jimmy Broad, whose goals won Stoke promotion in 1921-22

Stoke's promotion-winning side of 1921-22

Bob McGrory (second left) and Billy Tempest (third right) prepare for Division One

Chapter Two

~ *The Wilderness Years* ~

No 12. **MART WATKINS**
Debut: v Bury, 6 October 1900
Final Farewell: v Fulham, 18 April 1908

Although the defining strength of Stoke teams of the early 1900s was the half-back line, the one consistent goalscorer throughout those dark years was Walter Martin 'Mart' Watkins.

Born in Oswestry in 1880, Watkins was one of six sons of a Welsh farmer from Llanwnog in Montgomeryshire. Along with elder brother Ernie, Mart played for his local club, Oswestry Town, where Stoke spotted him. He signed in August 1900 and the Potters' horrific start to the 1900-01 season – one point from the first seven games – ensured a rapid first-team baptism.

Tall, slim, with a neat moustache, Watkins was described as a 'smart player', possessing a whiplash shot. He dictated Stoke's attacks, specialising in sweeping passes to his wingers, then racing into the penalty box to launch himself at the ensuing crosses.

Watkins helped Stoke avert relegation in 1900-01, scoring the only goal in each of the two final away games. In 1901-02, he finished top scorer with sixteen and repeated the feat with thirteen in 1902-03. Within eighteen months of his debut Watkins won the first of his ten Welsh caps. On 3 March 1902, he wore No 8 against England in a 0-0 draw at Wrexham. Alongside him were teammates Dickey Roose and Sam Meredith, brother of Watkins' wing partner, Billy. Watkins scored against England in March 1903 in a 1-2 defeat. However, a 0-1 defeat by Scotland in the next game meant wholesale changes and Watkins dropped from favour.

At Stoke, Watkins found a new inside-left partner in Arthur 'Sailor' Capes, signed from Nottingham Forest in June 1902. The burly Capes had scored twice as Forest beat Derby 3-1 in the 1898 FA Cup final. He and Watkins struck up a bulldozing partnership and Capes, although often described as 'workmanlike' or 'unpolished', also won a cap – for England against Scotland in April 1903.

Perhaps influenced by Watkins' international partnership with Billy Meredith, in January 1904 Manchester City offered £450 for Watkins' services. The deal collapsed, but with Stoke desperate for funds following the construction of the new Butler Street stand, Aston Villa secretary-manager George Ramsey signed Watkins for a 'high price'. Watkins followed England international Arthur Lockett, who had moved to Villa Park the previous summer.

Watkins returned to the international fray, scoring in a 2-2 draw with England in February 1904, a 3-1 win over Scotland, and a 2-2 draw with Ireland in 1905. In Wales' 0-1 defeat by Ireland at Bangor in March 1904, he played alongside his brother Ernie, of Southern League Millwall Athletic.

Watkins signed for Sunderland in October 1904, then Southern League Crystal Palace in June 1905. He played for Northampton in 1906-07 before being coaxed back to Stoke.

In his 1907-08 preview *Sentinel* columnist 'The Potter' described Watkins as 'an exceedingly clever forward on his day'. Sadly for Stoke, second time around, his days proved few. He missed numerous chances and failed to link with stand-in centre-forward Tommy Holford. Watkins scored just five times in twenty sporadic appearances and, in November, lost his place to Freddie Brown, although he did win a tenth Welsh cap in a 0-1 defeat by Ireland.

In 1908 cash-strapped Stoke resigned from the League, then folded. Their demise benefited Tottenham, who, having resigned from the Southern League and failed to be elected to the Football League, were left out in the cold in 1908-09. Spurs won a hastily arranged election by a majority of one over Lincoln City. According to the *Official History of Tottenham Hotspur*, written by vice-Chairman G Wagstaffe Simmons in the 1940s, an understanding existed which saw Spurs pay off some of Stoke's debts as a thank you for not contesting the election themselves.

As a free agent, Watkins moved on to Crewe, Stafford Rangers, and coached at Tunstall Park, before returning to play for the re-born Stoke club in August 1911. Although still only 31, Watkins failed to make the first team and retired in May 1914, with war-clouds looming. Mart passed away in the City General Hospital, Newcastle-under-Lyme on 14 May 1942.

Magic Moment: *With Stoke needing a point to stay up in the final game of 1901-02, Watkins, playing on the right wing, delivered a vicious cross which Manchester City goalie John Hillman dropped over the line for the equaliser in a 2-2 draw.*

Worst Nightmare: *In Stoke's first game of 1907-08, Watkins was presented with a glorious opportunity to win the match against Chesterfield. Fielding's pass left him with an open goal, but Watkins fell over the ball. The* Sentinel *commented, 'He will never get many opportunities like that one.'*

STOKE RECORD	Appearances	Goals
Football League	125	48
FA Cup	14	4

No 13. **Dr LR ROOSE**
Debut: v Blackburn, 19 October 1901
Final Farewell: v Wolves, 28 September 1907

The handsome and debonair Leigh Richmond 'Dickey' Roose, one of the most famous amateur players of the pre-World War I era, was known as 'a veritable Prince among goalkeepers'.

Born at Holt, near Wrexham on 27 November 1877, the son of a Presbyterian minister, Roose trained as a doctor of bacteriology, being briefly tutored by HG Wells. Helped by lecturing at teaching hospitals, Roose became independently wealthy and played football, in the Corinthian spirit, simply for his love of the game. On one occasion, when playing for Aston Villa, he even hired his own train to get him to the game on time.

As an amateur, Roose was able to register for different teams in different leagues and often played for more than one in a season. He won the first of his Welsh caps whilst playing for Aberystwyth Town in 1900. He also served the Druids club and London Welsh, winning a further three caps, before joining Stoke in October 1901, as part of an experiment by the board, who also engaged two other notable amateurs, Len Hales and Sam Ashworth.

Roose's tactics involved roaming all over his own half until the 1912 law change, which restricted goalkeepers to handling inside the penalty area. He showed 'several clever examples of the finest custodianship and was very smart in meeting rushes'. His bravery endeared him to the Stoke faithful, reared on Roose's fearless predecessors Rowley and Clawley.

Nine of Roose's 24 Welsh caps came during his two spells at Stoke. He played eight consecutive internationals from 1906 to 1908. In 1907 Wales won the Home International Championship for the first time with Roose pivotal to the success. In the clinching 1-1 draw with England at Craven Cottage, he made several wonder saves to frustrate the English forwards.

Roose's calming influence, boosted by the goals of Watkins and Capes, helped Stoke finish sixth in 1902-03. The construction of the Butler Street stand, bordering the River Trent, put the Victoria Ground in contention to stage an FA Cup final replay, if needed, although Bury's 6-0 demolition of Derby at Crystal Palace ruled the question irrelevant. Stadium development swallowed the season's £1,500 surplus and the team soon began to suffer. Players such as Lockett and Watkins were sold, prompting yet another relegation battle. In the run in, Roose conceded only five goals as Stoke recorded three wins and two draws in their last six games to survive.

Lecturing in London forced Roose to resign from Stoke in the summer of 1904, though this did not prevent him turning out for

Everton from November. With Stoke reeling under a £2,500 debt, Denny Austerberry coaxed Roose to rejoin Stoke in August 1905 and he assisted the Potters to a mid-table finish. The following season not even Roose could avert relegation, although Stoke's goals-against record of 64 was by no means the worst in the division. The meagre total of 41 goals scored, the lowest in the top flight, indicated where the team's problems lay.

Such was Roose's eminence that when the opus History of Football was published in twelve parts during 1905-06 (published in book form by Desert Island Books as *The Book of Football*), he was the obvious choice to write a chapter on goalkeeping. Roose was introduced to readers as being 'in the opinion of many eminent critics, the most brilliant goalkeeper who ever played the game'.

Roose's words support the notion that goalies were odd creatures, artistes even, unlike their rough, clumsy outfield brethren. He espoused the custodian's individuality. 'A good goalkeeper,' he began, 'like a poet, is born not made. He has to fill a position in which the principle is forced upon him that it is good to be alone – a position which is distinctly personal and decidedly individualistic.' He cited temperament, concentration and height as the key attributes for a top class custodian and, with a sideways glance to Stoke's always opinionated fans, continued, 'Leaving one's goal is looked upon as a cardinal sin by those armchair critics who tell a goalkeeper what he should and shouldn't do, and administer advice from the philosophic atmosphere of the grandstand. They wobble mentally, in proportion with the custodian's success in rushing out to meet an opponent even when the result is as inevitable as when a man's logic is pitted against a woman's tears. Never more than in this case is it true that he who hesitates is lost.'

In September 1907 Roose hurt his hand at Molineux while making a save. The Wolves club doctor discovered a dislocated little finger. Though Roose returned to complete the match at right-back, the injury sidelined him until the turn of the year. With Stoke's finances at crisis point in January 1908, Roose joined Sunderland, whom he assisted to third-place finishes in 1908-09 and 1910-11. His departure from Stoke sparked a stampede, as fifteen players jumped the rapidly floundering ship. Roose also played a few games for Huddersfield, Aston Villa and Woolwich Arsenal. He joined Llandudno in 1912 and was a regular before retiring, aged 37.

On one famous occasion, Roose's desire simply to play saw him fall foul of the burgeoning Potteries rivalry. On 23 April 1910, along with three other notable amateurs, he played for Port Vale at the Victoria Ground in the vital championship decider of the North Staffs & District League, in which Stoke's reserves competed. Vale swept to a 2-0 lead with Roose performing heroics. But the incensed

Stoke crowd objected to the tactics of 'packing' the Vale team. Some hot-heads poured onto the pitch, sweeping up former hero Roose and carrying him towards the River Trent intent on ducking him. Stoke Chairman Rev AE Hurst pleaded with them to calm down, and Stoke forward Vic Horrocks was knocked out in the scuffling. It took the arrival of the local constabulary to prise Roose from the clutches of the mob and remove him to the safety of the boardroom. The Staffordshire FA declared the championship void. Vale were fined ten shillings for their trouble, while Stoke had the Victoria Ground closed by the FA for the first two weeks of the 1910-11 season. A bewildered Roose claimed that he had been told the game was a friendly and not a winner-takes-all championship decider.

When war came, Roose joined the 9th Battalion of the Royal Fusiliers and as a Lance Corporal won the Military medal for action in Flanders. He was killed in action in October 1916.

Magic Moment: *On his debut, Roose gave 'a magnificent display of goalkeeping' capped by a 'flying, majestic save' to earn Stoke a draw.*

Worst Nightmare: *Roose's medical skills were needed when Stoke visited Liverpool in January 1902. Several players became ill after eating plaice for lunch. Roose, ailing himself, tended them, enabling Stoke to field a side. It didn't help. Roose succumbed after ten minutes with a pulse rate of 148. After half-time Stoke had just seven players fit to resume, although two later returned. Stoke lost 0-7.*

STOKE RECORD	Appearances	Goals
Football League	147	–
FA Cup	12	–

No 14. GEORGE TURNER
Debut: v Aston Villa Reserves, 5 September 1908
Farewell: v Port Vale, 29 September 1917

The summer of 1908 was a desperate time for football in Stoke-on-Trent. Burslem Port Vale had folded the previous season, and now the city's senior club, Stoke, faced a similar fate. Gate receipts from the 1,800 crowd at the penultimate home game against Barnsley totalled just £40 and the board put the entire squad up for sale. Most left, but few realised any significant cash. Chairman WA Cowlishaw appealed in the pages of the *Sentinel* for public support but, when none was forthcoming, he washed his hands of the ailing club. He resigned Football League membership on 16 June and liquidated the company. Mr CE Sutcliffe, secretary of the Football League, was moved to declare: 'Football in the Potteries is dead.'

But all was not yet lost. Twelve burghers of the borough, including former players Joe Schofield and Billy Dickson, were determined that football should stay alive in Stoke. They formed a new club, which took on the assets of its predecessor.

The consortium was put together by former Football League referee AJ Barker of Hanley, who became part-time secretary-manager. The Victoria Ground stood on land leased by the Church and Barker discovered a proviso in the deeds that dictated that the land be used for athletic purposes. This stopped the previous chairman selling the lease to the Territorial Army. It was bought by the new committee and Stoke (1908) FC was born. The Reverend AE Hurst was installed as the new chairman, confidently predicting 'a new and brighter era' for the club.

George Turner symbolised the rekindling of interest in football in Stoke. Born at Halmerend, Staffordshire, in 1887, he made his name locally as a speedy left-back with Halmerend Gymnastic. With the new directors scouring the district for players for a team to compete in the Birmingham & District and Southern Leagues, Turner, described in the *Sentinel* as a professional athlete when joining the club, was one of the first selected.

At just over 6ft, Turner was the tallest player on Stoke's books, and also one of the quickest. 'He fulfils every requirement of the full-back; is speedy, quick at recovery, a strong and sure kicker, a rare tackler and at all times cool and collected,' rhapsodised the *Sentinel*, although being renowned for an ability to recover may say much for his ability to err too!

Over 12,000 gathered to see Stoke beat Aston Villa reserves 5-3 in the new club's first game. The ignominy of facing the reserve teams of clubs with whom Stoke had founded the Football League just twenty years earlier receded and crowds of 4,000 soon turned up. Turner performed creditably until a leg injury against Birmingham sidelined him for a year.

Equally at ease with either foot, Turner switched between left and right-back, depending on the availability of others. The *Sentinel* declared: 'like a shuttlecock, Turner plays alternately in the left and right positions and his consistency does him credit.' He scored Stoke's sixth and final goal in the Southern League Division Two title decider against Eastern Division winners, Hastings St Leonards on 25 April 1910.

Following injury to Sam Baddeley in the summer of 1911, Turner, as one of only three survivors of the first game of the reborn club, assumed the captaincy. In 1910-11 he made 42 appearances, scoring nine goals from full-back, as Stoke cantered to the title again. The League deemed Stoke's second Division Two championship sufficient to warrant promotion, but the standard of the

First Division found Stoke wanting. Two seasons later they were relegated again.

Turner proved his versatility by switching to right-back for almost the entire season to accommodate the newly converted Alec Milne on the left. But Stoke's rampaging run of 48 goals in thirteen games was halted by events off the field. Turner was granted a testimonial in January 1914, but the board refused to guarantee him a £400 return on the gate money. Turner demanded a transfer, but his asking price was set at an astronomical £1,500. He was joined on the list by a fellow dissenter, Welsh international, Joey Jones, while many others openly supported Turner's position. The board lost patience with the rebels, and for a vital game against Brentford made six changes. But Turner was not one of them, and despite his dissent he performed well as Stoke won 2-1.

Although neither Turner nor Jones left the club, the episode sapped morale and Stoke finished a disappointing fifth, when it had appeared that the championship was theirs for the taking. The ill-feeling provoked the departure of two of the club's saviours, secretary Barker and chairman Hurst.

Called up in August 1917, Turner was posted to the front in April 1918. Within a week he was wounded and his leg was amputated. After the war he acted as Secretary for Podmore Hall FC.

Magic Moment: *In the vital home game against Brentford in 1913-14, Turner, belying the off-field rumpus which he had partially caused, crashed home the match-winning penalty.*

Worst Nightmare: *In April 1917 Stoke met Port Vale in a stormy match in the Lancashire Regional Section of the Wartime League. Turner and Vale skipper Tommy Holford carried on a running feud that spread to the main stand. Referee H Oxley was threatened!*

STOKE RECORD	Appearances	Goals
Southern League	176	17
World War I	72	3
FA Cup	13	–
Other	1	–

No 15. **ALEC MILNE**
Debut: v West Ham, 25 December 1912
Farewell: v Barnsley, 20 March 1926

Veteran Alexander James Milne set a pattern for ageing Stoke full-backs that would endure for a quarter of a century. Born at Hebburn-on-Tyne on 29 September 1889, Milne was spotted by scouts in the north-east coalfields playing for Hebburn Argyle. He signed for Stoke in October 1912 and was initially employed at left-half in an attempt to stem the goals conceded in the Southern League First Division.

Milne couldn't have enjoyed a worst start to his Stoke career – a 0-5 thrashing at West Ham. But his place was sealed when, with Milne injured, Stoke lost 0-9 to Northampton. He moved to his natural left-back slot, allowing George Turner to find his home at right-back after years of to-ing and fro-ing between flanks.

A small, muscular man of only 5ft 7½in, Milne proved to be a solid professional with a rugged tackle and a 'grand clearing kick'. A specialist spoiler, Milne used his strong body and arms to ward off his foes. However, his major attribute was zest. 'He tackles well and fearlessly and when beaten exhibits wonderfully quick recovery'. Milne became an integral part of the side, and in the 1914-15 championship season was ever present. Unlike Turner, Milne did not receive the call to arms, although wartime service restricted his appearances. He produced munitions in his native north-east.

1919-20 saw League soccer resume. Stoke, re-elected at the end of 1914-15, finally took their place in Division Two. They had a new secretary-manager, former League referee, Arthur Shallcross, and a new chairman, EB Reynish. The *Sentinel's* reporter 'Nimrod' was relieved to be back in the big time. 'I can speak personally of the chilling effect of playing in the Southern League. Many and many a match have the Potters played in those far away Welsh hills when the only supporters have been a secretary with a big moustache, a starved reserve and a humble scribe! Those days are over thank heavens!' Peacetime boosted crowds all over the country, and such fervour enabled Stoke to establish their first supporters club with over 1,000 'missionaries' joining up.

Milne was tactically astute, adept at exploiting the offside rule, for which he was described as the 'McCracken of the Stoke team'. This was a reference to the Hull manager who had instituted such an effective offside ploy that the powers that be eventually altered the Laws, reducing the number of defenders needed to avoid offside from three to two.

Stoke finished a creditable tenth in that first post-war season. Average attendances exceeded 13,000, and 27,000 watched the first League Potteries derby with Port Vale. After Tom Brittleton's decision to concentrate on coaching the reserves, Milne, as the club's senior professional, assumed the captaincy. Whether or not his influence was integral, a remarkable turnaround ensued as Milne led Stoke to promotion in 1921-22, helped by an unbeaten run that stretched from Boxing Day to Good Friday. The achievement provoked a congratulatory telegram from the Vale supporters club, which ended: 'May the public waken up and realise their responsibilities to maintain the thing they have desired so long.'

Sadly they didn't. The average attendance of 15,200, poor for a team chasing promotion from Division Two, only rose by 4,000. Stoke lacked the quality to make an impact in the top flight, limping to instant relegation. Milne carried a leg muscle injury through the spring and consequently lost the captaincy to Bob McGrory.

Milne missed the whole of 1923-24 but thereafter kept his place until the age of 36. A 0-3 defeat at Middlesbrough in February 1926 saw Milne carry the can for defensive howlers. The sprightly Billy Spencer replaced him, although Milne then filled in for the injured McGrory at right-back as the season drew to its horrific conclusion of relegation to Division Three (North).

Milne transferred to Doncaster Rovers in the summer of 1926, playing on until he was 41. He retired at the conclusion of 1929-30 and died in Doncaster in 1970.

Magic Moment: *Milne filled in for the injured Billy Tempest, who limped out on the wing, for most of Stoke's promotion clinching 3-0 win over Bristol City in May 1922. According to 'China Dragon' in the* Dispatch, *Milne produced 'one of the most entertaining and virile displays of football I have ever seen'.*

Worst Nightmare: *Missed a simple clearance and allowed Jack Peart to score the clinching second goal as Leeds City won the Wartime Championship decider first leg 2-0. Milne was dropped for the second leg, which Stoke could win only 1-0.*

STOKE RECORD	Appearances	Goals
Football League	192	–
FA Cup	19	–
World War I	11	–
Southern League	65	–

No 16. **JACK PEART**
Debut: v Ton Pentre, 1 September 1910
Farewell: v Reading, 2 March 1912

When John George Peart bagged a brace of goals on his debut in the Southern League Division Two, it signalled the start of the most prolific scoring run any player has achieved in a Stoke shirt.

Born in South Shields on 3 October 1888, Peart began his career in 1904 with three seasons with South Shields Adelaide before signing for Sheffield United in 1907, for whose reserves he scored nearly 50 goals in his first season. He already had mustered eight in 28 appearances in the first team when his career was disrupted by a broken leg sustained against Everton. He spent over a year recuperating.

Peart signed for Stoke with the country gripped by the infamous Dr Crippen murder case. Crippen, who had murdered his wife in London, fled aboard the transatlantic liner *Montrose*. The newspapers chronicled the use of telegraph for the first time to catch a criminal. Amid daily updates the *Sentinel* found space to remark upon Peart's arrival: 'his imposing presence should upset many a defence in the coming months.'

Although only 5ft 10in, the burly 12st north-easterner appears larger than his team-mates in contemporary team photos. Known as 'the nightmare of goalkeepers', Peart used his frame to good effect, hurling it at custodians and defenders alike. Clearly playing at a level below his talents, Peart entertained the crowd with back heels and flicks to colleagues. 'One noticeable aspect of his play was his heading to the wings. He rarely failed to place the ball well, his only fault is a tendency to hold onto the ball too long.' His showmanship occasionally saw Peart take on the opposition defence en masse, which often resulted in possession being lost.

Peart bagged 34 goals during his first 22 devastating appearances for Stoke. The fearsome forward line, with Peart at centre-forward between the unrelated Billy and Alf Smith, rattled in 97 of Stoke's 167 goals that season. Peart's most sustained spell of scoring brought him fourteen goals in seven games. He had also scored thirteen goals in seven games earlier in the season. In both cases he scored in seven consecutive matches, setting a peace-time club record which he held until John Ritchie scored in nine consecutive games in October and November 1963.

With Peart rampant, Stoke appeared invincible, but his scoring exploits were halted by a broken leg in December 1910, against Crewe, which kept him out until the opening day of the following season. His continued misfortune earned him the tag of 'the most injured man in football!'

Back from injury, Peart was selected for the Southern League in inter-league matches on three occasions. On the last, at Stoke on 9 October 1911, Peart lined up against a Football League side featuring Pennington of West Brom, Hampton of Villa, Roberts of Manchester United and Iremonger of Notts County.

But Peart never really recovered and in March 1912 the Stoke directors accepted a £600 offer from Newcastle for his services. The Toon sought a striker capable of scoring the goals to propel them to the Football League championship. On Tyneside Peart failed to live up to his fearsome reputation and Newcastle finished only third. He lost his place and in February 1913 was sold to Notts County.

During World War I, Peart guested for Leeds City and Rochdale. Indeed, his Leeds side beat Stoke in the Lancashire Wartime League title decider over two legs. With the return of peace he did the rounds as player, then manager, with Birmingham, Derby, Ebbw Vale, Norwich, Rochdale, Bradford City and Fulham. He stayed at Craven Cottage for thirteen years and guided Fulham to their first FA Cup semi-final in 1936, which they lost 1-2 to his former club Sheffield United.

Peart's Fulham won promotion as Second Division champions in 1948-49, but Peart had died early that season, on 3 September 1948, at his home in Paddington.

Magic Moment: *Against Brentford in November 1911 Peart scored the winner. He 'seized the opportunity the scattered Brentford defence afforded him and, racing through at an enormous speed, found the net with a fast, rising shot.'*

Worst Nightmare: *Peart netted the clinching second goal as Leeds City defeated Stoke 2-0 in the Wartime League North championship decider first leg.*

STOKE RECORD	Appearances	Goals
Southern League	44	38
FA Cup	3	3

No 17. **BILLY TEMPEST**
Debut: v Portsmouth, 7 December 1912
Farewell: v Bradford City, 26 April 1924

In the summer following Jack Peart's departure, Stoke signed 19-year-old William Tempest, a flying left-winger, who soon established himself as the fans' favourite.

Born in Stoke-on-Trent on 8 January 1893, Tempest was a pro at Huddersfield in their first season of League football, 1910-11, although he failed to make the first team. He signed for Stoke from local amateurs Trentham in 1912 but played only rarely for eighteen months. He was kept out by sporting icon Harold Hampton who won an Olympic Soccer Gold medal at the 1908 games in London.

Tempest's sunken eyes, dolefully staring out from beneath bushy eyebrows and high forehead, gave him a Chaplinesque look. His figure was not unlike Charlie's either at only 5ft 4in tall and a slender 10st. Tempest could not have been less clown-like on the field, however, using his lack of inches to advantage as he sped past lumbering full-backs. Known as a positive wing-player, with 'twinkling feet', the *Sentinel* declared 'when he has a back on toast –

metaphorically speaking of course – his runs along the touchline are a delight. His is a graceful progression, an immobile body being borne along on a very mobile pair of legs. He used to have a knack of taking the ball very cleverly across the toes of the man who tackled him and another characteristic of his play is to double back and centre with his right.' Though criticised for shooting from impossible angles when a cross was called for, his main centre-forward, Arty Watkin, thrived on Tempest's centres. The young Billy also gelled with his inside-left partner, the experienced Billy Herbert.

After starring in Stoke's 1914-15 Southern League Division Two title winning season, Tempest answered his country's call to arms. Being stationed in Luton, he was unavailable to Stoke and guested for various Southern clubs. Tempest scored 42 of his regimental team's 63 goals during the 1917-18 season as a centre-forward and was clearly a class act amongst such company.

With Stoke back in the League in 1919-20, Tempest, having turned professional, resumed on the left flank. After the War the club had erected a wooden shed to serve as dressing rooms on the corner between the open Boothen End and the main Boothen Stand. Its focal point was a wooden stove around which the players would gather to warm their hands after training. Chatterbox Tempest enjoyed nothing more than dissecting the previous week's game whilst supping Bovril, the preferred drink of sportsmen of the day. That same stove was in use well into the 1950s, although the hut itself eventually took on a more permanent appearance.

At the end of 1923-24 Tempest refused to accept the reduced terms on offer and was made available for transfer. After a final appearance in the North Staffordshire Infirmary Cup against Port Vale, which Stoke won 1-0, he signed for Stoke's Burslem rivals. The clubs argued over his price and the Football League stepped in to arbitrate a £1,000 fee. Thereafter Tempest took pleasure in wreaking revenge on his former employers; indeed, Port Vale won all four League encounters in which Tempest played.

Tempest made 45 appearances for Vale before being forced to retire through injury in May 1926.

Magic Moment: *In the most keenly awaited Potteries derby of the decade, the FA Cup first round clash of January 1922, Tempest shot Stoke 2-0 ahead with an 'acute-angled drive during a melée in the home goalmouth'. Stoke won 4-2.*

Worst Nightmare: *With the club sliding towards ignominious relegation in 1922-23, Tempest added to Stoke's appalling run of injuries when in early March he broke his collarbone in the first minute against Tottenham, ending his season.*

STOKE RECORD	Appearances	Goals
Football League	163	22
FA Cup	15	2
Southern League	38	6
World War I	24	1

No 18. ARTY WATKIN

Debut: v Llanelly, 18 October 1913
Final Farewell: v Chesterfield, 5 February 1927

Arthur Edward Watkin had the potential to be one of Stoke's greatest goalscorers. Unfortunately, he suffered from an Achilles heel that stopped him from achieving his full potential – nerves.

Born in Burslem in 1896, Watkin joined Stoke in 1913 from Hanley Swifts in the Southern League. The 18-year-old was a regular during 1914-15 and his 24 goals in twenty games propelled Stoke to the Southern League Division Two title. His pace and skill often took him round the final defender or goalkeeper to slot home. He completed a hat-trick of such goals against Coventry in January 1915 in the Southern League, one of five hat-tricks that season.

Watkin linked well with left-winger Billy Tempest throughout his career, but never more than in this first season. Despite being a lithe 5ft 10in, heading was not Watkin's forté. Tempest realised this and began to whip over crosses for Watkin to glance in at the near post, or slip the ball inside early to exploit his pace.

Eight points clear at the turn of the year, Stoke clinched the championship, and promotion back to Division One, on 5 April with a 10-0 home thrashing of Ebbw Vale. In a frenzied burst of scoring, Watkin notched a five-minute hat-trick and finished with another five-goal haul. Stoke were elected back into the Football League on 19 July, but the club's decision to pull out of the Southern League incurred a £500 fine, although it was made academic by the suspension of organised football for the duration of the conflict.

Such was the expectancy that accompanied Watkin's return to Stoke after the war that it was a tall order living up to his billing, and it proved impossible. A long-standing knee injury was treated by trainer William Peart, enabling him to return late in 1919-20, replacing the ailing Bob Whittingham. Watkin scored on his first appearance in the Football League, the decisive second goal in Stoke's 3-0 victory over Port Vale in the first ever League Potteries derby – which only served to intensify the burden of expectation.

Stoke spent heavily before the start of the 1920-21 season, signing centre-forward Jimmy McColl from Celtic. Secretary-manager Shallcross moved Watkin to inside-left, where he developed into a tricky linkman between McColl and another new signing, Harry

Crossthwaite. Watkin still retained an eye for goal, top scoring with sixteen. Of his hat-trick early on against Nottingham Forest the *Sentinel*'s Nimrod wrote: 'Stoke followers have waited patiently for a glimpse of the real Watkin and they were rewarded by an exhibition which very few forwards can surpass. How the mind went back to season 1914-15, when he struck terror to the hearts of opposing defenders!' But dreams of promotion faded. Watkin's goals tailed off and Stoke barely avoided the drop on goal-average from Coventry.

By this time Watkin had acquired a reputation for either scoring two or three a game or being anonymous. His patchy form saw him described as 'an enigma', an early example of that now well-worn cliché. 'The fact of the matter,' wrote the *Sentinel* 'is that Watkin is the victim of a nervous temperament and it is only when the physical joy of the game obsesses him that he is seen in his best form. A goal from his foot has a magical effect and if it should be done early in the game he is just as likely to get a crop'. Given that these symptoms surfaced after the war, it is possible that Watkin's Army experiences lay behind them. In post-war team photos he slumps uncomfortably forward, while his team-mates pose rigidly.

Watkin also had problems combining football with his job as a Pottery department manager at Grimwade's. Once Stoke were relegated his employers pressured him to quit top class football. He duly spent 1923-24 with Congleton Town. New Stoke manager Tom Mather, who arrived from Southend United in October 1923, identified Stoke's need for goals and persuaded Watkin to return on an occasional basis. It made little difference. Stoke barely avoided relegation, scoring just 34 goals, the second lowest in the Football League. Arty worked as a full-time manager at the Pottery until his retirement and he died in Stoke-on-Trent on 27 August 1972.

Magic Moment: *On the last day of 1921-22, Watkin, playing with a splintered ankle, scored twice as Stoke beat bottom-placed Bristol City, to clinch promotion ahead of Barnsley on goal-average.*

Worst Nightmare: *A factor in his return to Stoke from Congleton may have been a post-match beating Watkin received from opponents frustrated at their inability to get to grips with him on the pitch. The incident convinced Congleton that they needed separate changing rooms for both teams!*

STOKE RECORD	Appearances	Goals
Football League	137	36
FA Cup	14	6
Southern League	27	25
World War I	9	5

No 19. **BOB WHITTINGHAM**
Debut: v Preston, 4 September 1915
Farewell: v Clapton Orient, 20 March 1920

Arty Watkin's replacement during Stoke's prolific wartime period
was not actually a Stoke player at all.

Born in Goldenhill, Staffordshire in February 1889, Bob
Whittingham initially slipped through Stoke's fingers. He signed as
a 16-year-old from Goldenhill Villa in 1905, but, with little prospect
of first-team football at Stoke, Crewe snapped him up after only one
season. From there he moved to Blackpool in May 1908, where he
scored 27 League goals in 53 starts. In January 1909, First Division
strugglers Bradford City secured his services. His impact was
extraordinary: his eleven goals in nine games almost single-hand-
edly ensured that the Bantams survived, sending Machester City
down on goal-average.

An all-action, stocky centre-forward with a pronounced Roman
nose, Whittingham stood only 5ft 8in but weighed a colossal 12st,
which he used to good effect in crashing into opposing custodians.
One goalkeeper was moved to comment that he would 'rather face
his Satanic Majesty than Whittingham'.

In April 1910 Whittingham joined Chelsea for £1,300 and, by
the outbreak of war had totalled 70 goals in 119 League games.
During hostilities he returned to North Staffordshire – although
Chelsea retained his registration – to guest for Stoke. From the out-
set he was prolific, scoring at more than a goal a game. His 'clever
scheming play' set up numerous chances for his fellow forwards,
while his speciality was a cross-field pass to find one of the wingers,
Billy Tempest or Henry Hargreaves. But he was at his best as a finisher. Whittingham packed a powerful shot when he got his considerable weight behind the ball. An expert at shooting on the run,
it was estimated, perhaps conservatively, that over half of his goals
came from outside the penalty area.

Playing mainly at inside-right, Whittingham top scored in every
season bar 1917-18 and twice scored four times in a game. The second of these, in November 1917, was a 16-0 win over Blackburn.
Rovers arrived two men short and Stoke lent them a goalkeeper
and a full-back.

At the start of 1916-17 Whittingham caused a rumpus by agree-
ing to guest for Port Vale. Stoke complained to the FA and he was
suspended pending a decision. It took until Christmas for the FA to
pronounce that Whittingham, although a guest, *was* a Stoke player. After a slanging match in the *Sentinel* between club chairmen
Reynish of Stoke and Huntbach of Vale, Whittingham turned out
for Stoke again and immediately revived their fortunes, scoring

four minutes into his first appearance in a 7-0 hammering of Bolton in January. Whittingham rattled in nineteen goals in thirteen games, including one as Stoke beat Vale 2-1 in Hanley.

Whittingham finally earned overdue England honours, playing in a Victory international at the Victoria Ground against Wales on 18 October 1919, scoring the opener in a 2-0 victory. Although officially listed on the team-sheet as a Chelsea player, he played alongside Stoke's Charlie Parker and faced skipper Joey Jones.

After the war, conflict erupted again between Stoke and Vale over which of them had signed Whittingham from Chelsea. The player washed his hands of it all and returned to Stamford Bridge, but Chelsea were determined to sell. Eventually, in October 1919, Stoke stumped up £500, simultaneously signing centre-forward David Brown for £1,200 from Dundee.

The outlay wasn't successful. Although Stoke won five games on the trot, Whittingham was nowhere near as prolific in League football. He incurred an ankle injury against Rotherham, compounded by a further knock against Fulham. Secretary-manager Shallcross sent him to Cleveley's Hotel in Blackpool to 'recuperate his health'.

Whilst in Blackpool, Whittingham contracted a 'severe cold', which may actually have been the beginnings of tuberculosis. His health collapsed and he was forced to retire from the game in April 1920 within a month of leaving Stoke. In recognition of his efforts the club awarded him a benefit in October 1920, when a team of League stars including Bolton's Joe Smith, McNeil of Chelsea, and Peers and Harrison of Wolves opposed a combined Stoke and Vale eleven. Whittingham later recovered sufficiently to play non-league football for Stoke United, as well as occasionally for Wrexham reserves. In 1925 he rejoined his local club Goldenhill Wanderers.

On 9 June 1926 Whittingham, who never truly shook off his illness, collapsed and died at his home at the age of just 37.

Magic Moment: *On his debut against Preston, Whittingham clinched a 3-1 victory with a 'fine individual effort. He ran from just over the halfway line and beat man after man before drawing the right-back Rodway and scoring'.*

Worst Nightmare: *On April Fool's Day 1916, Whittingham and team-mate George Smart were sent off for 'apparently causing the referee some displeasure by their remarks'. Whittingham said later that their comments were not directed at the ref but at each other.*

STOKE RECORD	Appearances	Goals
Football League	18	8
World War I	84	86

No 20. **TOM BRITTLETON**
Debut: v Nottingham Forest, 28 August 1920
Farewell: v Blackpool, 11 April 1925

When secretary-manager Arthur Shallcross signed James Thomas Brittleton in the summer of 1920, Stoke acquired the services of one of the superstars of the age.

Born in Winsford, Cheshire on 23 April 1879, Brittleton made a late entry into the Football League with Stockport in December 1902, aged 23. He played 45 games as an inside-forward and top scored in 1903-04 with seven goals. His reputation as a 'clever' player brought him to the attention of top clubs and in January 1905 he signed for Sheffield Wednesday, champions in the preceding two seasons. His fee was £300 – setting a new club record for Wednesday. Towards the end of the 1905-06 season Brittleton converted to right-half, where his ferocious tackling soon earned him a reputation as the best No 4 in England, and hence the world.

He starred in the Owls' 2-1 FA Cup final win over Everton in 1907 and totalled a then club record 372 appearances for the Owls. Following a belated first appearance at the age of 33 in February 1912, Brittleton won a total of five England caps, which might have been even greater had it not been for the onset of war.

In May 1920, Wednesday mistakenly decided that 41-year-old Brittleton's career was coming to a close. He joined Stoke and was immediately made captain. As an instantly recognisable footballing hero, he replaced the recently departed Whittingham as the focus of press interest in the team. How would this ageing superstar fair in the hurly-burly of Division Two?

Brittleton's disposition was of 'the type to compel respect'. Playing in a new position, right-back, he led Stoke's young team by example, playing neat passing football when possible, and crunching into tackles where necessary. Despite his advanced years, the 5ft 10in Brittleton was lean and fit. He sported a moustache, more in the fashion of the Edwardian era in which he had begun his career than the Roaring Twenties in which he finished it. Indeed, a photograph of the proud FA Cup winner of 1907 shows little sign of the interceding thirteen years.

After Stoke sold fans' favourite, Charlie Parker, to Sunderland, Brittleton switched to half-back. The *Sentinel* was moved to comment: 'A player of his experience ought to know what to do with the ball when he gets it and method is usually seen in his play. Like many of the great half backs he very readily assumes the role of a sixth forward when the opportunity presents itself.'

Stoke's somewhat surprising promotion in 1922-23 was in no small part due to Brittleton's appointment as player-coach to assist

Arthur Shallcross. Brittleton actively believed in developing young talent and in this had the full support of the fans, particularly when Stoke put together a run of fifteen games without defeat from 27 December. Despite the heavy ball of those times, he also added to Stoke's armoury with an exceptionally long throw, which set up chances for Jimmy Broad, a superb header of the ball.

Early in the game on Good Friday at Blackpool, Brittleton ruptured a groin overstretching. He didn't play again until the following season, so missing the nerve-wracking run in as Stoke battled with Barnsley for promotion. In an open letter to supporters who, the week before the vital decider against Bristol City, questioned the board's desire for promotion, Stoke Chairman Reynish wrote: 'to lose our talented utility player T Brittleton, which lost us the game at Blackpool, and has greatly disrupted the side since, has been a hefty blow.' Stoke lost three and drew two of the next six games, but clinched promotion in the final match, thereby earning Brittleton a Division Two runners-up medal fourteen years after his FA Cup winners medal.

Following the resignation of short-lived manager John 'Jock' Rutherford, during the ensuing traumatic relegation season from Division One, Brittleton refused the offer of the hot-seat. He opted instead to regain his place in the team at the start of 1923-24. That season, at the age of 45, he played an astonishing 35 games, most of which were in the new position of left-back. Brittleton earned a benefit from the club after finally retiring, at the end of the following, 1924-25 season. He played his last match a fortnight before his 46th birthday, becoming in the process the oldest player to appear for Stoke – a record unsurpassed until the extraordinary longevity of Stanley Matthews.

Brittleton returned to Cheshire and played non-league football for Winsford United for a further season. His son, John Brittleton, played for Aston Villa and Chester. Tom died on 22 February 1955.

Magic Moment: *Brittleton scored the last-minute winner against West Ham – his first goal for Stoke – in a melée following a corner. The* Sentinel *noted: 'congratulations were showered upon him, the display being remarkable as an indication of his popularity.'*

Worst Nightmare: *Brittleton fractured his wrist v Chelsea in September 1924, which effectively ended his career at the age of 45.*

STOKE RECORD	Appearances	Goals
Football League	114	5
FA Cup	9	–

Harry Davies, the second man to pass 100 goals for Stoke

Billy Spencer, full-back throughout the halcyon 1930s

Joe Mawson, dangerous on his day, but notoriously inconsistent

The team of the late-1930s relax on the golf course, led by Bob McGrory (third left)

Chapter Three

~ *The Yo-Yo Years* ~

No 21. **BOB McGRORY**
Debut: v Barnsley, 2 May 1921
Farewell: v Huddersfield, 4 May 1935

Robert McGrory set numerous records during his distinguished playing career and, as manager, took Stoke to within one game of clinching a first ever League championship.

Born at Bishopton, near Glasgow on 17 October 1894, McGrory apprenticed as a joiner in a Clydesdale shipyard. In 1914 he signed for Dumbarton, despite only previously playing Boys Brigade football. He missed only two games in five seasons for the 'Sons'. After starring for the Home Scots against the Anglo Scots in March 1920, he attracted interest from Burnley, for whom he signed in August for £3,500. McGrory failed to become a regular at Turf Moor and joined Stoke on 23 April 1921, spotted by director Arthur Sherwin.

McGrory's arrival did not go to plan, as the 1948 *The Official History of Stoke City FC* recalled: 'The smoke of the Potteries was to blame. On the evening he [McGrory] arrived the pottery ovens were laying down one of the special "barrages". It was enough to daunt any newcomer. It was touch-and-go whether he took the first train back to Burnley. But he decided to stay a Scottish "wee while".' Indeed, Sherwin revealed that McGrory taciturnly said: 'I don't like the looks of this place'. It took him 31 years to leave!

Solidly built at 6ft tall and 12st 4lbs, McGrory was frequently described as 'stout-hearted' and played with 'an absence of flurry no matter what the situation'. He acquired a reputation as a fearless man-marker. And if 'dour' described McGrory's approach on the field, it aptly summed up the bluff Scot's personality off it.

After an early 1-7 aberration at Hull, Stoke, with McGrory a major influence at the back, lost only two of the next 27 games, with the defence conceding just six goals in thirteen matches. The run allowed Stoke to claim the 1921-22 runners-up spot.

McGrory proved to be one of the few Stoke players to cope with the step up to the First Division, even though, amidst a horrendous run of injuries, Stoke succumbed to relegation. He skippered the side during Milne's absences through injury, taking the job full-time in the summer of 1925. McGrory did not relinquish the armband for a further ten years, making him Stoke's longest serving captain. His full-back partners in that time included Tom Howe, Tom Brittleton, Arthur Beachill and Billy Spencer.

Although Stoke were relegated in 1926, McGrory's drive helped Stoke win the Third Division (North) title a year later. Famously consistent, he played 101 consecutive League games from March 1926 to September 1928 to become only the second Stoke player to reach that milestone.

From 1930, the 39-year-old McGrory began to coach Stoke's reserves, for whom he also regularly turned out from the summer of 1932. His replacement in the first team was long-time full-back partner Spencer, who deputised during the 1932-33 promotion season. Tom Mather's well-known sentimental streak meant that McGrory played in the 5-2 promotion clincher over Lincoln in late April, but to all intents it seemed as if his playing career was over.

By Christmas 1933, with McGrory-less Stoke floundering in the top flight, Mather recalled the 'old War-horse' to add his experience to a porous defence – and it worked. McGrory's return allowed Spencer to return to left-back and the defence was at once more balanced. During the second half of the season Stoke picked up more points than any other teams bar champions Arsenal and runners-up Huddersfield, finishing a respectable twelfth.

Promoted to assistant manager in 1934, McGrory appeared in all 42 League matches in 1934-35 at the age of 41, making him the oldest First Division player to complete a full season and earning him the nickname of 'Granpa'. His career then took a dramatic turn. He took up the offer from Stoke's board, now chaired by his champion Arthur Sherwin, to succeed Mather, who quit to manage Newcastle on 3 June 1935. McGrory's club record of 511 appearances for Stoke would stand for 24 years.

McGrory's managerial style was abrasive, contrasting starkly with that of his predecessor. Aware of the financial problems that had dogged the club in the past, McGrory implemented a policy of blooding local talent. He replaced himself with Charlie Scrimshaw, while Frankie Soo displaced Sellars in midfield and the emerging Freddie Steele edged out Sale. It was brave management and it paid off. The young imports gelled and Stoke developed into one of the most attractive teams of the 1930s. In 1935-36 they finished fourth with a new club record points total (47) in the top flight.

McGrory liked to relax on the golf course, having one of the lowest handicaps amongst professional footballers. He once proposed a national golf competition for football clubs, reckoning that in golf if not soccer Stoke could end up as champions. Club social outings revolved around eighteen holes and a prolonged stay at the nineteenth! Indeed, several former players recall McGrory's insistence on thrusting a hip-flask at each man, whether they drank or not, as they left the dressing room five minutes before kick-off, expecting each to take a 'snifter' of whisky before the game.

Cash was generated by dint of having a glamour player called Matthews on the right wing. Much in demand due to his international fame, Stoke played a number of friendlies against European sides during the '30s. In April 1934 Stoke played the Swallows club of Amsterdam in that city's Olympic Stadium, in what was the first game in Europe to be played under floodlights. The first foreign team to play at Stoke, Austria FC were defeated 1-0. Other visitors included Racing Club de Paris and Slavia Prague.

Tensions soon surfaced between the stern Scot and his star player. Under Mather, McGrory's room-mate, and best friend, Bobby Liddle had lost his place to Matthews. McGrory took every opportunity to avenge this injustice. In 1937 Matthews raised hackles by demanding the maximum signing-on fee, £650, which was £150 more than the sum offered. Frank Mountford, then an apprentice at Stoke, recalls: 'I remember walking down the corridor one day and Bob and Stan were in the office and they weren't half going at it hammer and tongs. There was never any love lost between them.' A stand off ensued with Matthews effectively on strike over the summer. He lost his wages, so that, when the board finally caved in, he was actually no better off. Matthews felt a point had been made, but feelings festered below the surface.

On Tuesday, 8 February 1938 the *Sentinel* screamed '*Stanley Matthews Bombshell for Stoke City*'. Matthews and McGrory were at loggerheads again. Clubs swooped like vultures for the chance to sign Matthews, among them Everton, Bolton and Derby. Former manager Mather, now of Newcastle, tabled an offer of £4,000 plus inside-forward JR Richardson. The package was equivalent to a £10,000 fee, which had only previously been surpassed twice.

McGrory cannily issued a statement to the effect that he had always sought to work harmoniously with Matthews, who received the same treatment as other players. Although this seemed fair, it was actually the root of the problem. Matthews knew his worth and wanted some return to reflect this. None was forthcoming.

The board dithered, but a mass protest of fans on 14 February, orchestrated by seven prominent local industrialists, prompted action. Supporter Reg Austin vividly recalls the sense of despair that pervaded 3,000 fans crammed into the King's Hall. 'Uproar. People were shouting, "Stan must not go" and "Matthews must stay". Oh aye, there was quite a to-do about it!' The following day the board, now chaired by Alderman Harry Booth, debated for two hours before denying Matthews' transfer request. Matthews forged an uneasy truce, but McGrory had proved his point – the most important person at Stoke was not Matthews but the manager.

Although renowned for his ability to spot local talent, McGrory proved less shrewd in the transfer market. After selling Charlie

Scrimshaw to Middlesbrough for £3,000, and Arthur Turner to Birmingham, he invested £1,300 in Rochdale's Arthur Griffiths and £5,000 in prize asset Patsy Gallacher from Sunderland. Both players picked up long-term injuries within a month and made just seven appearances between them.

World War II deprived Stoke's youthful talent of the best years of their careers. The players dispersed. Many were called up, although some of the more high-profile stars became physical training instructors and were exempted from active service. Stan Matthews, for example, was billeted in Blackpool and made more appearances for the Seasiders as a guest than he did for Stoke. McGrory's feud with the star resurfaced in 1946 when, with Stoke challenging for the championship, he picked George Mountford rather than Matthews. Blackpool manager Joe Smith cheekily enquired whether Stan was available and Stoke, believing that Matthews' career was winding down, took the £11,500 on offer.

When Matthews departed, Stoke were still battling Liverpool, Wolves and Manchester United for the title. The atrocious winter postponed matches well into June 1947. City went into their final game at Sheffield United knowing that, with their rivals having completed their programme, a win would secure the title. But City agonisingly lost 1-2, finishing fourth. This remains the nearest Stoke have ever come to winning the League. Perhaps the lack of Matthews' big-match temperament had cost the club the title.

Having come so close, McGrory ambitiously bid for England internationals Tommy Lawton and Wilf Mannion. He was rebuffed, but succeeded in signing Irish international Jimmy McAlinden from Portsmouth for £7,000 and Celtic's Tom Kiernan for £8,500, breaking Stoke's transfer record twice in a month. The newcomers were expected to signal another title tilt, but injuries ruled out six first-teamers by mid-September and Stoke finished fifteenth. Six players then handed in transfer requests. McAlinden and Kiernan were sold, with Stoke losing over £1,000 on each deal.

When veteran goalscorer Freddie Steele left in 1949, McGrory had trouble replacing him. The club record £9,000 lavished on Celtic's Les Johnston proved wasted as the player lacked an eye for goal. The following year Neil Franklin and George Mountford went AWOL in Colombia, leaving behind an ageing, one-paced team. Two consecutive relegation struggles left McGrory with his hands bound by a board who no longer trusted his judgment. In May 1952, he resigned in a typical huff, citing 'lack of support by the directors'.

In 1953 Merthyr Tydfil, an ambitious non-league side seeking election to the Football League, tempted McGrory out of retirement, although ill-health meant his tenure lasted just one season. McGrory died in his native Glasgow on 23 May 1954.

Magic Moment: *On 4 December 1948, McGrory selected a Stoke team to face Blackpool which cost nothing. All had come through the apprentice ranks at the club, costing only their £10-signing on fees.*

Worst Nightmare: *Stoke's 0-2 FA Cup fifth-round defeat by Third Division Hull in 1949 was down to McGrory's lack of managerial nous. That week he took the squad training on the Blackpool sands. On their return on Friday evening, the players, desperate for female company, dashed home. Not surprisingly they turned up for the game looking, and playing, as if they had been up half the night!*

STOKE RECORD	Appearances	Goals
Football League	479	–
FA Cup	32	–

No 22. **JIMMY BROAD**
Debut: v West Ham, 27 August 1921
Farewell: v Bradford City, 26 April 1924

Untypical of his generation, James Broad was a nomadic footballer. Born in Stalybridge on 10 November 1891, Jimmy came from footballing stock. His father, also James, was secretary/treasurer/trainer of Manchester City in the early twentieth century. Eldest brother William played for Manchester City and Millwall, while middle brother Tommy, a right winger, for Oldham and Manchester City.

Although he began as a goalkeeper in non-league circles with St Mark's, West Gorton, Jimmy Broad soon turned goalscorer, playing up front for Stalybridge Celtic, Manchester City and Oldham before guesting for Blackburn and Greenock Morton during World War I. Fresh from combat duty with the Royal Scots Guards, the kilted Broad arrived at Millwall Athletic unannounced and requested a trial. He impressed in an 8-1 reserve team win over Tottenham, scoring all eight Millwall goals, and proceeded to bag 37 goals in 48 Southern League games for the Lions.

Broad was brought to Stoke by the ambitious new chairman, John Slater, a former reserve-team player and now wealthy owner of both Berryhill and New Halden Collieries. Slater personally paid for the transfers of both Jimmy and his brother Tommy. Jimmy – who arrived at Stoke after spending the summer coaching Las Palmas in the Canary Islands – cost £2,500 in June 1921.

The brothers were barely distinguishable, although Tommy stood half an inch taller. Both used their physique to bulldoze past opponents, rather than relying on sheer skill. Compactly built at 5ft 8in and 11st 12lbs, Jimmy appeared short for a centre-forward. The tactics of the day, however, focused on inter-passing and running, qualities which he possessed in abundance. Despite his sullen and glowering expression, Jimmy led the social aspects of the club and soon became first-team tiddlywinks champion.

Jimmy's scoring renown travelled with him to Stoke and he did not disappoint, bagging four goals in his first four games. He was supremely confident and difficult to dislodge when in possession. He would rush 'like the wind' and used his pace to good effect, loving nothing more than to confront a goalkeeper one-on-one.

Broad's other favourite trick was to slip the ball past an opponent on one side and dash round him on the other. His rapacious shooting meant that he took over the mantle of free-kick expert and penalty taker from Bob Whittingham. Broad blasted home the winner from a free-kick in an early season Potteries derby, which was enough in itself to endear him to Stoke's fans.

His major weakness was failing to time his forward sprints, so that he often found himself offside. The *Sentinel* griped: 'a referee becomes so accustomed to blowing him offside that he will take it for granted that he is offside sometimes when he may not be.' With typical striker's tunnel vision, Broad would also 'shoot on sight even if a colleague were better placed'. On occasions, however, his willingness to try his luck from range paid off. Against Wolves in April 1922 from out on the left wing he found the net from 35 yards.

Jimmy bravely challenged for every cross, clattering goalkeepers, regularly getting hurt himself, but often emerging with another goal to his name. He thrived on Tommy's centres, driven in at pace, which allowed him glancing contact to direct the ball goalwards. His four-goal haul against Crystal Palace on 3 December 1921 was the first by any Stoke player in a Football League game. He rounded off the feat with a flashing header from a cross from his brother. The duo were now, to Stoke fans at least, known collectively as 'the famous Broad brothers'.

In 1921-22, with the Potters gunning for promotion, Broad contrived to miss a penalty in the closing minutes of the vital last game against Bristol City, shooting straight at keeper Vallis. No matter, Stoke won 3-0 and clinched promotion.

The top flight proved a hurdle too high, but Broad remained a class act in a struggling team, bagging 23 League goals, including two hat-tricks. His treble at home to Preston completed a burst of ten goals in five games. Arguably it was the cartilage injury he sustained in challenging Villa goalkeeper Spiers to a through ball in mid-February – which put him out for the season – that condemned Stoke to the Second Division.

On the previous Monday, at Millwall, Broad had played in the England v the South trial game, alongside Charlie Buchan of Sunderland. He did not do himself justice and was well policed by

Southampton's Titmuss. He was never selected again, although whether this was because of injury is not a matter of record.

That Easter, John 'Jock' Rutherford, former Newcastle, Arsenal and England right-winger, was appointed as Stoke's first manager, taking from the board responsibility for team selection. His time in charge was troubled. Stoke lost disastrously to Nottingham Forest and were relegated after a 0-0 draw with champions Liverpool. Rutherford, along with secretary Shallcross, quit soon afterwards.

Broad returned for the start of the following season but the team lacked confidence and he only scored fourteen goals, enough to finish again as top scorer. At the end of the campaign the Stoke board, constrained by financial difficulties, hit upon a plan to persuade certain players to depart – insisting that, if they stayed, they accept reduced terms on account of the club's demotion. Never a shrinking violet, Broad and co-conspirator 'big' Joe Kasher, led a delegation of eight unwanted team-mates. They surreptitiously arrived at the ground by taxi, broke into the club offices and ransacked them, causing 'great damage'. Not surprisingly Broad soon departed, acrimoniously, followed by Kasher, who signed for Accrington Stanley.

Tommy also left, signing in July 1924 for Southampton for £250. Jimmy guested for Sittingbourne before joining Everton for £1,400. For the start of the new Spanish season he accepted a position as a coach at Barcelona. He lasted a year in Spain, returning to sign for New Brighton, then Watford. After just three appearances at Vicarage Road, Broad was involved in an ugly training ground incident for which he was unceremoniously sacked.

Broad moved on to Caernarvon Town, Taunton and Fleetwood. He scored for every team he played for, and mingled goalscoring duties with coaching. He coached (Deportivo) La Coruna of Spain, as well as in Turkey, Switzerland, Italy, South Africa, Norway and Holland. In 1931, at the age of 40 the nomadic Broad finally settled down, taking up the post of groundsman at Chelmsford City. He remained in Essex until his death on 22 August 1963.

Magic Moment: *A flying header into the top corner against Leeds in October 1921, sliding along the turf afterwards in celebration.*

Worst Nightmare: *Failing to turn out for the final match of 1922-23. Broad had carried moth-ball pellets in his trouser pockets whilst out golfing. The brown paper bag holding them disintegrated in a downpour and the pellets dissolved into ammonia, causing blisters!*

STOKE RECORD	Appearances	Goals
Football League	108	62
FA Cup	8	5

No 23. **BOB DIXON**
Debut: v Blackburn, 22 January 1923
Farewell: v Grimsby, 22 September 1928

Admiring Jimmy Broad's hat-trick at Blackburn in 1923 was an 18-year-old keeper making his Stoke debut, Robert Hewitson Dixon.

Born in Easington, Whitehaven on 30 August 1904, Dixon was spotted by Stoke's north-eastern scouting network playing for West Stanley in County Durham – the club from which Stoke had signed another keeper, Dick Herron, in 1911.

Dixon's debut was not without blemish, despite the 5-1 score-line. 'The newly acquired goalkeeper gave an uneven display,' wrote the *Sentinel*, 'at times he impressed but at others he made slips which obviously showed him not to be completely at his ease.'

That nervy display convinced the directors that Dixon needed a spell in the reserves. He was replaced by Gilbert Brookes and played just one more game that season. Early in 1923-24 Dixon won his place back, this time from a new signing, Scottish international Kenny Campbell, who had been brought in to try to avert relegation. Dixon owed his reinstatement to the arrival on 12 October 1923 of new secretary-manager Tom Mather, the former Bolton and Southend manager, under whom Dixon became first choice.

Dixon modelled himself on Liverpool and England keeper Sam Hardy, a custodian widely revered as the most consistent ever seen. Despite his slight 5ft 9in frame, a spell that season in which Dixon conceded just three goals in three months banished memories of his awkward debut. Rarely seen without his trademark wide-brimmed cloth cap, Dixon's courage during the relegation battle of 1924-25 dug his errant defenders out of the mire on numerous occasions. He thought nothing of throwing himself at oncoming forwards' feet, often leading to personal injury.

Following errors in Stoke's 0-3 home defeat by Wolves in March 1925, Dixon was dropped. By the time he regained his place the following season, Stoke were deep in the relegation mire. The jittery defence struggled to cope with the new offside law, implemented that summer. Dixon twice conceded seven goals, against Oldham and Derby. Unsurprisingly, City were relegated from Division Two.

1926-27 proved the ideal pick-me-up. Dixon missed just one game as Stoke raced to the Division Three (North) title. Marshalled by Bob McGrory, the defence conceded just 40 goals, the best in all four divisions, and Dixon kept eighteen clean sheets, a club record that was not broken until Roger Jones kept twenty during Stoke's 1978-79 promotion season. In 1927-28 Dixon also missed just one game, as City cemented their place back in Division Two, finishing a creditable fifth, with only five clubs conceding fewer goals.

Perhaps unfortunately, early in the 1928-29 season Dixon lost his place to Dick Williams. During the championship season, Williams had on one occasion filled in for Dixon, saving a penalty in a 3-1 win at Lincoln. Having served the club for six years, Dixon earned a benefit which raised £500.

Dixon, 25, signed for West Ham in March 1929. He understudied England keeper Ted Hufton before taking over during 1931-32. West Ham's relegation that season saw him replaced by George Watson. Dixon left the Hammers that summer and returned to the Potteries to keep the Prince of Wales pub in Sandford Hill, as well as running a caravan park in Lytham St Anne's. His wife, Daisy Bates, played football and cricket for England Ladies.

Magic Moment: *With Stoke 2-0 up, Dixon saved a David Jack penalty, low to his right, in the 4-2 FA Cup 4th round win over First Division Bolton Wanderers in January 1928.*

Worst Nightmare: *On his debut at Blackburn, with Stoke 5-0 ahead, Dixon dropped a simple cross and Rovers' McKay tapped in.*

STOKE RECORD	Appearances	Goals
Football League	189	–
FA Cup	11	–

No 24. **HARRY SELLARS**
Debut: v Clapton Orient, 26 January 1924
Farewell: v Arsenal, 28 September 1935

A second youngster to be thrown into the fray as Stoke laboured in the mid-1920s was Harold Sellars. Born on 9 April 1902, at Beamish, County Durham, Sellars joined his local club, Darlington, as an amateur in 1919. The Quakers found him a job cleaning train carriage windows – an improvement on his previous employment as a miner. Remarkably, Sellars turned down a trial at Manchester United in favour of turning professional with Northern League club Leadgate Park, considering the munificent sum of his £2 per week wage more secure than the possibility of joining United.

Sellars arrived in Stoke by a circuitous route. Though recommended by a scout, Huddersfield manager Herbert Chapman decided against signing the 21-year-old on account of the glut of inside-forwards already at his disposal. The same scout caught the ear of a Stoke director, assuring him of Sellars' potential. Mather watched Sellars once and that was enough, securing his signature on 15 December 1923, thereby forging a long link between Stoke and the Sellars clan, which Harry's son John continued until 1960.

Tall, at 5ft 11in, Sellars' chirpy temperament earned popularity with his team-mates. He had a fighter's looks, with ears protruding at nearly 90 degrees from his head, while the scars of pro football left him with a broken nose, set at a jaunty angle to his workman's face. Sellars began his Stoke career at inside-left, replacing the injured Johnny Eyres, and scored on his debut in a 2-0 win at Clapton Orient. In and out for the next three seasons, Sellars converted to right-half – despite being naturally left-footed – during Stoke's relegation season of 1925-26.

Despite the drop, manager Mather's genial persona endeared him to supporters. The chirpy Lancastrian, never seen without his trademark bowler hat, wing collar and tie, stood only 5ft 5in and was towered over by almost the entire team. Oft seen patrolling the environs of the Victoria Ground with his cane, supervising training, his strength lay in identifying players' best positions. Sellars, now an automatic choice, established himself at right-half while Mather gambled on rearranging the half-back line. In came Cecil Eastwood from Preston North End and centre-half Tim Williamson from Third Lanark, and Mather was rewarded with the Third Division (North) championship.

Stoke's heavy spending, although rewarded with promotion, left the club with a £13,000 bank overdraft that forced the offloading of high-profile players. Sellars reverted to left-half, Len Armitage taking over the right side of midfield. Sellars had found his best position, from where his distribution was married to his tackling and ability to cover. He also developed a prodigious long throw with the old heavy ball which caused mayhem in many opposing defences.

In 1927-28 Stoke reached the FA Cup quarter-finals for the first time since 1899, but lost 1-4 at Herbert Chapman's Arsenal. The club consolidated in the League and Sellars was one of six players to play 40 or more League games. The reserves also won the Central League for the first time. But possibly the most important development came when the board, showing foresight, acquired the freehold of the Victoria Ground from the Church, giving the club sole ownership of their ground for the first time.

Sellars played a solid role in the 1932-33 promotion season, in which the half-back line of Sellars, Bill Robertson and Arthur Turner proved instrumental, and which was largely unchanged throughout the halcyon years of the mid 1930s. But early in 1935-36 Sellars injured his knee. He made way for the mercurial talents of Frank Soo and transferred to Port Vale in July 1937.

Sellars became the landlord of the Crewe Arms in Middleport before being tempted out of retirement to assist Congleton to win the Cheshire Senior Cup. During World War II he worked at the Potteries Motorised Transport bus depot in Stoke.

After the War, Sellars returned to Stoke, becoming McGrory's assistant manager and first-team coach. In this role he oversaw the development of his son, John. Harry later managed Dundalk in Ireland. He died in Stoke-on-Trent on 30 December 1978.

Magic Moment: *Off the pitch, gap-toothed Harry wore dentures. When Stoke stayed in a hotel at Middlesbrough, Sellars woke with a start, switched on the light, and saw a rat dart across the floor with his dentures in its teeth. Two seasons later, when Stoke stayed in the same hotel, Harry recovered his false teeth. The hotel had been restored and workmen had found them behind the skirting board.*

Worst Nightmare: *A leg injury that restricted Sellars' movement, allowed Reading's Bacon to score six of his team's seven goals in a 7-3 win on Good Friday 1931.*

STOKE RECORD	Appearances	Goals
Football League	369	18
FA Cup	25	1

No 25. **HARRY DAVIES**
Debut: v West Brom, 23 September 1922
Final Farewell: v Arsenal, 26 March 1937

Another youth to debut in Stoke's Division One season of 1922-23 was inside-forward Harold Augustus Davies. Born in Gainsborough on 29 January 1904, Davies was the son of Hull and Wolves full-back Harry. The family moved to Staffordshire after Harry senior retired. Stoke spotted Harry junior playing for Bamfords Athletic near Uttoxeter and he signed for Stoke in 1922. He was quickly thrust into a team struggling to stay afloat in the top division.

He announced his arrival in his second game by scoring the only goal to earn victory at West Brom, but the team's fortunes plummeted and, after a run of sixteen games, Davies lost his place at inside-right to the more experienced Fred Groves, who lacked his skill but possessed compensatory brawn, useful in the battle to avoid the drop. Davies flitted in and out of the side, not fully establishing himself until midway through the following season, by which time Stoke were back in Division Two.

Standing 5ft 8in tall, Davies was of unique appearance – short-cropped blond hair and ears which stuck out almost at right-angles to his head. He skipped about the field on skinny legs which bore his lean 11st frame. He became the schemer in the side which challenged for an immediate return to Division One, finishing as second top scorer with nine goals behind Jimmy Broad. A poor run of only two wins in the final thirteen games, including five matches without a goal, put paid to Stoke's hopes and marked the beginning of two seasons of struggle.

In 1924-25, Davies, although first choice, was handicapped by niggling injuries and with an ever-changing side full of young, inexperienced players Stoke finished one place above the drop zone. A year later, with Stockport, they were relegated to Division Three (North). Despite playing in a losing team, Harry drew plaudits for his own displays. His speciality was receiving possession in a tight situation and opening out the play with either an accurate pass or a turn and a quick pair of heels.

Down in Division Three, Stoke clicked, running away with the championship. Injury restricted Davies to 28 appearances, but he still managed fifteen goals, including two in the 5-1 demolition of fourth-placed Halifax on the last day as City celebrated promotion. Back in Division Two, Davies notched eleven goals. Mather had switched him to inside-left, exploiting his two-footed play, and allowing the naturally right-footed Bussey to play at inside-right.

Davies' skills were rewarded by two games for the Staffordshire FA against the Football League, while 1929 saw his selection for an England trial at Bramall Lane. The outcome was inclusion in an FA touring party to South Africa, where he played twice in victories against the home nation's full side.

He was 25 and in his prime when Huddersfield Town, seeking to recapture their Herbert Chapman-inspired dominance of the mid-1920s, signed Davies as a replacement for England international Clem Stephenson, who had stepped up to the manager's chair. Davies left for Leeds Road in April 1929 for 'a big fee'. His sale sparked protests against the Stoke board, accused of lacking ambition by selling star players such as Cecil Eastwood and now Davies.

In his first season with the Terriers, Davies top scored with nine and played centre-forward in the 1930 FA Cup final. Huddersfield lost 0-2 to Herbert Chapman's new club, Arsenal. Following that setback Davies fell out of favour. As he was only 28, in February 1932 Mather brought him back to the Victoria Ground. Davies was central to Mather's plans to propel Stoke back into the First Division. It was a popular decision and his return to inside-left coincided with a run of three defeats in fifteen games which saw Stoke come close to pipping Leeds for the second promotion place.

Davies added craft, guile and passing ability which provided chances for the likes of Joe Mawson and, latterly, Tommy Sale. Davies switched to inside-right midway through 1932-33, thereby becoming an early influence in the career of Stanley Matthews, whose dazzling wing play was already causing quite a stir. Due to the semi-retirement of Bob McGrory, Davies was honoured with the captain's armband, although the bluff Scot was back in the side in time to lift the Second Division championship trophy.

Back in Division One, Davies was a fixture in the side at inside-left with Bobby Liddle at inside-right. These were the glory days of Stoke with a forward line featuring Matthews and Johnson on the wings and Sale at centre-forward. Davies, now reaching the veteran stage, acted as schemer rather than goalscorer, although he became only the second player to pass one hundred goals for Stoke, after Charlie Wilson, when netting in Stoke's 1-2 defeat at Barnsley in the FA Cup in February 1936.

Latterly Davies' career was affected by a series of injuries which restricted his effectiveness and he lost his place to youthful new signing Jim Westland from Aberdeen. After a year in the reserves, in February 1938 Davies moved to Port Vale in exchange for centre-forward Tom Ward.

Davies retired from playing during World War II and won a Military Medal while serving with the Royal Army Service Corps. He kept the Priory Hotel in Abbey Hulton after the War and then the Plume of Feathers at Barlaston. Aside from his talents as a footballer, Davies was also a fine billiards player. He died on 23 April 1975.

Magic Moment: *On 13 December 1934, Davies scored the only goal of the game to defeat Stoke's first ever foreign visitors, Austria FC.*

Worst Nightmare: *At 1-1 against Everton in November 1933, Davies slipped whilst shooting and scooped the ball over the bar from close in with keeper Ted Sagar stranded. Stoke lost 1-2.*

STOKE RECORD	Appearances	Goals
Football League	390	102
FA Cup	22	9

No 26. **WALTER BUSSEY**
Debut: v Swansea Town, 26 December 1925
Farewell: v Manchester United, 27 August 1932

As Stoke were relegated to Division Three (North), Walter 'Wattie' Bussey emerged as a promising young inside-right.

Born at Eckington in South Yorkshire, 6 December 1904, Bussey was a typical South Yorkshireman – hard working and proud. Whilst employed as a collier, Bussey played amateur football for a number of teams in the Doncaster area, including Aughton Celtic and Dinnington Main. He signed for Stoke in March 1924, initially retaining his amateur status, so that he could also turn out for

Denaby United. Bussey declined full professional terms with the Potters until November 1925. In that season of turmoil, as Stoke plummeted towards the Third Division, Bussey was one of 34 players employed, but made only four appearances.

Compactly built at 5ft 7in and 10st, Bussey earned his reputation by overcoming his lack of height with his 'cleverness and skill. He can control the bouncing ball and make a perfect pass when on the run'. He began to break into the first team during the waltz to the championship the following season, making fifteen appearances and scoring eight goals, among them four in successive games in December 1926. His appearances remained sporadic until mid-season 1927-28, when Harry Davies converted to inside-left to partner Bobby Archibald. There is evidence to suggest that Davies' conversion was a result of manager Tom Mather's glowing admiration for Bussey.

Despite being primarily a playmaker from the inside-right position, Bussey still weighed in with his share of goals – averaging one every four games or so, with a best season's tally of eleven in 1928-29. He formed a devilish partnership with centre-forward Charlie Wilson, being responsible for a large proportion of his goals. On his day, Bussey could spray the ball around majestically, prompting through the centre and down the wings.

Though Bussey's star was in the ascendant he was notoriously inconsistent, being described in the *Topical Times Who's Who of Football Stars of 1933* as having 'spasms of form and scoring'. Mather gave him every opportunity to prove his worth, but the emergence of Harry Ware and Tommy Sale left Bussey in the cold and his last appearance for Stoke came in the opening game of the 1932-33 promotion season. Having been a late starter, his career was never going to be a long one and in October 1933 Bussey, desiring first-team football, moved to Blackpool for £1,500.

Further moves took Bussey to Swansea and Exeter before he retired from football at the outbreak of war. He put on nearly two stones in weight in his latter seasons and his effectiveness suffered. Bussey settled in the West Country, earning a living as a painter and decorator. He died in Exeter in January 1982.

Magic Moment: *The third goal of Bussey's hat-trick in Stoke's 4-0 hammering of Port Vale in September 1931 was 'a sharp, low drive from a partial clearance by Vale keeper Slater'.*

Worst Nightmare: *An example of Bussey's inconsistency occurred in his first Potteries derby. He lashed a dipping drive onto the bar. Following up, with keeper Matthews floored, he dithered too long and was denied the winning goal by Vale full-back Jack Maddock.*

STOKE RECORD	Appearances	Goals
Football League	185	36
FA Cup	12	4

No 27. **BILLY SPENCER**
Debut: v Portsmouth, 13 February 1926
Farewell: v Wolves, 7 December 1936

Born in Nelson, Lancashire on 15 May 1904, William Spencer worked in a mill in his home town. Spencer was one of two fine full-backs – the other being Charlie Scrimshaw, who joined Stoke from Hebden Bridge in the West Riding League – signing for the Potters as an amateur in December 1924. He continued to work at the mill, before turning pro four months later. Spencer established himself in the team at the same time as Charlie Wilson and Josh Williams arrived in a blaze of glory from Huddersfield.

At 5ft 8in and 10st 2lbs, Spencer's thin appearance was made all the frailer by sloping shoulders. He had a distinctive shock of blond hair, closely cropped at the side and brylcreemed to a tuft on top. During a game that tuft swayed wildly as Spencer beavered around the field. Cool under pressure, his play revolved around good positional sense and an ability to read the game.

Spencer replaced long-serving Alec Milne midway through 1925-26, slotting into a defence which had suffered horrendous reverses. Relegation was unavoidable, but the germ of Stoke's resurgence can be seen in the side which finished the season with a 1-1 draw with Southampton. Four of the regular forwards who would win promotion played that day, while Spencer's burgeoning full-back partnership with McGrory was the foundation on which Stoke built the championship challenge of 1926-27.

Spencer's positional play complemented the tough-tackling McGrory. Indeed, many consider that partnership to be Stoke's finest full-back pairing. Despite their on-field empathy, rumours abounded that Spencer and the Stoke captain did not get on. Spencer allowed himself to be easily riled by McGrory's gruffness, although he always publicly denied this. Irrespective of any off-pitch frostiness, the partnership lasted for ten seasons, although coincidentally both Spencer and McGrory missed the majority of the 1931-32 season through injury. Spencer did not survive the first game of that season, suffering a horrendous broken leg against Chesterfield which kept him out for over a year.

Ever present in 1927-28, Spencer also missed just one game in 1934-35. He won a Second Division champions medal in 1932-33, during which he confirmed his versatility by switching to cover McGrory's absence at right-back, with Arthur Beachill coming in on the left. Back in the First Division the switch looked vulnerable and Stoke took some fearful hammerings – Derby 0-4 at home, West Brom 1-5 and Middlesbrough 1-6 away. Spencer returned to the left once the immutable McGrory was restored around Christmas 1933. The veteran pairing, now totalling 68 years between them, helped Stoke remain in the First Division.

Not long after assuming managerial control, McGrory moved Spencer back to right-back to allow the emerging Scrimshaw to take over at left-back. Perhaps this was further evidence of the vindictive side of McGrory's nature. Spencer's form suffered, allowing McGrory to ease him out of the side, with Ira Winstanley taking over midway through 1935-36. After spending nearly two seasons in Stoke's reserves, Spencer moved to Crewe for £750 in June 1938. He retired from football, without a first-class goal, in 1940.

For recreation Spencer played bowls and was a leading light in the North Staffordshire League. He also loved tending his garden – and was expert in growing chrysanthemums. Stationed in Carlisle during World War II, he played in the same RASC regimental team as his long-term team-mate Harry Davies. At the end of the War he ran the Compasses public house in Newcastle before returning home to coach Nelson in the Lancashire Combination. He quit due to the onset of deafness, caused by his wartime service.

Magic Moment: *When Stoke beat Bolton 4-2 in the 1928 FA Cup 4th round, Spencer tackled David Jack and released Harry Davies for the killer third goal. Spencer was cheered for his 'unhesitant and effective interception'.*

Worst Nightmare: *Spencer was blamed for Stoke's shock 0-1 FA Cup 3rd Round loss to Doncaster in January 1930. He slipped while clearing, leaving keeper Norman Lewis facing two Rovers forwards.*

Stoke Record	Appearances	Goals
Football League	338	–
FA Cup	16	–

No 28. **BOBBY ARCHIBALD**
Debut: v Stockport, 29 August 1925
Farewell: v Bury, 13 February 1932

Tom Mather's big summer signing in 1925 was Robert F Archibald, a genial Scot bought to fill the left-wing slot that had seen six occupants in the year since the farewell of long-serving Billy Tempest.

Born in Coatbridge, Glasgow on 6 November 1894, Archibald, like fellow Scot Bob McGrory, played Boys' Brigade football before signing professionally for Third Lanark. He hawked his services around Scotland, playing for Albion Rovers, Aberdeen, Rangers and Raith Rovers before returning to Third Lanark. During and just after World War I, Archibald played football for his regiment in France, Denmark, Italy and South America.

In August 1925, aged 29, Archibald's wanderlust brought him to Stoke City. The 'City' was added after the Potteries' six towns were granted City status. Archibald's arrival followed that of centre-forward Dick Johnson for £1,200 from Liverpool, and inside-left Joe Clennell from Cardiff. The opening of 1925-26 boded well, with Archibald scoring on his debut, in a 3-0 win over Stockport, but the season soon turned sour as the team failed to blend. Injuries played their part. Johnson lasted just two games before succumbing and his replacement, Jack Paterson, managed just six games. Mather failed in his attempts to forge a motley crew of experienced players, and Stoke slumped unceremoniously towards relegation.

Tiny at 5ft 4in and weighing just 10st, Archibald's physique earned him the nickname 'Steve' due to his resemblance to top jockey Steve Donoghue. His stylish play on the wing marked him out as one of the few class acts in the team relegated from Division Two for the first time in Stoke's history. He was renowned for his consistency. Starting with his debut, he played 58 consecutive matches before pulling a muscle against Rochdale in November 1927 and missed just six games in the ensuing six seasons.

Archibald's hobby was tinkering with wireless sets for hours on end and in 1927 he eventually produced one for the home dressing room at the Victoria Ground. A gadget fiend, Archibald was also one of the few Stoke players to run his own car.

During Stoke's push for the Third Division (North) title, Archibald's neat footwork set up numerous chances for Charlie Wilson to notch 25 goals. Partnered for several seasons by Harry Davies – after his conversion to inside-left in 1927-28 – Archibald continued to score classy goals, averaging five or six a season. After six years service, he was awarded a benefit game, choosing the final home match of 1930-31 against West Brom. The second highest League crowd of the season, 26,064, paid £1,540 6s 2d, not only to bid farewell to Archibald, but also to see the highly successful Albion side. Their 1-0 victory now clinched promotion to add to their FA Cup final triumph of the previous Saturday.

Archibald played for a further season at the Victoria Ground, during which he lost his place to Harry Taylor. Once Mather had secured the signature of Bristol City's Joe Johnson in April, he released the 38-year-old Archibald to Barnsley.

Archibald played just seven games for the Tykes. After spending several seasons in the reserves he retired through injury in May

1937 at the age of 42. He returned to his native Glasgow where he became an insurance agent and scouted from time to time for Bradford City manager Fred Westgarth. Bobby's younger brother John, oddly much taller at nearly 6ft, played in goal for Albion Rovers, Reading, Chelsea, Newcastle, Grimsby and Darlington. Bobby died circa 1966.

Magic Moment: *On the day after his 37th birthday, Archibald laid on a goal with a whiplash cross for Sale as City beat Bury 3-2.*

Worst Nightmare: *In his second game for Stoke, a Potteries derby at the Old Recreation Ground, Archibald missed three gilt-edged chances, including one open goal, as City slipped to a 0-3 defeat.*

STOKE RECORD	Appearances	Goals
Football League	242	37
FA Cup	14	3

No 29. **CHARLIE WILSON**
Debut: v Clapton Orient, 13 February 1926
Farewell: v Charlton, 28 February 1931

When Charles Wilson arrived at the Victoria Ground late in 1925-26, hailed as the man who would save Stoke from relegation, Tom Mather secured the services of one of the superstars of English Football. Wilson had been leading scorer in Huddersfield's championship sides of 1923-24 and 1924-25 under Herbert Chapman.

Born in Atherstone, Warwickshire on 13 March 1897, Wilson began playing football for Atherstone, before joining Southern League Coventry just before the outbreak of World War I. After being demobbed he played six games for Tottenham during 1918-19, although for unknown reasons he shrouded himself in secrecy. In four of these games he played under the name 'C Williams', being described as a 'colt from the midlands', and in another the pseudonym of 'C Forshaw'. Only in the sixth did he finally take the field as Charlie Wilson.

Wilson eventually notched 47 goals in 72 games for Tottenham. As one of the sharpest shooters around, Herbert Chapman signed him for Huddersfield in 1923, the final piece of his jigsaw.

Wilson plundered 57 goals in 99 games for the Terriers, but never won an international cap. This was surprising, given that the England selectors switched centre-forwards from game to game, with the likes of Vivian Gibbins of Clapton Orient and Thomas Cook of Brighton awarded caps. Despite Huddersfield homing in on a record third consecutive title, Wilson, struggling with injury, was put up for sale. Mather swooped, with right-winger Josh Williams also arriving from Leeds Road, Mather's last desperate fling as Stoke stared into the abyss of relegation to Division Three.

Relegation prompted Stoke chairman John Slater to propose a merger between with Port Vale 'to safeguard local football'. He was shouted down by partisan opposition from supporters of both clubs and resigned, taking his sizeable financial backing with him.

The bustling Wilson was difficult to knock off the ball and loved to shoot on sight at every opportunity. Not surprisingly for a goalscorer of his quality he thrived in the Third Division (North) and racked up 25 goals in 31 League games, including five against Ashington in a 7-0 win. This made him the first Stoke player to score five in a Football League game. He revelled in the crossing of Archibald from the left and Williams from the right and his championship medal completed the first full set of Divisions One, Two and Three to be won by any player.

Back in Division Two, Wilson scored 38 goals (32 in the League and six in the FA Cup), to set a club record for a season which has yet to be broken, although he finished well short of 'Dixie' Dean's record-breaking 60 goals for Everton. Wilson also top scored the following two seasons, becoming the first player to reach 100 goals for Stoke. He collected four more hat-tricks, including a four-goal haul against Bristol City at Ashton Gate in February 1930.

Due to frequent absences through injury, Wilson lost his place in 1930-31 to new-signing Wilf Kirkham who signed from Port Vale in a blaze of publicity. Wilson fought his way back after October, scoring ten goals in sixteen games, but with the squad full of young talent the 34-year-old was released in the summer of 1931. As no League club sought him, he played for Stafford Rangers while keeping the Doxey Hotel, within walking distance of Rangers' ground. He then played for Wrexham, Shrewsbury and Alfreton Town, also moving pubs in Stafford to the Noah's Ark. Wilson died in 1971.

Magic Moment: *In the FA Cup 5th round against Manchester City in February 1928, Wilson sent 'thousands of Stoke fans who had made the journey delirious with delight' when he fired home a spectacular late winner.*

Worst Nightmare: *In the Potteries derby of 13 December 1930, Wilson, clear of the Vale defence, was about to score Stoke's second and clinching goal when referee AE Fogg, blew the final whistle.*

STOKE RECORD	Appearances	Goals
Football League	164	113
FA Cup	11	8

No 30. **JOE MAWSON**
Debut: v Swansea Town, 16 February 1929
Farewell: v Portsmouth, 9 September 1933

Born at Brandon Colliery, County Durham, on 26 October 1905, by the age of 24 Joseph Spence Mawson had already spent several years at the coalface at Washington Colliery when he became one of a number of players discovered by Stoke's north-eastern scouts. Mawson had previously played for Crook Town and Durham City before turning professional with the Colliery team, as had Bobby Liddle, who he joined at Stoke in January 1929.

Raw, but eager, the 5ft 8in, 10st Mawson was presented with his debut, in which he scored, on account of injuries to Charlie Wilson and Joe Shirley. His lack of guile and wayward passing quickly relegated him to the reserves, but his never-say-die-attitude in his occasional first-team appearances kept him in Mather's thoughts. Eventually Wilf Kirkham's horrific leg break on the opening day of 1931-32 handed Mawson his chance in his preferred centre-forward role. His style was to run with the ball and he scored the majority of his goals in a head down thrust through the middle, only looking up to beat the goalkeeper, whom he generally took on to try to walk the ball into the net. Despite averaging more than a goal every two games, Mawson's self-centred approach was not necessarily in the best interests of the team and he wasted numerous opportunities for tap-ins for colleagues by attempting to beat everyone himself. Described by the *Topical Times 1933 Who's Who of Football Stars* as having 'no frills about him', Mawson's effervescent challenging of defenders, however, did him eternal credit and numerous colleagues profited from blocked clearances.

Stoke started 1931-32 poorly but Mawson's reintroduction against Manchester United, along with Tommy Sale and left-half Bill Robertson, with centre-half Arthur Turner debuting just three games later, brought an immediate turnaround. Stoke defeated United 3-0 and won five out of their next six with Mawson bagging six goals, rendering Tom Mather's interest in Huddersfield's experienced centre-forward Joe Robson needless. Mather now found a consistency which enabled him to select the same eleven for fifteen consecutive games – during which Stoke lost just three times – a club record unlikely ever to broken. Mawson's intuitive partnership with Bobby Liddle, his inside-right partner, realised 31 goals between them. Stoke were unbeaten in fourteen matches from 14 November 1931 to 6 February 1932 and boasted the best defensive record in the division, although they finished two points shy of promotion. After Mawson's brace saw off First Division Sunderland in round four of the FA Cup, City became one of only two Second

Division sides to reach round five. The other, Bury, defeated Stoke 3-0 at Gigg Lane.

Stoke clearly had a squad capable of challenging for promotion and the following season Mawson finished top scorer with sixteen goals in 26 games, as Stoke won the Second Division championship. However, his inconsistency still worried Tom Mather and, with the season coming to its climax and Stoke tenuously one point clear at the top, he found himself dropped after a poor performance at Plymouth when he missed three easy chances.

Mather plumped for fresh blood for the final push, signing Jack Palethorpe for £3,000 from Reading in early March. At this crucial stage, Palethorpe crashed home eight goals in ten games, which effectively guaranteed promotion. That rush of goals put paid to Mawson's career at the Victoria Ground.

Mawson moved on to Nottingham Forest, Stockport, Linfield and Crewe before World War II broke out. He died in Stoke-on-Trent on 10 September 1959.

Magic Moment: *Mawson had a hand in all of Stoke's goals as City hammered Preston 4-1 in September 1931. He scored the first himself 'rounding Kerr to make a sharp dash for goal and, although attended by both Kerr and Ward, dashed through in fine style to fire into the corner of the net'.*

Worst Nightmare: *In September 1931 Mawson bungled an easy chance to set the seal on Stoke's biggest ever Potteries derby win. With Stoke 4-0 ahead he handled in front of an open goal before scoring. The goal was disallowed.*

STOKE RECORD	Appearances	Goals
Football League	86	46
FA Cup	7	4

Matthews, Steele, and Johnson help Frank Soo (right) coach his son

Pre-season training in 1935

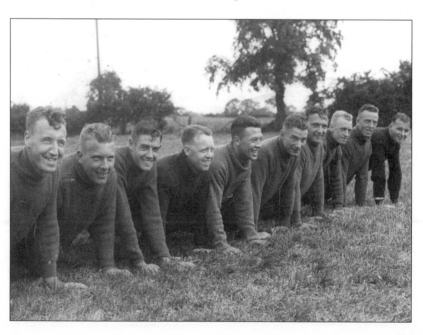

Tutin, Soo, Steele and Johnson complete another training lap

The Division Two Championship-winning team of 1932-33

Stoke's greatest ever half-back line of Arthur Tutin, Arthur Turner, and Frank Soo

`McGrory plots the downfall of Manchester United in the FA Cup (January 1936)

Chapter Four

~ *Back in the Big Time* ~

No 31. **BOBBY LIDDLE**
Debut: v Nottingham Forest, 25 August 1928
Farewell: v Derby, 24 September 1938

Stoke re-established themselves in the First Division with a blend of experienced professionals and homegrown youthful talent, and embarked upon a halcyon era that extended for over fifteen years. Central to this golden age was didactic manager Bob McGrory and, particularly, his mistrust of the elevated status of his star players. Robert Liddle unwittingly became the pivotal figure in the war between McGrory and his brightest star – Stanley Matthews.

Liddle was born in Gateshead on 11 April 1908. At the age of nineteen he was working as a miner at Washington Colliery, playing in the works team, when, like Joe Mawson, he was persuaded by Stoke's scouts to move to the Potteries, signing in January 1928.

A tricky right-winger, 5ft 6in tall and 10st, Liddle's effervescent character, broad smile and Geordie wit endeared him to colleagues and supporters alike. He also impressed on the field, scoring on his debut in a 5-1 win over Nottingham Forest. Despite this good start, his dark, sharply brylcreemed hair was not seen regularly in Stoke's first team until the latter part of the 1929-30 season.

Blessed with lightning pace, Liddle also boasted a sweet right foot and a more than adequate left. This two-footed ability allowed manager Tom Mather to play him anywhere in the forward line, as and when necessary. Liddle became used to playing out of position, spending much of 1929-30 and 1930-31 at inside-left.

The 1933 Topical Times Who's Who of Football Stars describes Liddle as 'a go-ahead wing man, with skill and speed and a shot'. Indeed Liddle's star rose so quickly that in 1930-31, his most prolific season, he finished equal top scorer on fourteen goals with Wilf Kirkham. The emergence of Mawson and Sale as goalscoring forces in 1931-32 gave Liddle, now back on the right wing, targets at which to aim his crosses. He was a major provider of Mawson's twenty goals, bagging eleven himself.

Being primarily a right flank player, Liddle established a good rapport with right back, and captain, Bob McGrory. The pair lodged together and got on well. When the young Stanley Matthews burst on the scene in 1932, wresting the No 7 shirt from Liddle, McGrory took offence. Liddle himself seemed less concerned by Matthews' arrival, since he happily switched to inside-right. After all, he was accustomed to being shuffled about the forward line and was quite glad simply to play.

But when McGrory occupied the managerial chair, Liddle still did not return to a wide position. In truth he was losing his zip and faded from the scene, losing his place to George Antonio.

Ironically, it was the outbreak of war, with Matthews billeted in Blackpool, that extended Liddle's career. It seems, with half a century's grace, as if McGrory was making a point by playing Liddle on the wing, rather than inside. Once hostilities ceased, and those between Matthews and McGrory resumed, Liddle found himself back in the reserves. In 1947, after the departure of Hubert Nuttall, he hung up his boots to become Stoke's trainer.

Typically for the period, Liddle had a simplistic approach to fitness. Ex-Stoke player Don Whiston recalls: 'Pre-season training meant just doing double laps around the ground. It felt like it never ended and we used to plead with him [Liddle] to do something different – it was driving us crazy. Eventually he said "Oh go on then. Run the other way round." His treatment didn't amount to much either. I remember lying on the bench in the dressing room with a leg muscle injury, and Bobby just came in, switched on the heat lamp, pointed it at my leg and lit up a fag!'

After completing 25 years service at Stoke, Liddle left in the summer of 1953, just after his great friend McGrory, to become a newsagent in Nottingham, where he died in April 1972.

Magic Moment: *Against Barnsley in March 1932, Liddle hit a low shot which seemed covered by goalkeeper Capstick. The keeper dropped to his knees, but the ball eluded him and rolled slowly into the back of the net 'sending the crowd wild with excitement'.*

Worst Nightmare: *An eye injury, sustained v Leeds in March 1932, forced Liddle to miss the next match at Bury. The directors used the opportunity to give the young Stanley Matthews his debut.*

STOKE RECORD	Appearances	Goals
Football League	297	61
FA Cup	16	3
World War II	155	32

No 32. TOMMY SALE

Debut: v Bradford City, 25 December 1930
Final Farewell: v Sheffield United, 8 April 1946

Nobody has scored more goals whilst wearing Stoke's red and white than Thomas Sale. Born in Stoke-on-Trent on 30 April 1910, Sale worked in a Pottery from the age of fourteen. In his spare time he played for Stoke's nursery side, Stoke St Peters. On one occasion St Peters, with Tommy in the side, won 44-0.

Sale signed professional forms in May 1930 but had to wait patiently for his chance. Although Sale was originally a half-back, manager Tom Mather found a more natural home for his mountainous 6ft 4in, 12st bulk at inside-left. Initially limited with the ball at his feet, he scored only four goals in twenty games in his first season and started 1931-32 in the reserves. It took Kirkham's broken leg and a 0-3 defeat by Burnley for him to be given a prolonged run in the team. Sale even assumed penalty taking duties from Len Armitage, although his style from the spot owed little to technique – he simply blasted the ball left-footed. His method proved successful and he is believed only to have missed twice.

Although a regular for most of the season, Sale still lacked consistency and the return of Harry Davies from Huddersfield saw him back in the reserves. Eight games into 1933-34, Mather converted Tommy to centre-forward to replace Jack Palethorpe. Sale had found his natural home. Nourished by the crosses of Matthews, Liddle and Johnson, Sale top-scored with fifteen goals, the first of three consecutive seasons as leading scorer.

Sale developed good ball-control for such a big man. Allied to his strong physique, this made him a potent weapon. Don Whiston recalls: 'Tommy had a tremendous shot in his left foot and he was really hard to play against, big, strong and awkward.' His job was simply to score goals. He notched eighteen in the first twenty matches of 1934-35, netting twice in Stoke's 8-1 defeat of Leeds. City topped the League for one week in late October and were in the top five for most of the season, but a bad run from February meant they finished tenth. Sale's form mirrored the team's, although his total of 24 goals in 36 games proved to be his best League tally.

Midway through 1935-36 Joe Johnson's injury forced new Stoke boss Bob McGrory to blood youngster Freddie Steele and, laughably given his immense frame, move Sale to left-wing. Sale still notched fifteen goals, but in the close season Blackburn tempted Stoke with an offer of £6,000 and Sale was happy to go, although his spell there did not prove fruitful.

In March 1938, with Stoke facing a battle to stay in the First Division, McGrory bought Sale back for £3,000 as cover for the injured Steele. Tommy scored five goals in his first three games back, including a vital match-winning hat-trick against Bolton. The climax to the season was tense with nine teams vying to avoid the drop. Four successive defeats was not helped by City's injury jinx. Steele, Arthur Turner, George Antonio and Arthur Tutin all missed the majority of the run in, while Sale injured himself in a 1-2 home defeat by fellow strugglers Leicester. Stoke survived, but in May Sale and young forward Jim Westland both underwent cartilage operations in Liverpool.

Seemingly as good as new the following season, Sale and Steele played in tandem, and, with Matthews and Frank Baker supplying the crosses, the pair bagged 45 goals between them. Sale grabbed two more hat-tricks, the second against Wolves in a 5-3 win. His third goal in this game took his total for Stoke to 100 and by scoring once in each of the next three games Sale reached second place behind Charlie Wilson in Stoke's all-time goalscoring chart.

In his prime and averaging a goal every two games, Sale lost potentially the best part of his career to World War II. Employed at the Michelin Car plant in Stoke, Sale's listed profession meant that he was not called into the forces. Therefore able to run amok on the football field, in six seasons Sale plundered 179 goals. If added to his peacetime total this would make him Stoke's record goalscorer by a considerable distance. In 1941-42 he bagged 55 goals in 37 games. On 3 January 1942 Sale cracked six in an 8-0 League Cup win over Walsall. Twelve hat-tricks in that campaign alone contributed to a total of 22 during the war years.

Of course, these tremendous feats occurred at a time when football was deprived of the regular services of the majority of its stars, called to arms and only able to play occasional games as a guest. Sale's records therefore must not be taken at face value. However, the goals still had to be scored and that he did so with aplomb is in no doubt.

In the summer of 1947, after being released, Sale joined non-league Northwich Victoria. He finished his career with Hednesford Town and continued to coach his Michelin works team. Sale now stands eighth in Stoke's all-time goalscoring chart. He died in Stafford on 10 November 1990.

Magic Moment: *In September 1931, Sale chased a punt upfield, dashed past both Preston full backs, Hough and Lowe, and chipped the ball over the advancing goalkeeper under heavy challenge.*

Worst Nightmare: *Whilst vying for promotion to Division One in 1931-32, Stoke visited Port Vale. Early in the second half Sale missed a glorious chance when put clean through. Stoke lost 0-3 and missed out on promotion by two points.*

STOKE RECORD	Appearances	Goals
Football League	204	98
FA Cup	19	5
World War II	241	179

No 33. **ROY JOHN**
Debut: v Bradford PA, 7 May 1932
Farewell: v Sheffield Wednesday, 5 May 1934

William Ronald John's arrival at Stoke finally ended Tom Mather's search for a goalkeeper, begun after the departure of Bob Dixon.

Born at Briton Ferry, Glamorgan on 29 January 1911, John began as a centre-forward for Briton Ferry Athletic. After failing to make the grade at Swansea, he converted to left-back, although he still could not win a place in the Swans' Second Division side and, despite being only seventeen, was handed a free transfer. After a trial with Manchester United he moved to Walsall in 1928.

John only began to play in goal during an injury crisis in early 1929, but he proved a success, winning his first Welsh cap in a 3-2 win against Ireland in April 1931. John's performances brought him to the attention of North Staffordshire neighbours Stoke, and Mather swooped to acquire his services in April 1932, once City's chance of promotion had gone.

At 5ft 11in and 12st 2lbs, the solidly built John appeared mean and moody, with brooding eyes below thick dark brows. With the season effectively over, the Football League granted Stoke permission to play him and fellow newcomers Joe Buller and Joe Johnson in the meaningless last game of the season. John made a lasting impression after producing a magnificent display culminating in a stupendous last-minute save in a 1-0 win.

His stunning start condemned previous incumbent Norman Lewis to the reserves. John made 40 appearances in Stoke's Division Two championship-winning season in which his form was described in the press as 'brilliant'. Stoke had the best defensive record in all four divisions of the League by some distance. John, who came from the school of goalkeepers which believes that a good game is measured by how few saves need to be made, excelled at organising his defenders with vociferous instructions, although when called upon, he proved his class with agile saves.

John played in all three games in 1932-33 as Wales won the Home International Championship. However, despite remaining first choice throughout City's first season in Division One, he showed signs of fallibility, slipping to let in a 30-yard shot from Warren of Middlesbrough in a 1-6 defeat. He was dropped following a mistake against Manchester City in the next game, when he allowed a Toseland shot to squirm through his hands, although he recovered to stop the ball crossing the line.

Having regained his place after three months in the reserves, John played against Manchester City in the FA Cup quarter-final. The match caught the imagination of the footballing public, enticing the largest club crowd, 84,569, ever to attend an English football match, outside Wembley, to Maine Road. Stoke fans never forgave John for his mistake which cost the club the game. 'It could have been Stoke' brooded the *Sentinel* as Manchester City beat Portsmouth 2-1 at Wembley two months later. The club did make a handsome profit that season, £13,422, causing Chairman Sherwin to remark that 'never in its history has Stoke been in such a good position financially'.

It did not help John, though. Reputations counted for nothing. Although he had become Stoke's first choice because of one brilliant save, that blunder at Maine Road cost John his job. In June 1934 Mather unceremoniously sold him to Preston.

The following September Stanley Matthews made his debut for England against Wales with ex-colleague John lining up against him. Before the game John sought out Matthews and found him sitting nervously in the England dressing room at Ninian Park. Matthews remembers: 'Roy placed one of his large arms round my shoulder and said kindly "Don't be scared, Stan. You won't want to come off at the finish." John suggested we exchange jerseys after the game.' England won 4-0 with Matthews cutting in to hammer home a Westwood pass a minute after half-time.

At the final whistle John handed Matthews his Welsh jersey as promised, twinkling: 'Next time I open my big mouth and waste my sympathy on the likes of you, just shut me up will you.'

John moved on to Sheffield United, Manchester United and Newport, before Swansea bought him back, eleven years after signing him as a forward! He retired in November 1939, but turned out for Blackburn, Bolton, Burnley and Southport during World War II. In 1942 he performed so well for a Welsh XI against an RAF XI, defying his tormentor, Matthews, that he announced his retirement immediately after the game. John became a hotel manager and ran a pub in Swansea before working as a manager for British Steel. He was also a fine wicketkeeper/batsman, and played cricket for Briton Ferry CC. He died in July 1973 in Port Talbot.

Magic Moment: *John's save from Bradford's Geldard made such an impression on Tom Mather it cemented John's place in the side.*

Worst Nightmare: *In the FA Cup quarter-final at Maine Road in March 1934, blinded by the brilliant sunshine, John allowed an Eric Brook corner to fly directly into the net for the only goal.*

STOKE RECORD	Appearances	Goals
Football League	71	–
FA Cup	5	–

No 34. **NORMAN WILKINSON**
Debut: v Wolves, 7 December 1935
Farewell: v Huddersfield, 15 March 1952

Following the departure of Roy John, Stoke's Achilles heel was the lack of a top-class replacement. Norman Lewis, the demure and error-prone custodian of the early 1930s wasn't the answer, but when, straight after becoming manager, Bob McGrory acquired Norman Wilkinson, the gap was filled.

Born in Tantobie, County Durham on 9 June 1910, Wilkinson, a collier, began with junior side Tannfield Lea as a centre-half. He played for West Stanley on the Durham coalfield, where he took up the gloves in an emergency. Wilkinson never looked back. At the age of twenty he signed for Huddersfield, where he played second fiddle to England international Hugh Turner. McGrory, conscious of Stoke's deficiency in goal, plucked Wilkinson from Huddersfield's reserves for just £100 in July 1935, believing the 25-year-old, but still slightly green, keeper could develop into a fine player.

At 5ft 11in and just 11st, Wilkinson had a slightly sullen look, with heavy eyebrows and a balding pate. Not unlike Lewis, he would wander around his penalty area nervously pulling up his woollen gloves. Although he did not inspire confidence to look at, he proved adept at shot-stopping. His weakness was a penchant for dropping crosses under challenge. Admittedly, the pressure which custodians of the day faced from no-nonsense centre-forwards far exceeded that of modern times. Wilkinson liked table tennis, which helped his sharp reactions and reliability in one-on-one situations.

Wilkinson remained first choice until war broke out, with Stoke specifically training him to improve his catching. He missed only one game in 1936-37. Ironically that was the then club record 10-3 win over West Brom, when the young Doug Westland deputised. In truth, the team's strength was its attack rather than its defence. Wilkinson conceded almost two goals per game in 1938-39. The blame, however, must surely lie with the much-disrupted defence in front of him. Six players filled the full-back positions, with only Harry Brigham considered an automatic choice at left-back.

After the declaration of war, Wilkinson returned to the coalface, turning out for Hull, Sheffield Wednesday, Nottingham Forest and Doncaster, closer to the Yorkshire coalfields. On being demobbed, Wilkinson, having suffered hardship underground and also seen action in France, weighed two stones under his normal weight. His poor condition led the Stoke directors to attempt to terminate his employment. Wilkinson protested to the FA. The law stated that all returning servicemen should be entitled to their old job. He won his case, although aged 35 he became fourth choice, behind Dennis

Herod, Manny Foster and Arthur Jepson. The war had affected Wilkinson in other ways too. Herod remembers him as 'aloof. He did not help me with my goalkeeping and he kept himself to himself'. Wilkinson seemed to be drifting into retirement, but Herod's knack of injuring himself handed him a belated chance of glory.

Thrown into the fray in the penultimate fixture of 1948-49, Wilkinson helped Stoke defeat Blackpool, Stan Matthews and all, 3-2. When Herod was injured on Boxing Day the following season, Wilkinson filled his boots, playing 22 games at the age of nearly 40.

Wilkinson moved to Oswestry Town in the summer of 1952, having signed off with a clean sheet on his final Stoke appearance, a goalless draw with Huddersfield. Wilkinson was aged 41 years and 275 days – the fourth oldest player ever to appear for Stoke. He had served Stoke for seventeen years, though for all but three of these he was never sure of his place.

Magic Moment: *In his comeback against Blackpool, ten years and one day after his last First Division game, the 38-year-old Wilkinson flung himself to tip a rocket from Stanley Mortensen over the bar.*

Worst Nightmare: *In September 1936 Wilkinson finger-tipped a piledriver from Leeds' centre-forward Stephenson onto the angle. The ball bounced across, hit the other post, and flew into the net.*

STOKE RECORD	Appearances	Goals
Football League	186	–
FA Cup	12	–
World War II	14	–

No 35. **ARTHUR TURNER**
Debut: v Cardiff, 21 March 1931
Final Farewell: v Chesterfield, 17 May 1941

Commentators who had bemoaned Stoke's lack of a commanding centre-half since the sale of Charlie Parker in 1920, finally got what they wanted with the arrival of Arthur Owen Turner.

Born in Chesterton, Staffordshire on 1 April 1909, Stoke initially overlooked this roughly hewn diamond lying on their doorstep. In the late 1920s Turner played for Wolstanton PSA and Downings Tileries FC in Stoke before signing as an amateur for West Brom. He moved to the Black Country, working as an upholsterer, but he never made the Baggies' first team. Fortuitously for Stoke, Turner lost his job after his factory burnt down and he found work in his native Potteries. He applied for a trial with Stoke, signing amateur forms in November 1930, quickly turning professional.

Turner broke into the first team near the end of his first season, replacing Peter Jackson after a 3-7 hammering at Reading, in one of Mather's occasional culls. Turner performed steadily as Stoke lost just once in their final six games and appeared to be City's first choice centre-half within six months of joining the club.

Mather had other ideas. In August 1931 he pulled off the high-profile signing of Blackpool's Hughie McMahon. Turner, though, was reprieved by McMahon's dithering start, encapsulated by a shocker at Burnley in a 0-3 defeat. Reinstated alongside fellow reserves Mawson, Robertson and Sale, Turner's form enabled the board to offload McMahon to Wrexham in February 1932.

Turner's massive 13st, 5ft 11in frame seemed to dominate the pitch. Not shy of using his physique to advantage, his rugged self put the frighteners on opponents. Future England forward Dennis Wilshaw, then a young Stoke fan, remembers him vividly: 'He was strong, tall and raw-boned. A stopper who tackled well, but had no finesse. Quite the opposite of Franklin who followed him.'

Turner's physical prowess, however, belied a broad, beaming smile which captivated team-mates and bonded the players. A keen cricketer, he also played for Staffs League club Silverdale CC. When Stoke were elevated to Division One in 1932-33 on the back of a mean defence, much was down to Turner, who played in all 42 games, earning himself the tag of 'Mister Consistency'.

Following the retirement of Harry Sellars and the sale of Billy Robertson to Manchester United, a new half-back line emerged with Turner as its pivot. Even today the names Tutin, Turner, and Soo trip off the tongues of North Staffordshire football fans. The trio complemented each other perfectly. Alongside Turner's bulk, the workhorse Tutin beavered, enabling Soo to show the silky skills of a master craftsman.

Following his appointment to the manager's job in the summer of 1935, McGrory bequeathed the captaincy to Turner, who excelled as a motivator. From April 1935 to March 1938 he played 128 consecutive games for Stoke – a then club record, surpassed only once since. In seven years between April 1931 and March 1938 Turner missed just twelve games.

At the start of the 1938-39 campaign Turner began to focus on coaching the reserves, although an injury to Billy Mould meant a recall to the first team. Once Mould recovered, in February 1939 Turner was sold to Birmingham for £6,000 – a large sum for an ageing defender. Typically Turner put the club before personal interest and moved on gracefully, helping to ease Stoke's financial problems in the process. In recognition of his service, Turner received a specially struck Staffs Cup winners medal after Stoke's reserves defeated Kidderminster in the final in May 1939.

Turner captained Birmingham to the Football League South Championship in 1945-46. After losing his place, aged 38, he moved to Southport, before becoming player-manager at Crewe in October 1948. In July 1952 Turner returned to Stoke to become assistant to new manager Frank Taylor.

His remit included the recruitment of young players. One of his finds was Don Ratcliffe. 'I was frightened of him,' remembers Don. 'He caught me smoking in the changing rooms one day. We were about to play a youth cup final and he loomed over me and said "If we lose today come and see me." We went 0-1 behind early on and I was terrified and ran around geeing up the rest of the team. Thank heavens we won 3-1. On the bus on the way back I tried to avoid him by sitting at the back, but he sat down beside me and said "I'd like to offer you terms". Brilliant.'

Stoke's slide towards relegation, caused by the same financial constraints that had forced his own sale fifteen years earlier, meant Turner soon moved on. He took up the reins at another of his former clubs, Birmingham City, whom he guided to the Second Division title and the 1956 FA Cup final – lost 1-3 to Manchester City. Turner also became the first manager of a British team in Europe. Birmingham, representing the City of Birmingham, reached the semi-finals of the first Inter-Cities Fairs Cup.

Replaced in an unsavoury manner by reserve coach Pat Beasley, Turner joined Headington United and began his seminal reign by persuading the board to change the club's name to Oxford United. Turner guided Oxford into the Football League in 1962 and within four years – with a team costing only £14,000 – had won the Third Division title. Turner stepped down in favour of Ron Saunders in February 1969, becoming general manager. In 1972 Oxford decided they could no longer afford such a luxury and dismissed Turner, who took the decision badly. He scouted for Rotherham and Sheffield United in the early 1980s and died in January 1994.

Magic Moment: *Although still only 29, for the 1938 campaign Turner, realising that his place was threatened by young Billy Mould, nobly handed the captaincy to Frank Soo.*

Worst Nightmare: *At home to Arsenal in September 1935, before Stoke's then record crowd of 45,470, Turner fluffed a challenge on Alex James, who laid on a goal for Cliff Bastin. Stoke lost 0-3.*

STOKE RECORD	Appearances	Goals
Football League	290	17
FA Cup	22	–
World War II	12	–

No 36. **ARTHUR TUTIN**
Debut: v Middlesbrough, 4 November 1933
Final Farewell: v Crewe, 5 September 1943

Alongside the robust Turner, Arthur Tutin's tiny figure buzzed around picking up scraps of possession with which to feed his forwards. He was the least feted of Stoke's famous half-back line but wielded considerable influence on City's style of play in the heady years of the mid to late-1930s.

He was born in Coundon, County Durham in 1907 and played for Bishop Auckland, Spennymoor and Crook Town in his native north-east. After trials with both Sheffield clubs and Bradford Park Avenue he joined Aldershot in 1932. By November 1933 Tutin's form persuaded Mather to pay £500 for him.

Having received rave reviews, much was expected of Tutin. He immediately displaced Billy Robertson, but his debut saw Stoke lose 1-6, despite scoring after 30 seconds. After a run of five defeats Mather turned to more experienced players to see Stoke safe.

Described in the club programme as 'lacking inches', Tutin features in a comical early Reuters newsreel. The camera pans along the half-back line, having to tilt down sharply to discover Tutin alongside the hulking Turner. Tutin, however, put his 5ft 4in frame to good use. As a stocky, powerful, tackler his aggression was ideally married to Soo's ball skills. Although Tutin could pass accurately and often supported attacks, he had the speed to rapidly retreat when necessary. His consistency almost matched Turner's, missing only four games from August 1934 to March 1938.

On 27 October 1934, following a 2-0 win over Chelsea, Stoke hit the summit of Division One for the first time in their history. Sadly, a lean spell from the forwards and three five-goal thrashings in four games late in the season exploded expectations. Supporters voted with their feet and only 9,965 turned up for the final home game of the season against Huddersfield.

The following season proved more stable as Bob McGrory took over and inspired City to their best finish in Division One. Stoke's back six were unchanged a club record 30 times from 14 December 1935 to 14 September 1936. A knee injury forced Tutin to miss two matches, but his return launched thirteen more unchanged games for Stoke's defence, now intact for 43 out of 45 fixtures. This defensive stability was the basis for City's success. Ultimately it was the inability to score goals which denied them a serious tilt at the title. They scored just 57, the second lowest total in the division.

The great half-back line earned Stoke the sobriquet 'the Arsenal of the North'. Indeed, Stoke's progress can be measured by being considered rivals to Herbert Chapman's treble title winners of the mid-1930s. The Gunners, now managed by George Allison, visited Stoke on Easter Monday 1937, drawing a record crowd of 51,373. The goalless game would be the only occasion in which more than 50,000 people packed into the ground.

A relatively late starter in top-flight football, the chirpy Tutin's career ended sooner than he would have liked. Replaced by Jock Kirton early in 1938-39, he faded from the scene during World War II when he opted to play for Crewe, rather than Stoke, in order to be nearer his workplace. Tutin retired in 1945.

Magic Moment: *At Birmingham in September 1935, Tutin landed an inch-perfect cross on the head of Tommy Sale whose flick landed perfectly for Matthews to half-volley past Harry Hibbs.*

Worst Nightmare: *Tutin allowed left-winger Ferguson to twice score unmarked, in identical fashion, on the far post as Stoke collapsed 1-6 at Middlesbrough on his debut.*

STOKE RECORD	Appearances	Goals
Football League	183	3
FA Cup	15	–
World War II	9	–

No 37. **FRANK SOO**
Debut: v Middlesbrough, 4 November 1933
Farewell: v Derby, 2 April 1945

The other debutant, alongside Tutin, in the Ayresome Park debacle was the youthful Hong Yi 'Frankie' Soo.

Soo was born at Buston, Liverpool on 8 March 1914 of Chinese immigrant parents. Having been recognised as a brilliant schoolboy player, he drifted into non-league football with Prescot Cables in the Cheshire County League. Soo worked as a clerk before being spotted by an alert scout and he signed for Stoke in January 1933. On making his debut he became the first player of Chinese descent to play in the Football League.

His ball skills garnered numerous admirers once he had debuted for the reserves at inside-left. Many called for his inclusion in the first team, but that would be delayed for nine months. Supporter Peter Haynes recalls: 'When he delivered a ball the pass was perfect and it rarely rose above a couple of inches above the turf.' Built like a natural athlete, the swarthy-looking Soo stood 5ft 7½in and weighed 10st 10lbs.

The winding down of Harry Sellars' long career early in 1935-36 enabled the classic half-back line of Tutin, Turner and Soo to come together. The trio became synonymous with the range of attributes required by a great midfield, previously exemplified by Arsenal's Crayston, Roberts and Copping. Soo's ball-playing magic complemented the grit, determination and industry of Turner and Tutin. Soo received plaudits from around the footballing world, but perhaps the most telling came from Alex James, who described him as 'modern for his time', strong praise indeed from a player to whom the term perfectly applied.

On successive Saturdays in March 1936 City defeated title challengers Derby and Huddersfield 1-0. In early April, Stoke stood third after a 2-1 win over Everton. City eventually finished fourth – a performance the club have yet to better.

Soo became Stoke captain in 1938, in succession to Arthur Turner, and thereupon produced a string of performances which challenged Arsenal's Wilf Copping and Everton's Joe Mercer, England's regular, if workman-like left-halves. In 1937 the *Book of Football Stars* declared: 'Soo is certain of international honours in the near future,' though in fact the selectors persisted with less mercurial talents. It may even have been the case that Soo's international career was hampered by that of his team-mate Stanley Matthews. Picking more than one ball-artist undermined the 'progressive football', based on a strong work ethic that the selectors sought to nurture.

It took the War before Soo finally won overdue England recognition, appearing in seven wartime and one Victory internationals. Posted near Liverpool from the summer of 1941, Soo's availability for Stoke was hampered, so he guested for Southport, Chelsea, Everton and Reading amongst others.

No longer a regular at the Victoria Ground, Soo fell victim to manager McGrory's tongue and his pathological dislike of star players. At the end of the War, amidst a furore almost as great as that which would greet the sale of Matthews, Soo joined Leicester – managed by former Stoke boss Tom Mather – for £4,600.

Soo later played for Luton – his fee £5,000 – and non-league Chelmsford. After retiring in 1950, he briefly coached the Israeli national team. In April he moved to Italy to manage Padova, before his travels took him to Sweden, where in 1955 he won the League title with Djurgaardens. He returned home to manage Scunthorpe in 1959-60, one of a number of short-term managers in that club's embryonic League career. One notable success in his single season at the Old Show Ground was a 3-1 win at the Victoria Ground – then recognised as marking one of the darkest days in Stoke's history. Soo also managed St Albans City before returning to Scandinavia with IFK Stockholm and AB Copenhagen. He returned to his native Merseyside where he died in January 1991.

Magic Moment: *Soo rattled home a short Matthews free-kick off the underside of the bar from 25 yards against Preston. That goal secured Stoke's first home win of the season in mid-October 1938.*

Worst Nightmare: *With Stoke 1-2 down v Everton in November 1933 Soo fired through a ruck, beating keeper Sagar. The ref, seeking a clear view, was hit by the ball, which deflected for a goal-kick.*

STOKE RECORD	Appearances	Goals
Football League	173	5
FA Cup	12	4
World War II	81	17

No 38. Sir STANLEY MATTHEWS
Debut: v Bury, 19 March 1932
Final Farewell: v Fulham, 6 February 1965

Stanley Matthews could not head the ball, rarely tackled and seldom used his left foot – and yet his reputation is cemented as one of the greatest exponents of the art of playing football.

Born on 1 February 1915, Matthews had a spartan upbringing. His father, Jack, known as the 'Fighting Barber of Hanley', ensured his sons grew up fit. 'From the age of ten my father insisted I join my brothers and himself in what I termed the "dawn torture" – morning exercises of deep breathing before an open window, followed by a spell with a chest expander. I am forever grateful.' Matthews inherited a life of abstinence. A teetotal, non-smoking vegetarian, his fitness undoubtedly helped him prolong his career.

The young Stan spent endless hours playing alone in his back garden, although his mother put a stop to this after Stan smashed the ball through the kitchen window, landing the offending leather in the stew she had been preparing.

Matthews grew up a Port Vale fan, hero-worshipping centre-half Bob Connelly, and played in that position for England Schoolboys against Wales in 1929. In one game he scored eight of his school's thirteen goals from defence. For this feat he received a sixpence from his headmaster, Mr W Terry, which led Matthews later to joke that he was the youngest ever professional footballer.

Another teacher, Mr J Slack, prompted Matthews to try outside-right, believing his speed and dribbling skills suited that position. He blossomed, and from the age of fifteen he worked in Stoke's club offices 'licking stamps, answering telephone calls and attending to any jobs the manager Mr Tom Mather might require.'

Aston Villa also took a shine to Matthews, and Stoke officials took up residence in the pub opposite the Matthews household from where any car with a Birmingham registration plate could be spotted. After numerous 'courtesy calls' Mather persuaded Stan to sign professional forms for Stoke.

On his seventeenth birthday Matthews signed on at £5 per week during the season and £3 per week in the summer. He was soon in the team and scored his first goal, the vital second in a 3-1 win at Vale, with 'a narrow angled shot'. Indeed, Matthews was a goalscoring winger in his youth. In Stoke's first season back in the top flight he cracked eleven goals in fifteen games from January to March.

At 5ft 9in Matthews looked like a sleek greyhound. His hair, brylcreemed back, flared behind him as he exploded past his fullback. His strength was his supreme dribbling ability. It was as if the ball was tied to his feet with elastic. Nat Lofthouse believes 'The "Wizard of Dribble" was the perfect nickname for Stanley. That's just what he was – a wizard who bamboozled defences with his ball control.' Tom Finney agrees: 'He could send an entire defence the wrong way with a shimmy, a sudden surge and clever dribbling. He laid on hundreds of goals.'

Broadcaster Stuart Hall recalls Matthews' particular method of destroying his opponent. 'Stanley was the matador caping the bull. The bull, the full-back, knew at 3pm that his reputation would be shattered. I picture the poor fellow trapped like a rabbit in a car's headlights. Matthews is balanced on the balls of his feet, perfect balance, that of the matador, as if suspended on gossamer. The twinny-toed shuffle continues – Matthews with the ball curled on his right foot, feints to the left, inside the back. The back counters with a move to follow, he is off balance. On the instant Matthews, with the outside of his right boot, flicks the ball past the back and is in flight. His body has leaned so far to the left that it defies gravity. The full-back vainly gives chase.'

Former *Observer* journalist Alan Ross wrote:

'The greatest of all time,' meraviglioso Matthews
Stoke City, Blackpool and England.
Expressionless character, weaving as on strings
Conceptual patterns to a private music, heard
Only by him, to whose slowly emerging theme
He rehearses steps, soloist in compulsions of a dream.

Any opponent who played outside the rules would be denied the much-vaunted Matthews handshake at the final whistle and would instead be the recipient of a withering stare. In 1945 Moscow Dynamo defeated an Arsenal side, containing Matthews as a guest, 4-3, although they subjected him to shirt-pulling and obstruction. Dynamo coach Yakushin challenged Matthews' whole approach to the game: 'His individual qualities are high, but we put collective football first and individualism second, so we do not favour his style as we think the teamwork would suffer.'

Eddie Hapgood, the Arsenal and England captain, whom Matthews applauded as his hardest opponent, agreed: 'Sometimes Stan dribbles for the sake of it. He likes to beat his opponent several times to demonstrate his skill.' Matthews counters: 'Not true. I dribble to get on top of the defence, hoping to destroy the confidence of my opponents. Once I have the opposition in two minds the path is clear to make openings for my colleagues.'

Matthews began the 1934-35 season by scoring four in an 8-1 demolition of Leeds. The England selectors could no longer ignore him and he won his first cap against Wales in September 1934, becoming the first Stoke player, since Tommy Holford over 30 years earlier, to don an England shirt.

A personal nightmare against Germany in 1935 – Matthews missing an open goal – resulted in his being dropped until 1937, in which year he notched a left-footed hat-trick in the 5-4 win over Czechoslovakia. At the end of that season Matthews dazzled in England's 6-3 triumph in Berlin, after the team had been instructed to perform the Nazi salute. Matthews made two goals and cut in off the wing to hammer home a cross-shot.

By now Matthews had become a cult figure. His image appeared everywhere, eclipsing that of Alex James of Arsenal, his predecessor as media darling. Although he never smoked, Matthews was pictured in *Charlie Buchan's Football Monthly* extolling the virtues of Craven A cigarettes. He also endorsed his own brand of football boots. This had more basis in truth as Matthews had his famous 'slipper' boots made for him in London by a master cobbler.

The cult was made all the easier to massage by the fact that Matthews played on the wing and thus was always close to the cameras of Pathe or Reuters, whose lenses focused on his magical shimmies, often using slow-motion techniques and music to highlight his graceful destruction of yet another full-back.

Despite his international renown, author Arthur Hopcraft described Matthews the man as 'the opposite of glamorous: brought up among thrift and the ever looming threat of dole and debt ... he came from that England which had no reason to know that the Twenties were Naughty and the Thirties had style.' Matthews acquired a reputation amongst his peers as thrifty, or simply plain mean. The reality was that Matthews had never needed to carry cash on his person. Throughout his life his travel had been laid on and, often, so was food and drink. Therefore on those occasions that he was required to have money, he rarely did. Many were happy to put their hands in their pockets just to say they had bought Stanley

Matthews a drink. Others took umbrage, whingeing about his reluctance to share his not inconsiderable wealth.

As Stan's fame spread, so did the golden image of his club, and Stoke were able to make lucrative trips abroad. For the first time in its history, the club's balance sheet was glowing with health. The canny Matthews recognised this and demanded his share, antagonising manager McGrory and the Stoke board in the process. With Matthews' star at its brightest, uproar followed the announcement that he wished to leave. The board refused his persistent transfer requests, citing his reasons as 'not sufficiently convincing'. For the moment, Matthews remained a Stoke player.

Matthews spent the War in the RAF, stationed near Blackpool, but in October 1946 the spat flared up again. Following a persistent leg muscle strain, Stan refused his manager's request to 'prove his fitness in the reserves'. The Stoke team was rumoured to have sent a deputation to the board requesting that George Mountford keep his place at the expense of Matthews, as they had won five successive games without him. The saga took Hermann Goering's suicide at the Nuremburg war trials off the front pages.

Coincidentally, Matthews' England place was threatened by the emergence of the Preston Plumber, Tom Finney. Manager Walter Winterbottom asserted: 'The only game plan I have is: We've got Matthews on the wing. How do we time our moves to give him service?' Matthews' various problems provoked one newspaper to waggishly declare: 'Matthews or Finney – Is Matthews Finis?'

He clearly was not. Once restored, his form inspired Stoke to challenge for the League title and he shone in England's 10-0 win in Portugal. The selectors had appreciated that Finney's two-footed ability meant they could include both wingers in the same team.

Back at Stoke, the board finally accepted Matthews' transfer demands, negotiating a £11,500 fee with his adopted Blackpool, whose manager, Joe Smith, had been monitoring the situation. The Stoke directors had been pledged to silence, but within a week the news leaked. Uproar ensued, but, on 10 May Matthews departed.

The incentive of the move for Stan was the chance to express his genius unfettered, which Smith promised, as opposed to the control which McGrory insisted upon. Matthews revelled in the change of scenery, winning the first Football Writers' Footballer of the Year award, presented on the eve of the 1948 FA Cup final.

Blackpool lost that final 2-4 to Manchester United and also lost 0-2 to Newcastle in the 1951 final. By now Matthews had won the hearts of British sports fans. Jimmy Armfield, who played behind him at right-back for Blackpool in the late 1950s remembers: 'On his 42nd birthday we played at Charlton and when we ran out the 40,000 crowd sang 'Happy Birthday to You.' When Blackpool reached the FA Cup final in 1953, the whole country (Bolton supporters aside) willed 38-year-old Stan's Blackpool to victory. With twenty minutes left Bolton led 3-1. Matthews got to work, weaving his magic down the right, inspiring the 'comeback of the century' as Blackpool won 4-3. The match is forever known as 'the Matthews Final' and ranks among Wembley's most treasured memories.

But Matthews' career was far from finished. He won his 54th and final cap against Denmark in May 1957, making him the oldest player ever to appear for England, was named the first ever European Footballer of the Year, and was awarded a C.B.E. to boot.

In October 1961, following a season in Blackpool's reserves, he accepted an offer to return to Stoke. Tony Waddington signed the 46-year-old in front of BBC Sportsview's cameras but cannily delayed his debut so that he could make his triumphal return at the Victoria Ground. The prodigal son's homecoming quadrupled the attendance to 36,000, with the extra gate money instantly covering the transfer fee! Stoke won 3-0 and Matthews withstood a physical buffeting to run rings round Huddersfield left-back Ray Wilson, although England's World Cup-winning full-back begs to differ: 'I coughed twice and the referee blew!'

In 1962-63 Stoke won the Second Division Championship, earning Matthews another medal to go with the one he won 30 years earlier. One of his greatest games in a Stoke shirt came at Chelsea in a top-of-the-table clash in May 1963. Matthews humiliated two of the most fearsome hatchet men in the game – Eddie McCreadie and Ron 'Chopper' Harris. Stoke full-back Tony Allen recalls: 'I have never seen anything like it. For the first five minutes they just kicked lumps out of him, but then, for 85 he ran them ragged. There was one moment when he left both of them sitting on their backsides on the pitch while he sprinted off.' With Stoke needing a nerve-settling second goal to clinch the title against Luton later that month, Stan hared across the muddy Victoria Ground pitch, onto Jimmy McIlroy's through-ball, and waltzed round the keeper.

Matthews made his final appearance in the First Division, his 701st League game, five days after his 50th birthday, making him the oldest player to appear in the top division of English soccer and the oldest outfield player in any division. His goal against Swansea in an FA Cup-tie in February 1964 made him the oldest player ever to score for Stoke. In April 1965 the club organised a special farewell – a Stan Matthews XI against a Rest of the World team containing Di Stefano, Puskas and Yashin. An estimated global TV audience of 112 million watched as Matthews walked onto the muddy Victoria Ground pitch for the last time, led by a lone piper. He later claimed he had retired too early and could have gone on for at least another two years! His retirement yielded a knighthood.

After a brief spell managing Port Vale, Matthews coached around the world, primarily in Africa, where he had spent the summer breaks of his playing career. He was feted in South Africa as 'the White Pele' and crowned King of Soccer in Ghana in 1956. He returned to the UK in his later years and became Life President of Stoke. The City council erected a statue in Hanley, although the shy Matthews did not like to walk past it.

On 23 February 2000 Matthews passed away, shortly after his wife, Mila. An estimated 100,000 lined the streets of Stoke-on-Trent to say farewell to their favourite son. Matthews' ashes were buried under the centre spot of the Britannia Stadium in a private ceremony. In the summer of 2001 a lifesize statue was cast which now stands at the entrance of the Britannia Stadium – a reminder to visitors of the genius of Stanley Matthews.

Magic Moment: *Accepting his second Footballer of the Year Award in 1963, Matthews entered to a standing ovation, which turned to laughter at the sight of the false grey beard and walking stick which Stan sported as he shuffled down the aisle to collect his Trophy.*

Worst Nightmare: *Matthews was denied a goalscoring start to his career when in his second game, against Barnsley in March 1932, he headed in Mawson's cross. The ref blew for Mawson being offside.*

STOKE RECORD	Appearances	Goals
Football League	318	54
FA Cup	37	8
World War II	69	8

No 39. **JOE JOHNSON**
Debut: v Bradford PA, 7 May 1932
Farewell: v Birmingham, 28 August 1937

Whilst Stan Matthews was tormenting full-backs on Stoke's right, there was no respite on the left, where England international Joseph Alfred Johnson posed a devastating threat.

Born on 4 April 1911, Johnson began life as a fishmonger in his native Grimsby, playing recreationally for local side Cleethorpes Royal Saints. He quickly attracted the attention of Second Division Bristol City and signed in July 1929. At the end of the desperate 1931-32 season, when Bristol won only three of their first 32 games, the Robins stumbled into serious financial problems and put their entire squad up for sale.

Stoke visited Ashton Gate on 16 April 1932, when the Robins' directors asked Tom Mather to buy whoever he wanted. By chance

Johnson, picked for just five games all season, was now chosen for his sixth. By half-time Mather had singled him out and the 21-year-old's signature was wrapped up for a mere £250 – one of the best bits of business in the club's history.

Johnson joined Stoke with Mather scheming an all-out assault on promotion. He slotted in quickly, replacing Bobby Archibald, and soon left his mark with his penetrating running style, which differed markedly from his wing-partner Matthews. Johnson would set off at full pelt, relying on speed and an agile body swerve to carry him past full-backs. He loved nothing more than to run from deep, using team-mates as decoys as he charged onwards, finally cutting inside to shoot at goal.

Johnson had wide, slightly doleful eyes in a large, bulbous head, which he sought to minimise by having his brown hair cropped tightly against his temples. A slim 5ft 7½in, weighing 10st 8lbs, Johnson's initial burst of speed could carry him past immobile full-backs, although his crossing lacked the consistency of Matthews. Like Matthews, he was severely one-footed, although happily for Johnson his good one was his left. Cultured and accurate, it also packed a rocket shot. Although primarily a provider, Johnson hit fifteen goals as Stoke secured promotion, and year on year his seasonal totals consistently reached double figures.

Johnson's attacking play was integral to that halcyon era in the club's history, although his on-field dynamism hardly reflected his leisure pursuits – reading and fishing. Johnson spent his summer breaks trawler fishing from his native Grimsby, declaring that the River Trent around Stoke was no place to fish!

By November 1936 Johnson verged on an international cap. On the day the eleven lucky names were announced he went to the cinema. It is said that as he emerged into the fading daylight he heard a newsboy calling 'Stoke players in England team!' Johnson bought a paper to discover that he was amongst them.

His first England game, against Ireland at the Victoria Ground, saw Johnson line up alongside club-mate Freddie Steele and the pair manufactured two goals in a 3-1 win. In his next, against Scotland, Matthews completed a trio of Stoke forwards – only the second occasion that three Potters had represented England simultaneously. That international also drew a record 149,547 crowd to Hampden Park. The threesome received a royal homecoming with a civic reception at Stoke Town Hall and an open-topped motorcade through a crowd estimated at 60,000. England, though, despite Johnson laying on the pass for Steele's opening goal, had lost 1-3.

Johnson, unlike Matthews, retained his place. Selected to tour Scandinavia during the summer of 1937, he won three further caps, against Norway, Sweden and Finland, scoring against the last two.

True to England's chaotic selection policy of the time, he was then replaced by Manchester City's Eric Brook.

Johnson's fortunes did not improve on his return to Stoke. He was plagued by an ankle injury sustained in the first game of 1937-38 at Birmingham. McGrory took advantage of an offer from West Brom's manager, Fred Everiss, in November 1937 of £6,500, realising a tidy profit on the player. Johnson's place at Stoke went to the young Frank Baker. Johnson played for the Baggies for nine years, scoring 47 goals in some 145 League games. During the War he guested for Crewe, Leicester and Notts County, and afterwards joined Hereford and Northwich Victoria. Johnson retired in 1950 to open a refreshment area in the vicinity of the Hawthorns, which he ran for many years. He died in West Bromwich on 8 August 1983.

Magic Moment: *Johnson sealed a 3-1 victory over Preston in December 1934, taking the ball past three players, seeing his initial shot come back off the post and then netting past Arthur Holdcroft.*

Worst Nightmare: *Johnson's England career might have begun brilliantly. In the first minute of his first cap, Irish full-back Fulton cleared off the line after Johnson's shot had beaten keeper Breen.*

STOKE RECORD	Appearances	Goals
Football League	184	54
FA Cup	9	3

No 40. **FREDDIE STEELE**
Debut: v Huddersfield, 22 December 1934
Farewell: v Aston Villa, 23 April 1949

A footballing phenomenon from a young age, Frederick Charles Steele built a reputation as one of the finest of all English centre-forwards. Born in Hanley on 6 May 1916, Stoke spotted Steele playing for Downings Tileries, Arthur Turner's old club. Freddie worked in Stoke's offices until he was old enough to sign professional forms at the age of seventeen.

During 1934-35 Steele established himself in Stoke's struggling attack at centre-forward at the expense of Tommy Sale. Steele soon became known as 'Nobby' due to his ability to jump to meet a ball from any angle. His prowess in the air was legendary, although at just 5ft 10in, he spent hours under the direction of trainer Tommy Vallance perfecting leaping from a standing start to head a ball tied to a rope beneath the Boothen Stand.

Steele had a square forehead, with thick black hair brylcreemed back off it. This seeming concrete slab met the ball thunderously with a twitch of the neck muscles to send it flying goalwards. His 12st frame allowed him to fend off the robust challenges which defenders of the day thrust at him. He took the buffeting which came his way and gave it back with interest.

In his prime the bulldozing Steele was 'fast, direct – a lightning deadly shot in each foot'. Stan Matthews believed Steele 'had a change of pace which makes him a great player. He could hit the ball with his right just as well as his left.' In later years Matthews would often voice the opinion that Steele was as good if not better than Lawton, Dean and Lofthouse.

With Matthews and Johnson whipping in the crosses, Steele had plenty of service. In 1936-37 he plundered five hat-tricks, including five goals against West Brom in a 10-3 win which was the first, and to date only, occasion that Stoke have reached double figures in the League. He finished the season with 33 League goals, setting a club record which still stands.

Steele's piracy of the penalty area brought him to the attention of the England selectors, and he won the first of his six caps against Wales in October 1936. Retained against Scotland at Hampden, Steele put England ahead just before half-time with a ripping shot from twenty yards. That game, however, turned on the will of the crowd, whipped up by the pipe band during the interval. Scotland delayed their return to the pitch, allowing the hapless England players to be intimidated by the cacophony. Three second-half goals ensured England's defeat. But as a mark of the assistance he had received from Bob McGrory, Steele gave his commemorative medal to the Stoke manager.

Steele toured Scandinavia with England at the end of the season, scoring seven goals, including a hat-trick against Sweden in a 4-0 win. Astonishingly Steele was never considered again, with Ted Drake or Tommy Lawton regularly preferred as England's No 9.

At club level, Steele continued his rampaging form, bagging five goals in September 1937 as Stoke thrashed Derby 8-1 to sit proudly atop the First Division for only the second time in their history. When war broke out, 23-year-old Steele had scored 90 League goals in 135 games for Stoke.

Steele had picked up a bad knee injury in 1937. Medical science was not as advanced as now, when the likes of Alan Shearer can battle back from two such operations to rebuild a career. Despite examination, Steele's cartilage damage remained undetected for several days, severely hampering his rehabilitation.

Although physically on the mend, Steele confessed to depression and announced his retirement, aged just 24. The shocked directors ensured he received attention from a psychiatrist, who employed 'new-fangled' hypnotism to coax Steele back to his former self. Stan

Matthews recalled in his book *Feet First*: 'The room was darkened. Freddie sat on one side of the fire-place while the specialist, who always wore a dark suit, sat on the other side. All that Steele could see were two piercing eyes staring at him. Day after day the voice behind the piercing eyes assured him he was a great footballer.' Before long Steele would arrive at the ground in the morning, whistling and believing the nets looked larger than ever before. Confidence restored, he scored in four successive games. Matthews observed: 'I wouldn't have believed it was possible had I not seen it for myself.'

Steele lost his best years to Hitler, returning to the Victoria Ground from his East Midlands billet whenever possible to produce numerous fabulous performances. He bagged six goals against Wolves in a 9-3 win on New Year's Day 1944. Four more came in an 8-2 win at West Brom as Steele notched twenty goals in nine games. But his coup de grace came in 1945-46 when he rattled in 43 goals in 44 games, including another five hat-tricks.

Possibly Steele's greatest season was 1946-47 when his goals helped Stoke challenge for the championship. The first goal of his hat-trick against Grimsby on 4 April carried Steele past Charlie Wilson's all-time club record of 121 goals.

Early in 1947-48 Steele suffered a broken leg against Charlton, almost ten years to the day since his earlier injury. It cost him four months out of the game. Without him, Stoke scored just 41 goals that season, against 90 the previous campaign. Unable to fully recover, Steele intended to enter semi-retirement, coaching Stoke's emerging youngsters. But McGrory had no ready-made replacement and Steele soldiered on, scoring nineteen goals in 1948-49.

In the summer of 1949 McGrory released Steele to become player-manager at Mansfield for a fee of £1,000. He finally retired from playing in May 1953 with career totals of 192 goals in 302 games. As manager it did not take long for Steele's superstitious nature to come to the fore. During crucial games, if his team were hanging on for a result, he often left the dug-out before the final whistle, hiding out in the dressing rooms with a towel over his head.

In December 1951 Steele transferred himself to Port Vale, the first case of a player-manager doing so in the Football League. He set about creating the most successful side Vale had then produced, surprisingly for such a prolific striker by using defensive tactics. His back five became known as the 'Iron Curtain' and conceded only 56 League goals in two seasons from 1952.

Although tactically astute, Steele's sides were thought boring to watch. He withdrew both wingers into midfield and played Roy Sproson as an Italian-style sweeper twelve years before Alf Ramsey 'thought up' the idea for England to win the 1966 World Cup.

But the tactics worked. In 1953-54 Vale defeated Cup holders Blackpool 2-0 in the fifth round and became only the second Third Division club to reach the semi-finals. Vale took the lead against West Brom at Villa Park, but eventually lost 1-2. Vale won promotion to Division Two that season with a record low 21 goals conceded, but Steele failed to counter the problems of an ageing squad and resigned in January 1957 with Vale propping up the table.

Steele returned to manage Vale a second time from October 1962, although his second coming was less successful and he quit in February 1965. Uncle to David Steele, the Northants and England cricketer, Freddie died on 23 April 1976.

Magic Moment: *In May 1938 Steele chose the final day of the season for a secret wedding. His bride was given away by captain Arthur Turner, the only team-mate in the know. Steele rushed from the morning service to the Victoria Ground and headed the clinching last-minute goal as Stoke beat Liverpool 2-0 to avert relegation.*

Worst Nightmare: *Clattered by Charlton's combative keeper, Sam Bartram, in September 1947, Steele received knee ligament damage which undoubtedly shortened his career.*

STOKE RECORD	Appearances	Goals
Football League	224	140
FA Cup	27	19
World War II	95	82

The mountainous Tommy Sale scored more goals for Stoke than any other player

The oldest man to appear in goal for Stoke, Norman Wilkinson

Arthur Tutin does one of his high kicks while posing for the camera

George Mountford's form allowed McGrory to offload Stan Matthews in 1947

Chapter Five

~ *The £10 Team* ~

No 41. **FRANK BAKER**
Debut: v Liverpool, 26 December 1936
Farewell: v Manchester City, 15 October 1949

Stoke's talented post-War side became noted throughout the country for being built upon local talent. Indeed, as City challenged for the first post-War championship, 1946-47, only two regular first teamers hailed from outside the Potteries. As the local lads had cost the club no more than their £10 signing-on fees, Stoke became known as the '£10 team'.

Born in Stoke-on-Trent on 22 October 1918, Frank Baker earned his living driving a laundry van, whilst turning out as an amateur left-winger for Port Vale reserves. His form caught the eye of a number of clubs, among them Wolverhampton. McGrory heard that Baker was to sign for Wolves boss Major Frank Buckley at 6pm one evening. In typically bluff fashion McGrory arrived at 5.30 and in half an hour persuaded the lad to plump for Stoke.

That was in 1935 and Baker turned on the style in the reserves. For the moment, England international Joe Johnson barred his progress to the first team. Baker made occasional appearances during 1936-37, but the door finally opened one game into 1937-38. Johnson hurt an ankle and Baker grasped his chance. It was not long before he was earning flattering comparisons with Matthews.

These, however, were misplaced. Like Johnson, it was Baker's pace that overcame his full-back. He possessed good ball skills, but none to compare with the mesmerising Matthews. Either way, their crosses, chipped towards the penalty spot or the far post, fed the voracious appetite of Freddie Steele. The only similarity seemed to be the slender frames of the two wingers, comically kitted out in enormous baggy shorts reaching down to their knees. Baker stood 5ft 7in and weighed 10st 8lbs. His boyish good looks were set off by brown, brooding eyes and he kept his dark, wiry hair very short.

A major asset of Baker's play was his goalscoring. In his first full season he bagged eleven, generally arriving late into the area to pick up any pieces. In 1938-39 he scored a further ten.

On account of his youth Baker was called up in the early months of the War and thus played few Wartime League games for Stoke. Desperate for football he requested permission, along with fellow players Syd Peppitt and Alec Ormston, to play as a guest for Middlesbrough in February 1941. Stoke refused, but relented the following season, allowing Baker, Billy Mould, Peppitt, and Ormston all to play for Sunderland.

In 1942 Stoke were advised that if their players joined the Territorial Army they would be stationed at nearby Meir and thus would be available most Saturdays. Half of the first team joined up and were promptly despatched to Northern Ireland! There Baker, Peppitt, Ormston and Mould assisted Linfield to win the Irish Cup. Baker even played for the Irish League against the Army in 1944.

With the coming of peace, Alec Ormston – Baker's main rival for the left-wing berth – was the first to be demobbed, staking his claim with a run of form after Christmas. Baker returned to the Potteries just before the season closed, and the pair, both in their prime at 28, vied for the position.

McGrory's solution to the Baker v Ormston conundrum was to move Baker inside to replace the retiring Tommy Sale. The move paid swift dividends. Baker's darting runs kept Steele and Ormston well supplied, although his own eye for goal suffered and he scored just six. Many fans considered Baker and Ormston to be the finest left-wing combination in the country and in any other era international honours would surely have been forthcoming. Neither, however, won selection for the England team. Baker was in a queue behind Middlesbrough's Wilf Mannion, Chelsea's Roy Bentley, and Sunderland's Len Shackleton, tough acts to follow. Baker and Ormston got on off the pitch as well as on it. 'They drank like fish – most of the time together,' recalls colleague Dennis Herod.

A crop of injuries ended Baker's career. In August 1947 he broke his arm against Liverpool and missed most of a bad Stoke season. He broke his leg against Manchester United in October 1948 and fractured it again at Wolves five games into his comeback in April. In all, Baker broke bones five times in two years.

After spending over a year in rehabilitation, the 33-year-old Baker called it a day in the summer of 1951. He ran a fish and chip shop in Fenton for many years, coached Stoke's 'A' team, and managed local non-league side Foley. Baker died in late 1989.

Magic Moment: *Baker scored the winning goal at Sunderland in November 1946 after dribbling through the entire defence.*

Worst Nightmare: *The last straw for Baker proved to be yet another broken leg, suffered at Maine Road in October 1949.*

STOKE RECORD	Appearances	Goals
Football League	162	32
FA Cup	12	1
World War II	17	1

No 42. **ALEC ORMSTON**
Debut: v Sunderland, 20 November 1937
Farewell: v Fulham, 12 September 1951

In December 1936 Stoke manager Bob McGrory spied on a local non-league game after a tip-off. His intended target did not excite his interest, but two other youngsters did, one of whom was a dashing 17-year-old left-winger, Alexander Ormston.

Born in Stoke on 10 February 1919, Ormston attended the same school as Stanley Matthews, Wellington Road in Hanley. He represented Hanley Boys and Stoke-on-Trent Schools with such panache that he was called to a trial with England schoolboys, although he wasn't selected. He joined Stoke from his junior club, Summerbank.

Ormston's peculiar crouching style, huddled over the ball with his body arced forward at a seemingly impossible angle, stemmed from physical impairment – he was a hunchback. Fan Chris Lowe remembers: 'It was incredible. You would just see this pair of shoulders coming towards you.' His opponents sympathised little with the 5ft 6in winger once he had skipped past them. Ormston's major strength was his crossing, but he could also tackle back, unusual for a winger in those days and unheard of in the case of Matthews.

Ormston, denied his natural wing position by Frank Baker, was picked occasionally in the problematic inside-left berth, following injuries to George Antonio and Jim Westland. Following Tommy Sale's return from Blackburn in April 1938, Ormston's opportunities became further restricted.

He was called up in the summer of 1940 and made just a few wartime appearances for Stoke, although these tended to be in his preferred left-wing berth. In 1939-40 Ormston cracked the winner in the championship decider against Manchester United as Stoke clinched the Wartime Regional Western League by two points.

In 1946-47, benefiting from early demobilisation due to a chest complaint, Ormston returned to Stoke as first choice left-winger. As Stoke challenged for the League title, he scored twenty goals. These included a hat-trick in a 5-2 win at Chelsea, making this by far his best season. His pace suited the way manager McGrory wished Stoke to play. The ball was conveyed quickly to the wingers with both Matthews and Ormston then expected to beat their men and deliver for Steele to show his aerial power. Ormston scored the goal as Stoke lost 1-2 to Sheffield United to miss out on the League title that June day at Bramall Lane.

During that season Baker and Ormston garnered many admirers. Both were probably in the reckoning for full England honours, but Preston's Tom Finney and Blackburn's Bobby Langton kept possession of the No 11 shirt. Ormston was consoled by three rep-

resentative games for the Football League against the League of
Ireland from 1946 to 1948.

In 1949-50 the chest complaints that first surfaced in the forces
restricted Ormston to just five appearances. When it became clear
that his condition was serious, McGrory moved to sign a permanent
replacement – Harry Oscroft from Freddie Steele's new club,
Mansfield. Ormston did return to play most of 1950-51, although
following the arrival of another club record signing, £9,000 inside-
left Les Johnston from Celtic, he found himself switched to the
right wing. His new role, allied to his loss of pace, diminished his
effectiveness. Now 32, he moved to Hereford at the end of the season as the £10 team split up. He finished his career at Stafford
Rangers and Runcorn.

Ormston spent a time recuperating in Loggerheads Sanatorium
in Shropshire before becoming landlord at the Fountain Head in
Hanley, later working in the offices of a colliery. During these years
he helped out part-time in Stoke's promotions office. After his death
on 12 July 1975, Eastwood Hanley FC played a Potteries All-Star
XI in a benefit game for his family.

Magic Moment: *In November 1940, on leave from the Army,
Ormston, turned up at the Victoria Ground on a whim. As Bobby
Liddle was unfit, Ormston was told to get kitted up. He scored twice,
and Frank Mountford thrice, in a 5-0 win over Birmingham.*

Worst Nightmare: *Ormston fluffed the chance of a fourth goal in
Stoke's 5-2 win at Chelsea in October 1946. Clean through with only
Robertson to beat, he shot tamely wide.*

STOKE RECORD	Appearances	Goals
Football League	172	29
FA Cup	20	1
World War II	59	19

No 43. **BILLY MOULD**
Debut: v Wolves, 19 March 1938
Farewell: v Huddersfield, 15 March 1952

The other player picked up by McGrory from that scouting mission
to Summerbank was centre-half William Mould.

Born at Great Chell, Staffordshire on 6 October 1919, Mould's
playing style conformed to the classic physical centre-half of the
1930s. He crunched into tackles and concentrated on clearing his
lines effectively. Don Whiston, a young fan at the time, believes
'Billy Mould was the finest kicker of a ball I have ever seen. He was

so clean in his clearances and he had a lovely balance while making tackles.' Mould provided continuity to Arthur Turner at centre-half as the Stoke captain's career neared its close. Mould had a short run in the first team late in 1937-38 following Turner's injury at Blackpool and the pair shared duties the following season.

The 5ft 9½in, 11st Mould seems to have a sheepish smile on his moon-shaped face in every photograph. With a high balding forehead, topped with dark curly hair, and stocky build, he bore resemblance to England captain Billy Wright.

During the War, Mould served in the Royal Artillery. Wounded in the leg by shrapnel whilst serving in Normandy after D-Day, 1944, he recovered enough to play twice for Stoke in March 1945. He also captained an FA XI against the Army in November 1946 at the Victoria Ground. The War cost Mould his place in the Stoke side, for afterwards he had to contend with the emerging genius of Neil Franklin. Mould had to accept reserve-team football until, following a 0-3 home defeat by Wolves, Bob McGrory lost patience with right-back Harry Brigham and re-cast Mould as a full-back.

Mould was at first reluctant to change position and tabled a transfer request, but he soon grasped the opportunity to kick-start his career, displacing Brigham, who joined Nottingham Forest for £4,000. Marshalled by the bullish Mould and stylish Franklin, City conceded only two goals in eight games as they forced themselves into contention for the championship. Mould's experience of playing at the hub of the team stood him in good stead as he organised his hot-headed left-back partner, John McCue. Indeed Mould's general influence was such that he captained the side whenever Franklin played for England, being handed the honour permanently in 1947 after Franklin handed in his own transfer demand.

Mould suffered a cartilage injury in a 2-1 win over Burnley in December 1948 and missed almost the whole of 1949. Now aged 31, he spent most of 1949-50 recuperating in the reserves and it was not until Cyril Watkin broke a leg in September 1950 that Mould regained his place at right-back.

Despite his recovery, Mould was freed by Stoke in July 1952 and signed for Harry Catterick's Crewe. In fact, the break-up of that great post-War team, who had lost so many years to the conflict, caused enormous on-field problems for Stoke. The lack of adequate local replacements, unavailable for recruitment during the war years, meant that Stoke had no on-going regeneration of the team. The inevitable relegation ensued in 1952-53.

Mould made 66 appearances for the Railwaymen, scoring his only League goal, before retiring in May 1954 to concentrate on his sports outfitters shop in Newcastle-under-Lyme. Diagnosed with a form of Alzheimer's disease late in life, which some think was exacerbated by incessant heading of a heavy football, Billy died in 1997, the same year as fellow £10ers Neil Franklin and Frank Bowyer.

Magic Moment: *In November 1946, Mould's last-gasp mistake allowed Sunderland's Burbanks a free run on goal. Mould recovered with a superb sliding tackle to clear the danger. Stoke won 1-0.*

Worst Nightmare: *Mould left Sheffield United's veteran inside-left Jack Pickering unmarked in the second minute of the title decider at Bramall Lane in June 1947. Pickering scored from close range.*

STOKE RECORD	Appearances	Goals
Football League	177	–
FA Cup	17	–
World War II	69	–

No 44. JOHN McCUE
Debut: v Mansfield, 21 September 1940
Farewell: v Scunthorpe, 26 March 1960

John William McCue appeared in more games in a red and white shirt than any other Stoke player.

Born in Stoke-on-Trent on 22 August 1922, McCue was spotted playing for Longton Schools and joined Stoke's groundstaff as an amateur in 1937. He signed professional forms in April 1940 and, due to his wartime occupation as a PT instructor, which kept him in the locality, he made the left-back spot his own from 1942-43 onwards, missing only one game from February 1943 to May 1945.

The left-footed McCue's style was uncompromising. Described as a 'grand kicker of the ball', should his winger get the better of him, however, McCue was not averse to the odd kick or two to rectify the situation. Frank Mountford chuckles: 'We used to call him "Chopper" because no one got past him. Or if they did they were lucky!' Thus McCue earned the moniker 'Chopper', before Chelsea's infamous Ron had even been born. His impetuous tackling did lead to mistakes, and a slip in attempting to intercept a long clearance let in Sheffield United's Rickett to score the decisive second goal in the title decider in June 1947.

McCue looked as hard as he played. His crew-cut blond hair topped an angular, drawn face. His nose, broken on numerous occasions during his career, took several different turns as it made its way to a bony point. Several team-mates allude to McCue's tunnel vision once he entered the arena, with his stark staring eyes displaying a total lack of comprehension of anything, aside from his own particular tasks.

McCue staked his claim for the England left-back spot in the immediate post-War years, although his weakness, a lack of constructive use of the ball, left Middlesbrough's George Hardwick and Manchester United's John Aston to contest the No 3 shirt. His only first-class honour came when selected for an FA tour to Australia in 1952, playing four games against the host nation.

Once demobbed, McCue played as a part-time professional, working for the British Coal Board as a PT instructor for miners in North Staffordshire pits. He trained on Tuesday and Thursday nights, running the sessions with his sergeant-majorly manner. Tony Allen, a latter day full-back partner, recalls: 'He didn't half sort you out. Nobody took the mickey out of him.'

By 1948 Stoke's team-spirit was beginning to disintegrate. The loss of the championship in 1947 and the departure of Matthews, coupled with the failure of McGrory's big-money signings caused rumblings of discontent. McCue, along with five other first teamers, handed in transfer requests. Each was denied, although the downward spiral continued as Stoke suffered relegation for the first time in over a quarter of a century.

First choice until 1957-58, at the stately age of 35, McCue's consistency remained legendary. Over the seasons in Division Two he fought off the challenges of Des Farrow and Jack Short, both bought in the belief that McCue's career was entering its twilight. It took the emerging prodigious talent of Tony Allen to put him in the shadows, but from October 1957 when Frank Mountford retired through injury, McCue's experience saw him switch flanks, coping admirably with the fact that he was not right-footed. It is a sign of his indelible professionalism that McCue remained first choice for a further 2½ years, exploiting his experience, aggression and commitment to the full.

By the time of his retirement McCue had set a new appearance record for the club. He still holds the record for overall appearances in a Stoke shirt, though as so many of these were made during the War he lies second in the 'official' appearance chart to Eric Skeels. In gratitude for his staunch service, the club granted him an overdue testimonial in October 1961.

By that time though, McCue had joined Oldham on a free transfer, part of the clear-out undertaken by Tony Waddington, the newly appointed manager of Stoke City. McCue made 56 appearances at Boundary Park before joining Macclesfield Town. He appeared in local charity games until the age of 60.

Towards the end of his life McCue suffered delusional flashbacks which his wife firmly believed were connected with so much heading of the heavy leather balls in the 1940s and 50s. He died in November 1999.

Magic Moment: *On one occasion when Stan Matthews returned to Stoke with Blackpool, manager McGrory pulled McCue aside saying 'You know what to do today don't you John, you know what to do'. McCue proceeded to kick Matthews black and blue. Stoke won 3-2.*

Worst Nightmare: *McCue was sent off against Port Vale in a 'friendly' Supporters Club Trophy for using 'improper language' as Stoke drew 2-2 in the second leg in October 1959.*

STOKE RECORD	Appearances	Goals
Football League	502	2
FA Cup	40	–
World War II	132	–

No 45. **DENNIS HEROD**
Debut: v Walsall, 28 December 1940
Farewell: v Sunderland, 28 March 1953

The goalkeeper who completed the back three of the £10 team was Dennis John Herod.

Born in Tunstall on 27 October 1923, Herod came to Stoke's attention rather fortuitously. He replaced the injured Trent Vale United goalkeeper just in time to play in the Sentinel Shield final, a competition for non-league clubs organised by the local paper, at the Victoria Ground. Although Trent Vale lost 1-5 Herod impressed the watching Bob McGrory and signed as a Junior in 1940. Due to the departure of first-choice Wilkinson to the North Yorkshire coal-fields, Herod quickly graduated to the first team, making his first appearance as an amateur in a 1-5 defeat by Walsall. His next two games ended 2-6 and 3-5, but despite this inauspicious start Herod was offered a contract.

His wartime appearances were restricted once called up to the 44th Royal Tank Regiment. Whilst training in Hampshire, Herod guested for the all-star Aldershot side, alongside Lawton, Mercer and Cullis. From 1943 Herod saw action in North Africa and Italy and escaped with his life when his tank received a direct hit in Normandy in August 1944, receiving only cuts and a fractured jaw.

With dark hair, thick eyebrows and sallow cheeks, Herod always looks rather preoccupied in photographs, as might befit a goal-keeper who played behind as flamboyant a figure as Neil Franklin. In fact, Herod admits that he suffered terribly from pre-match nerves, an affliction widespread amongst his team-mates. 'Stan Matthews was the worst. We only had one toilet in our dressing room, but we needed two because he occupied it for the last twenty minutes before the game!'

Ever present in 1945-46, Herod vividly remembers the Burnden Park disaster on 9 March 1946. Stoke visited Bolton's ground in the FA Cup quarter-final, second leg (that season Cup rounds were played over two legs). Although the reported attendance was 65,419, it is thought another 15,000 forced their way in as the game kicked off. Barriers gave way in the ensuing crush and 33 spectators behind Herod's goal died, with a further 520 receiving crush injuries. 'They were actually laying them out on the ground while the match was taking place. There was a policeman near me and I said "What's the matter?" He said "Oh they've fainted." Well, I'd seen a lot of dead people in the war and I knew they hadn't fainted. I knew they were dead.'

Stoke fans, feasting on the title challenge of 1946-47, soon dubbed Dennis 'Herod the King', although he is more circumspect as to his value to the side. 'I was probably the weakest link in the team. I had not got the physique to be a really top class goalkeeper like Frank Swift or Ted Ditchburn. I did, however, have fast reflexes and I could move quickly.' He played in the title decider at Sheffield United – and blames himself for Pickering's first goal: 'I was slow to get down to it and it has given me nightmares ever since, because winning the championship of the First Division is the highlight of any professional footballer's career. We penned them into their half for the second 45 minutes, but they broke away and scored a second goal.'

At 5ft 9½in Herod was small for a goalkeeper, in fact one of the smallest custodians Stoke has ever fielded. He made up for his lack of inches with acrobatic agility and bravery which bordered on foolhardy. His fearless diving at the feet of oncoming forwards became a feature of his game. On Boxing Day 1949 he crumpled under a heavy challenge by Sunderland's Trevor Ford. The ball ended up in Stoke's net and the goal stood. Bob McGrory spent the entire journey home chuntering away to himself while the concussed Herod lay prostrate on the back seat. Eventually McGrory leapt to his feet and shouted towards the back of the bus: 'Why didn't you punch it, Dennis?' To add further insult, the catatonic Herod was dumped off the coach at his mother's house to recover.

Herod admits to smoking heavily and gambling, vices which led him into comradeship with Neil Franklin. Herod acted as groomsman at Franklin's wedding, and received an offer to accompany him to Colombia. Herod declined, not wanting to leave his beloved Potteries, where his wife ran a successful grocery business.

In the summer of 1950 McGrory signed Donald Clegg from Bury to replace Herod. Stoke lost their first two games and Clegg found himself unceremoniously dropped. Indeed, Herod saw off numerous challengers, including Arthur Jepson, Fred Elliott and Manny

Foster in his fourteen years at Stoke, although his shortcomings meant McGrory was constantly seeking to replace him.

On 16 February 1952, Herod broke his arm in a brave challenge at Villa Park and finished the game on the right wing, as his team-mates defended a 2-1 lead. Shortly after half-time the ball was cleared upfield. Neglected by the Villa defence, Herod found himself one-on-one with keeper Con Martin. 'He didn't come out so I just placed it past him. *Fait accompli.* Marvellous!' Herod remains the only goalkeeper to have scored a first-class goal for Stoke. It sealed Stoke's first win in nine games as they battled to stay up.

This new-found prowess cut little ice with Stoke's new manager, Frank Taylor, who made his intentions clear with his first signing. In July 1952 he bought keeper Bill Robertson from Birmingham for £8,000. In December Robertson broke a leg and Herod was recalled, although he himself broke a leg against West Brom a month later.

Already the subject of interest from Preston, Herod was transfer listed. The act provoked a threat to sue, as Herod maintained it was illegal to transfer an injured player. Although removed from the list, the disenchanted Herod felt it best to move on, becoming part of the clear-out which followed relegation. Herod signed for Stockport for £750 in July 1953, playing 33 times, before retiring aged 32. He became a popular greengrocer in the markets around Manchester and the Potteries. He stood as a local councillor for the Conservative Party and assisted Newcastle Town for a short time.

Magic Moment: *A treble save from Sunderland's Len Shackleton in March 1948 saw Herod get up quickly to smother his efforts each time. After the game Shackleton declared Herod a 'Jack in the Box'.*

Worst Nightmare: *In September 1945 Stoke visited Newcastle. Herod recalls: 'Someone told us Newcastle's centre-forward, Albert Stubbins, couldn't head the ball any more. By half-time it was 1-6 and he had scored five past me with his head'. Stoke lost 1-9.*

STOKE RECORD	Appearances	Goals
Football League	191	1
FA Cup	24	–
World War II	125	–

No 46. **NEIL FRANKLIN**
Debut: v Everton, 18 May 1940
Farewell: v Arsenal, 6 May 1950

Indisputably one of football's greatest centre-halves, had it not been for Cornelius 'Neil' Franklin's decision to turn his back on England, perhaps he, and not Billy Wright, would have become the first player to pass a century of international caps.

Franklin was born in Shelton, Stoke-on-Trent on 24 January 1922 and emerged through the nursery side, Stoke Old Boys. At fifteen he won schoolboy international honours in his original position of right-half and signed professional forms in January 1939. The outbreak of war soon gave opportunities to Stoke's apprentices and Franklin made his first-team debut at the end of 1939-40, before volunteering with the RAF in February 1941. His conversion to centre-half soon followed, due to the continued absence of Billy Mould, whom he also replaced as captain.

A perfectionist, blessed with exceptional ball control, Franklin possessed superb positional sense. At 5ft 11in and 11st 4lbs, the slim Franklin's timing was immaculate in both tackling and aerial work. The typical big 'stopper' centre-half of pre-War years, such as Derby's John Barker, Arsenal's Herb Roberts, and Huddersfield's Alf Young, were bulkily built to deal with the likes of the Herculean Lawton, Dodds and Lofthouse. Franklin eschewed this stereotype, but could still outjump anyone, relying on his timing and muscular upper body. His grace on the ball showed that it was possible for centre-halves to be constructive as well as destructive and Franklin continued the trend begun by his predecessor in the England team, Stan Cullis of Wolves. Franklin developed the role as the creative hub of the team and could be called the first *libero*, preceding Franz Beckenbauer's leggy runs from the German back four by twenty years.

Franklin's assuredness on the ball brought early recognition by England. He earned four wartime international caps, the first in a 3-2 defeat of Scotland at Villa Park in February 1945, followed by appearances in all six Victory internationals.

Stanley Matthews likened Franklin to Bobby Moore, believing he was even more constructive in his play: 'Neil used to break up attacks and deliver the ball perfectly as I liked it to my feet.' Legend has it that Franklin was so unflappable that the parting of his thick dark hair was rarely disturbed as he languidly dribbled out of defence before distributing the ball to the forwards.

Goalkeeper Dennis Herod, who suffered many fraught Saturday afternoons, saw Franklin's genius from a different perspective: 'He was a great player, but so unpredictable. If he was under pressure he would shout to me "Dennis, come on" and I would come out expecting him to give me the ball. Nine times out of ten he would do a U-turn and trot off up the field. It was like playing in a minefield. He didn't believe he could have a bad game and he was the only one of us who didn't suffer with nerves. He didn't give a dog's dinner for anything.'

Following the sale of Matthews, his bête-noir, McGrory turned his ire on Stoke's remaining star performer – Franklin – stripping him of the captaincy early in 1947-48 in favour of Billy Mould. Franklin's style of play also infuriated McGrory, who wanted him to deliver the ball early, rather than carry it forwards himself. But Franklin refused to part with the ball unless he was certain that doing so would improve his team's position. McGrory also urged Franklin to be more physical in his defensive work, an idea which Neil rejected: 'I have never understood why I should be expected to hurt a fellow player. Any lout can knock a man off the ball. It needs a footballer to take the ball off an opponent.'

His imperious defending won Franklin a then world record 27 consecutive caps to April 1950, plus a further ten stretching back into the War – astonishing figures in the era of selectorial whims which regularly saw the likes of Matthews and Finney ignored.

But McGrory's campaign soon had its effect. In the summer of 1949 Franklin shocked Stoke by stating his intention to leave. He cited the deterioration of his wife's health, caused by the thick smog belched out by the kilns and furnaces of the Potteries. A world record £30,000 bid was mooted by Raich Carter, player-manager of Hull and one of Franklin's closest friends. Stoke's directors, conscious of the uproar that would ensue if another high-profile player left, blocked Franklin's request. Although he re-signed four games into the new season, he was not at ease with himself and it was only a matter of time before another opportunity arose.

Franklin was another inveterate gambler but, unlike his fellow addict Dennis Herod, he had a lucky streak. In January 1950 Stoke hosted Manchester United. At half-time Franklin asked the injured Herod to place a bet on his behalf. 'It was £250 each way on Simon de Montfort at Sandown. And it came in! He gave me £100 out of the winnings and that was a lot of money in those days.'

Franklin's gambling left him with assets in excess of £10,000 and that wealth gave him the confidence to make an astonishing announcement to the football world. He declined the FA's offer of a place in the squad for the 1950 World Cup in Brazil, saying that his wife was due to give birth that summer. Instead, he intended to spend a season playing for Independiente Santa Fe in Bogota, Colombia, for a reported King's ransom in wages.

Santa Fe's President, Luis Robledo (no relation to the footballing Robledo brothers of Newcastle United), had studied at Cambridge University. He believed that providing high-quality football might put paid to the continuing civil disobedience in Colombia, known locally as *la Violencia*, with British stars forming the main attraction. Franklin was offered £60 per week plus a £2,000 signing-on fee, more than four times the maximum wage at home.

Although the money seemed too good to be true, other consider-
ations also played on Franklin's mind: 'It wasn't really the money.
I was unhappy at Stoke. The manager wanted me to change my
style of play but I reckoned if it was good enough for England then
I should have been good enough for Stoke.'

Franklin's insubordination outraged the FA. England manager
Walter Winterbottom tried on three occasions to persuade him to
change his mind, but Franklin simply shrugged his shoulders and,
on 8 May, accompanied by team-mate George Mountford, set off for
South America. In Bogota they joined Manchester United's Charlie
Mitten, who had arrived from his team's tour of North America.
With Colombia having been expelled from FIFA for poaching players from around the world, the rebels found themselves suspended
from playing anywhere within FIFA's jurisdiction.

On arriving in Colombia, Franklin was full of bravado: 'There's
no future in Britain,' he told waiting reporters. 'We'll live finer than
any footballers in the world.' Despite a good start, with Santa Fe
winning 3-2 and the three English rebels leaving the pitch to cries
of 'Long Live Britain', problems soon arose. A 6.30pm curfew meant
that they could not socialise, not to mention problems with the language and the diet. Franklin was back in England by August.

There he faced the wrath of an FA determined to make examples of the 'Bogota Bandits'. Despite Players' Union leader Jimmy
Guthrie threatening to serve a High Court writ, Stoke suspended
Franklin indefinitely and in February 1951 sold him to Hull for
£22,500.

Damaged knee ligaments restricted Franklin's movement and
he failed to re-establish his former high standards. In February
1956 he joined Crewe, for whom he finally scored his first League
goal, and in October 1957 moved on to Stockport. In 1958 Franklin
emigrated to New Zealand to become player-manager at Wellington
Town, retiring as a player at the age of 40.

Franklin returned to Europe to manage Appoel in Cyprus before
taking charge of Colchester. His managerial philosophy was simply
summed up: 'I still don't believe in any of that defensive stuff.' He
won his only honour as a manager, promotion from Division Four,
in 1965-66, but was sacked in 1968.

In 1981 Franklin offered his views on the modern era of professionalism: 'Money has killed the game now. Players are paid to be
defensive. There's too much fear in the game, which doesn't help
spectators to make it more enjoyable.' Many football followers who
had seen him in his prime agreed. In later years Franklin kept a
pub in Oswaldtwistle, near Blackburn, and later the Dog and
Doublet at Sandon, Staffordshire. He died at his home in Stone,
aged 74, on 9 February 1996.

Magic Moment: *At Molineux in 1950, Franklin faced two Wolves forwards bearing down on him. Without glancing behind him, he leant back and flicked the ball in a perfect arc into Norman Wilkinson's arms, leaving his opponents dumbfounded.*

Worst Nightmare: *Prior to the title decider at Bramall Lane in June 1947, Stoke had a three-week break in Ireland. On arriving at Holyhead, Franklin found he had forgotten his boots and passport.*

STOKE RECORD	Appearances	Goals
Football League	142	–
FA Cup	20	–
World War II	186	3

No 47. **GEORGE MOUNTFORD**
Debut: v Crewe, 5 December 1942
Final Farewell: v Cardiff, 27 September 1952

The other Stoke player to be lured by the shiny Colombian peso was right-winger George Frederick Mountford.

Born in Kidderminster on 30 March 1921, Mountford joined Stoke from Kidderminster Harriers in December 1942. His fee was £40. From his natural right-wing position he provided ammunition for Tommy Sale and namesake Frank Mountford (no relation). For a winger, Mountford maintained a healthy scoring ratio and – with Stan Matthews on wartime duty in Blackpool – made the No 7 shirt his own. In fact, Matthews had a hard time winning back his place as McGrory favoured the hard working, if less talented Mountford.

At 5ft 9in, the stockily built Mountford had narrow shoulders on top of which stood a thinly thatched head with large jug-like ears. He loved to take on opponents and possessed a good turn of speed, which often took him into goalscoring positions as he burst in from the touchline to shoot. Mountford earned media praise for his direct running, a style entirely different to Matthews, carrying the ball at speed rather than imitating the wile and guile of the maestro.

Throughout 1945-46 the pair vied for selection. When Matthews pulled a leg muscle in September 1946, Mountford came in and the team embarked upon a five-game winning streak which included a 5-2 hammering of Chelsea. Even when Matthews was fit Mountford kept his place. This did not please Matthews, although no one blamed Mountford, who was playing out of his skin in a team challenging for the League championship. But the rift between Stoke and Matthews this time proved irrevocable.

Although Matthews' sale began Stoke's unstoppable decline, in Mountford they had a sound enough replacement. He grabbed the

winner in the nervy penultimate game at Villa Park, which left
Stoke needing only to beat Sheffield United to be proclaimed champions. But Stoke lost 1-2 with Mountford ably contained by the
Blades' Albert Cox. Perhaps the final, crucial, difference between
the pair lay in Matthews' big-match temperament, which may have
tipped the balance that day in Stoke's favour.

As one of the few Stoke players of the period not to hail from the
Potteries, it was Mountford's torn arm ligaments sustained in
December 1948 that allowed McGrory to field the famous all home-
grown £10 team. After the departure of messianic Freddie Steele,
Mountford converted to centre-forward and scored twice in a 3-1
win over Manchester United.

Upon the completion of the 1949-50 season, the lustrous peso
lured Mountford to Independiente Santa Fe in Bogota, Colombia,
as player and assistant coach to Neil Franklin. Mountford was a
star from his very first practice match when he netted a hat-trick,
his pace earning him the moniker of 'Bald Arrow'. He did not find
Colombia as alien as did Franklin and remained for the whole season. His year did not pass without incident. In one game, as the two
captains joined with the referee to toss up, the opposing skipper
pulled out a knife and muttered murderously to the dumbstruck
official "We win or else". Mountford also played in a Colombian
national team hastily cobbled together from the pick of the guest
players – including Charlie Mitten, Hector Rial and Alfredo Di
Stefano – that defeated newly crowned World Champions Uruguay
3-1 in July 1950.

Back in the Potteries, Mountford found himself suspended both
by Stoke and the League. His exile ended in September 1951 when
he returned to first-team duty in an effort to stem Stoke's atrocious
start of five consecutive losses. Injuries to Frank Bowyer and Willie
McIntosh, a £10,000 signing from Blackpool, disrupted Stoke's
attack. Only the arrival of Wolves' Irish inside-left Sammy Smyth,
who top-scored with twelve goals, enabled City to finish one place
clear of the relegation zone.

New manager Frank Taylor was determined to stamp his mark
on the Stoke personnel. The 31-year-old Mountford moved to
Queen's Park Rangers in mid-October 1952 in exchange for left-half
Des Farrow, with Rangers also receiving £4,000. The deal turned
sour for Taylor, as did many others for the dour Yorkshireman, who
lacked the necessary transfer acumen. Farrow made just eight
appearances over two seasons.

In September 1953 Mountford returned to his roots to play for
non-league Hereford, ending his playing days with Kidderminster
Harriers and Lockheed Leamington. He retired from football to
become a GPO engineer.

Magic Moment: *The first of his four goals on 5 May 1945 in a 6-0 Wartime League (North) win against Port Vale saw Mountford put Stoke ahead with a fierce drive following a solo run. His fourth goal made it nine in three games against Vale inside three months.*

Worst Nightmare: *Mountford tore ankle ligaments in a 0-1 home defeat by Preston early in 1947-48. The injury restricted his appearances to just over half of the League programme.*

STOKE RECORD	Appearances	Goals
Football League	148	25
FA Cup	10	4
World War II	95	37

No 48. **FRANK MOUNTFORD**
Debut: v Tranmere, 13 May 1940
Farewell: v Huddersfield, 28 September 1957

Frank Mountford, another of the bevy of talent to emerge from the Potteries during World War II, served Stoke City for 38 years.

Although born in Askern, near Doncaster, on 30 March 1923, Mountford hailed from a Potteries family forced to travel to seek work in the austere 1930s. Shortly after his birth the family moved back to Stoke, where Frank's father had secured a job in a local pit. Frank captained Bradeley Junior School as a goalscoring centre-forward and played for Stoke-on-Trent schools.

Mountford signed professional forms with Stoke on his seventeenth birthday and found a job as a collier, a listed occupation, so he was not called up. His foreman, a Stoke fan, allowed Mountford time off whenever necessary to play. On Frank's second appearance, against Notts County in the first game of 1940-41, he bagged a hat-trick and went on to top score with 23 goals and again in 1942-43 with twenty. This led McGrory, not one for public praise, to describe Frank as 'another Freddie Steele'. Mountford seemed set for a career as a prolific goalscorer until he arrived at a momentous decision. He remembers: 'I loved playing at centre-forward when I was younger, but when I played professionally and found out what it was all about I wanted to play in defence, where I could kick people rather than get kicked. My mother was all for it!'

Revered by Stoke's fans for his energetic approach to the game, Mountford stood just 5ft 9in. He had thick black hair, with bushy eyebrows, and always appears to have a twinkle in his eye in photographs. Strong and two-footed, Mountford's speciality was diving to head clear from opponents. Fan Brian Calvert remembers: 'For consistency, determination and commitment he has, in my opinion, never been surpassed. He never gave a mediocre performance and never knew when to give up.'

His trademark was to receive the ball, trap it, then take a little skip as he looked up, before laying it off. His committed approach meant that he often required the services of club trainer Norman Tapken. Brian Calvert recalls: 'I have memories of Frank clutching a sponge to his head, refusing to leave the pitch.' Mountford admits that his apparent bravery had a rather more prosaic motivation: 'I didn't want to come off as I might lose my place. I'd play anywhere to get a game.' This hints at the disparity in earnings between regular first teamers and those players consigned to the reserves. In an era when the alternative to a career in football was shiftwork at the local colliery, players fought tooth and nail to keep their cherished first-team places.

Both Peter Doherty and Nat Lofthouse paid tribute to his ability by describing Mountford as their most formidable opponent. 'I loved playing against these stars,' Mountford says. 'It was relatively easy as I didn't have to do anything else except not let them have a kick.' Mountford frequently took star rating in the press, despite the team containing the likes of Matthews, Steele and Franklin, and he was soon being described as the 'best uncapped player in the country'. Surprisingly, given the selectors' liking for committed, wholehearted types, Mountford never achieved representative honours, having the misfortune to have Billy Wright ahead of him in the queue for an England place.

Alongside Franklin and Kirton, Mountford formed a formidable post-War half-back line, the foundation of Stoke's title challenge in 1946-47. He tore a leg muscle in the 0-3 defeat by Derby in January and McGrory drafted in Johnny Sellars in his place. Mountford's was arguably as important a loss to the team, although for entirely different reasons, as was Matthews. He returned for the penultimate game of the season, but, suspecting that Sellars was now McGrory's favourite, rocked the club by requesting a transfer just two days before the final game at Sheffield United. His petulance meant he had to watch from the sidelines as Stoke missed numerous chances to win the title decider. Mountford remembers: 'Bob McGrory was distraught when we lost and he blamed me for losing – even though *he* dropped *me!*'

Although born outside North Staffordshire, Mountford grew up in Stoke and had a thick Potteries accent, and thus qualifies as one of the £10 team – although Bob McGrory blew his top when he discovered that his precious 'all-local lads' had, technically, a Yorkshireman amongst their number! Mountford took over the mantle of penalty taker from Alec Ormston, due to the winger's absence through injury, late in the 1947-48 season. Frank scored sixteen spot-kicks, believed to be most ever for a Stoke player. He did not, however, relish the task, considering it thankless.

In 1950 Mountford took over the centre-half role vacated by the renegade Neil Franklin and enjoyed one of his finest seasons, being ever present. But the appointment of Frank Taylor as Stoke manager in the summer of 1952 caused Mountford, and others, particular anguish. 'We played against each other many times when he [Taylor] played as right-back for Wolves and we hated each other on the field. He was arrogant and he hadn't changed much when he became manager.' Taylor intended to revamp Stoke, and after chasing Manchester United and England international Allenby Chilton, signed Aberdeen's Ken Thomson, pushing Mountford to right-half.

Following right-back George Bourne's broken leg, which ended his career, Mountford converted to full-back and the switch prolonged his career. He played alongside another veteran, John McCue, until retiring a few games into 1957-58 following a sequence of torn muscles. He stands tenth in Stoke's all-time appearance chart, although if wartime matches are included he played more games in a Stoke shirt than anyone else, bar McCue.

Having learnt at first hand of the value of the trainer, it came as no surprise when Mountford became assistant to Norman Tapken. He was promoted to head trainer in June 1960 when Waddington took charge and served Stoke throughout his reign.

Alan Durban was appointed to the Stoke hot seat in 1977 and, realising that the new manager would want to install his own backroom staff, Mountford retired, becoming groundsman of Trubshawe Cross playing fields in Burslem. Now a cheeky elderly man, Frank is another of the £10 teamers to suffer from a form of Alzheimer's disease, believed to have been exacerbated by years of heading the heavy, laced footballs of the 1940s and 50s.

Magic Moment: *Whilst trainer in the 1970s Mountford, sitting on the bench, picked up the intercom phone to take instructions from Tony Waddington, who watched the first half of games from the directors box. Mountford felt Waddington was posturing within the directors' hearing and dumped the handset into his bucket of water.*

Worst Nightmare: *During the 0-2 FA Cup home defeat by Third Division (North) Hull in 1949 Mountford was kicked by Hull's player-manager Raich Carter, leaving him a passenger for 80 minutes.*

STOKE RECORD	Appearances	Goals
Football League	391	21
FA Cup	34	3
World War II	183	54

No 49. **JOCK KIRTON**
Debut: v Chelsea, 26 December 1936
Farewell: v Charlton, 22 November 1952

The senior member of Stoke's £10 team did not hail from the Potteries – although Stoke fans believed that if you cut John 'Jock' Kirton you would find red and white stripes running through him like a stick of rock.

He was born in Aberdeen on 4 March 1916 and played for St Marchers and the Banks o' Dee, winning several Scottish schoolboy caps. Bob McGrory's Scottish scouting network persuaded Kirton to sign in 1935 and he made a number of appearances as cover for Frank Soo over the following two seasons.

A hunky 5ft 9½in and 11st, Kirton had a large bulbous nose and wiry black hair. His habit of wearing his long baggy shorts, typical of the era, rolled tightly up to his waist exposed muscular thighs, rather like the similarly Herculean John Charles in the 1950s.

Kirton's chance to claim his own place arrived when Soo moved to right-half to cover Arthur Tutin's retirement in September 1938. Kirton made the No 6 shirt his own, although, as with many of his generation, he lost his youth to the war. His early call up restricted his availability for Stoke, so he guested for Nottingham Forest, Leeds and Notts County. By chance, he ended up in the same battalion as Steele, Wilkinson, Challinor, Antonio and Jim Westland. Not surprisingly the unit's team, captained by Kirton, prospered in the Army Cup, winning its first two games 15-0 and 15-1.

Kirton made numerous representative appearances for British forces during the War and won a wartime cap for Scotland in a 2-6 thrashing by England at Wembley in February 1944 – although he was played out of position at centre-half. Association with such humiliation tarnished his reputation and the selectors turned thereafter to Middlesbrough's Baxter.

Kirton lead Stoke's 1946-47 title challenge. A wholly different type to the departed Soo, he broke up attacks and distributed the ball simply. His spirit and unceasing thirst for Stoke's cause marked him as the heart of that great side. Don Whiston recalls Kirton as 'a hard player. In a practice match he scissor-kicked George Mountford to the ground after they had an argument.'

Stoke reported record profits in 1946-47 of £32,207, as against Liverpool's £17,000 and Wolves' £11,000, although these figures proved something of a wolf in sheep's clothing. Discontent simmered in the ranks of the playing staff, and Kirton, suffering from a bad ankle injury that restricted him to only one appearance in the next eighteen months, handed in a transfer request in the summer of 1948, along with five other players.

Kirton settled his differences and fought back from injury to regain his place. The flight to Colombia of Neil Franklin meant he inherited the captaincy in the summer of 1950 and he missed only six games that season and just one, at the age of 36, in 1951-52.

As Stoke tumbled out of the First Division in 1952-53 Kirton lost his place to Johnny Sellars. He sought a free transfer as his wife's health had suffered from the smog from the pot banks. In July 1953 he moved as player-coach to Bradford, where he made just eight appearances, under player-manager Ivor Powell, before retiring from the professional game. Kirton continued playing in non-league circles, appearing for both Hinckley Athletic in the East Midlands and then Downings Tileries, once he had returned to his adopted Potteries to earn a living in the building trade. He died in the City General Hospital, Stoke in March 1996.

Magic Moment: *In the record 10-3 demolition of West Brom, his fifth game for Stoke, Kirton had a hand in six goals. For the third of Freddie Steele's five, Kirton masterminded a neat passing move.*

Worst Nightmare: *Kirton's status as captain did not solve his accommodation problems. In 1950 Stoke refused to provide a club house for his family, so he put in another transfer request. When engineering a quick goal in his next home game, a wag in the crowd shouted 'Good old Jock. Thee canst come and live over my way!'*

STOKE RECORD	Appearances	Goals
Football League	219	2
FA Cup	30	–
World War II	65	2

No 50. **JOHNNY SELLARS**
Debut: v Derby, 17 April 1943
Farewell: v Bolton, 15 February 1958

Born in Trent Vale, Stoke-on-Trent on 28 April 1924, four months after his father Harry had signed for Stoke, Johnny Sellars grew up enveloped by the game.

He joined Stoke in October 1941, along with several other promising youngsters. Taking advantage of the opportunities the War afforded young players, Sellars played as an inside-right or right-winger and notched his first goal in March 1944 at Leicester. Despite playing in half of Stoke's games in 1945-46, Sellars was kept out of the side by George Antonio as City contested the League title the following season. Frank Mountford's injury at the Baseball Ground in January handed the 22-year-old his chance. He filled in ably at right-half, playing an integral role as Stoke fell just short of a first ever League championship.

A natural athlete, the 6ft 2in Sellars had great speed and stamina which allowed him to cover every blade of grass on the pitch. Although much taller than his father, Sellars inherited his characteristic tough-tackling physical attributes. As an accurate passer of the ball, he was potentially more talented then Harry, although as the junior member of Stoke's half-back line, he dutifully stayed back during Neil Franklin's forays upfield.

In 1947-48 Sellars filled in around Stoke's injury-ravaged team at full-back, right-wing and even centre-forward, before finding a home at left-half, replacing Kirton. This despite Sellars being predominantly right-footed. McGrory called him a 'manager's dream' for his willingness to play in any role. Here was his ideal player, unlike the self-aggrandised stars Matthews and Franklin. Known for his reliability and consistency, Sellars was ever present in 1948-49 and missed only three games over the next two seasons.

Incredibly, given his voracious appetite, Sellars was only a part-time pro. He designed ladies shoes for the Lotus shoe Company in Stone, ten miles south of Stoke, while his pace and employment status allowed him to often compete in the famous Powderhall Sprint events which featured sizeable cash prizes.

His relative wealth and good looks meant Sellars came to fancy himself as a ladies man. Team-mates Don Ratcliffe and Johnny King recall Sellars' wife, a Doris Day lookalike, whom Johnny loved showing off to. His blond hair, a curly bush atop a strong-jawed smiling face, attracted many converts to his personal following.

His persona could not prevent Sellars from picking up injuries. He missed the first half of 1951-52 with a slipped disc and his career was ended by an eye injury received in the fifth round FA Cup-tie at Bolton in February 1958. His eyesight never fully recovered and he suffered from recurring double vision for the rest of his life. He hung up his boots in May 1959, retiring to run his own business in Bristol. He was in the process of selling up and emigrating to Spain when he collapsed and died in his mother's house in Stoke-on-Trent on 24 June 1985.

Magic Moment: *Stoke defeated Liverpool 4-2 on 5 March 1955, their first victory at Anfield at the 26th attempt. Sellars had a blinder in midfield and released Oscroft for the killer third goal.*

Worst Nightmare: *In the last match of 1952-53 with the score 1-1 and Stoke having to win to stand a chance of avoiding relegation, Sellars missed his kick, allowing Jackie Stamps to give Derby a 2-1 lead. Stoke lost and suffered relegation for the first time since 1926.*

STOKE RECORD	Appearances	Goals
Football League	384	14
FA Cup	29	1
World War II	45	13

No 51. **FRANK BOWYER**

Debut: v Manchester United, 20 January 1940
Farewell: v Sheffield United, 23 April 1960

When Frank Bowyer scored on his debut he started as he continued, becoming one of the greatest goalscorers in Stoke's history.

Born at Chesterton, Staffordshire on 10 April 1922, Bowyer played for Stoke-on-Trent Schoolboys before joining Stoke's groundstaff at the age of fifteen. He signed professional forms in July 1939 – just prior to the German invasion of Poland – and played 28 games in 1940-41 in a team packed with fellow starlets such as Herod, McCue, Franklin and Frank Mountford.

The teenage Bowyer also guested during the War for Derby, where he fell foul of the legendary arrogance of Raich Carter: 'I played the ball straight to him. He controlled it, stopped and then kicked it out of play over the touchline! He shouted at me "Play it in front of me. I want it two yards in front of me, not to my feet".'

Bowyer hadn't the temperament to confront the likes of Carter. His shy smile testifies to a placid man, who lived for the delight of playing football. He combed his jet black hair into a quiff which fell over his right temple, but it could not hide his bucket ears, the root of much friendly joshing. At 5ft 10in he was tall for an inside-forward, but in his twinkling feet lay a dazzling ability.

Due to his National Service, Bowyer remained unavailable to Stoke for all of 1946-47. No less than that of Matthews and Frank Mountford towards the end of that campaign, Bowyer's absence for the whole season robbed City of a valuable source of goals to take the pressure off Freddie Steele. The newly demobbed Bowyer made his belated League debut two months short of his 26th birthday. In doing so he created a remarkable record as he debuted nearly nine years after signing as a professional.

Blessed with a rocket right-foot, Bowyer had supporters behind both goals ducking for cover as the net ballooned towards the terraces. Frank Mountford remembers that Bowyer was 'a wonderful volleyer of a ball. His goals always seemed to be sweetly timed on the half-volley.'

In 1947-48 Bowyer top-scored with 21 goals. His tally put him in the ranks of the country's top scorers, and was only overtaken late in the season by Bolton's Bill Moir who finished with 25. Despite his success in Stoke colours, Bowyer requested a transfer which, surprisingly, was granted. McGrory expressed interest in a player-exchange deal. Bowyer, however, changed his mind and remained at Stoke for a further twelve years, regularly finishing as leading scorer.

His goalscoring feats won him selection to tour Canada with the FA in the summer of 1950, alongside Nat Lofthouse and Johnny Hancocks. On that tour Bowyer found the net ten times, including four goals in a 19-1 defeat of the Saskatoon All-Stars.

In January 1951 Bowyer scored a last-gasp winner in the first competitive Potteries derby for eighteen years in Stoke's 1-0 FA Cup third round replay – a typical right-footed half-volley. For this goal alone many City fans of the period fondly remember Bowyer. After so many years without direct competition, rivalry between both sets of supporters had acquired a keen edge.

Bowyer acted like a responsible uncle to the raucous youngsters who populated Stoke's teams during the 1950s. Both Tony Allen and Don Ratcliffe remember him as a steadying influence. Bowyer eschewed a lifestyle of carousing in favour of a settled home and doting wife. Being the sensible type, he also kept pigs at his home in Newcastle-under-Lyme. Johnny King recalls: 'Frank was shrewd and he had this sideline going, selling his pigs to local butchers. He did very nicely.' Don Whiston recalls: 'He was one of the few of us to be able to afford a car and he used to give me a lift to training. Otherwise I'd have to go on the bus.'

His generosity stretched to fans too. Donald Lawton remembers meeting Bowyer in the most inauspicious surroundings. On leave from National Service in the RAF, Mr Lawton called in at the Globe Café in Newcastle for lunch. He was joined at his table by his hero, Bowyer, who, once he realised that Mr Lawton was heading for the game, refused to allow him to pay the 2s 6d for his meal, stumping up the cash himself – despite earning only £12 per week.

In March 1954 Bowyer scored twice as City hammered Bury 6-0 at Gigg Lane, still Stoke's biggest ever away win. Just over a year later he shot Stoke to the top of the Second Division with the winner in the first local derby played at Vale Park. But Stoke's 1-0 win proved inadequate. City lost out on promotion due to Birmingham and Luton's last-gasp victories.

In later years Bowyer dropped deeper and became a provider of goals with incisive long passing well before Johnny Haynes came to the fore at Fulham. Bowyer earned three separate benefits from Stoke, the last being a straight payment of £1,000 in recognition of his service to the club.

Despite top-scoring in 1959-60 with fourteen goals, Bowyer did not feature on new boss Tony Waddington's retained list. Although 38, Bowyer's release sparked a storm of protest, partly because he stood just three goals short of Steele's club goalscoring record. Bowyer ranks ninth in Stoke's all-time appearance chart, although if wartime matches are included he lies third, behind McCue and Mountford.

Frank played for two seasons with non-league Macclesfield, latterly as player-manager, before retiring from the game in 1962. His wife contracted a rare blood disease and the Bowyers moved to the cleaner air of Newquay on the south coast, where Frank became a school caretaker. He died in hospital in Truro after a short illness in November 1999.

Magic Moment: *In January 1954 Bowyer scored a first-half hattrick against Hartlepool in the FA Cup third round home tie. 'I got a standing ovation as I went off at half-time,' he smiled.*

Worst Nightmare: *After the 0-1 defeat at Third Division (North) Halifax in the FA Cup in 1953 'everybody felt deflated', said Bowyer. 'We came back on the coach and nobody spoke.'*

STOKE RECORD	Appearances	Goals
Football League	398	137
FA Cup	38	12
World War II	162	56

In 1945, Stoke's tattered wartime kit shows signs of the period's auterity

Billy Mould, full-back of the 1946-47 championship-challenging team

The baby-faced assassin, Frank Mountford

Tony Allen, on the far post, watches anxiously as Blackburn hit the crossbar

Chapter Six

~ *The Bad Lads* ~

No 52. **KENNY THOMSON**
Debut: v Middlesbrough, 6 September 1952
Farewell: v Ipswich, 3 October 1959

Kenneth Gordon Thomson captained Stoke City, founded the first of a dynasty of salacious drinking dens amongst Stoke players – and spent two months in jail.

Born in Aberdeen on 25 February 1930, Thomson played for Caledonian Thistle and Banks o' Dee, which had previously yielded Jock Kirton to Stoke. Bob McGrory's scouts had spotted Thomson as a 17-year-old, though he then signed for his local club, Aberdeen.

Considered one of the best pivots in Scotland during his two seasons at Pittodrie, in September 1952 Thomson became one of Frank Taylor's first signings. He cost £22,000 and was hailed as the answer to the problem posed by Neil Franklin's flight to Colombia.

The 6ft Thomson hurled his athletic frame into tackles, often two-footed, and his competitive spirit drove the team on from the middle of the field. Away from football his dark good looks, with full lips and hazel eyes, endeared him to the ladies and Thomson revelled in the lifestyle which playing in the Potteries afforded him.

Stoke and England left-back Tony Allen recalls 'a stopper, pure and simple. A good tackler who always gave you plenty of help. He always covered for me. You need a player like that in any team. I think he was the best centre-half I ever played with' – high praise from a player whose England caps were won alongside Leeds' Jack Charlton and Birmingham's Trevor Smith.

As the teak-hard bulwark of the Stoke defence, Thomson's commanding presence marked him out as a natural leader and he succeeded Jock Kirton as captain early in 1952-53. In those pre-substitute days Thomson is said to have had a unique method of motivating his players to get up after a knock. If a player lay injured on the pitch he would walk over and, allegedly, insert his finger under their shorts and sharply up their backside. 'You soon got up!' winces Don Ratcliffe, 'and if he'd done it to you once and you were down and saw him coming over, you got up bloody quick I can tell you!' Thomson so perfected the trick that to the casual observer it seemed that he was enquiring as to his victim's health!

In charge on the park, Thomson began to arrange social activities off it. He founded a band of renegades within the team – christened by their colleagues as the 'Bad Lads'. Nicknamed 'Thompo',

Kenny was the self-styled leader of the rebels, whose early recruits included Harry Oscroft, Bobby Cairns, Tim Coleman and Bobby Hutton. Hi-jinks included nights on the town, lewd behaviour, and baiting other players. Latter-day member Don Ratcliffe recalls: 'When we had team drinks we would split into defenders on one side of the room and attackers on the other – aside from Thompo that is. We'd always end up telling the defenders that if they were any good they'd be over here with us – it caused several fights!'

Despite burning the candle at both ends Thomson was one of Stoke's few consistent performers as Taylor's side sought to climb out of Division Two. The closest City came was in 1954-55 when they finished two points shy of second place. The crunch came at high-flying Rotherham on 18 April, but Stoke lost 1-2.

Thomson was equally voluble in his dealings with the military-mannered Frank Taylor. They were often eyeball to eyeball and Thomson gave as good as he got. He knew his worth to the team and felt on safe ground in challenging the manager. However, the blame for Stoke's stagnation in the 1950s cannot be laid solely at Taylor's door. It must, in part, be down to the off-field antics of the better part of the team, led by Thomson.

Having won selection as a reserve for the Scottish national side on three occasions whilst at Pittodrie, Thomson failed to win the expected bevy of full caps which as a teenager had seemed his for the taking. Dundee's Doug Cowie and Rangers' George Young kept him in the international wilderness. 'Anglos' were frowned upon. Had he stayed in Scotland things might have been different.

Thomson developed eyesight problems at the age of 28 which the use of contact lenses – then new and bothersome, unlike the easy-to-use gas permeable lenses of today – failed to solve. Thomson's performances suffered in the early part of 1959 and following a 0-4 hammering at Ipswich he lost his place. Taylor reluctantly released him to Middlesbrough for £8,500 in December 1959.

Thomson joined Hartlepool in October 1962 and had played 28 games for them before football was rocked by the infamous match-fixing scandal of 1963. To the footballing public, the most famous culprits were Tony Kaye and 'Bronco' Layne, but others were jailed too, including Kenny Thomson, who was sent down for two months, but not before selling his story to the papers. After his release he met Don Ratcliffe and offered a bizarre explanation. 'He told me that he never fixed any match in his life. He only told the papers he did so he could make some cash.' Thomson found himself banned from involvement in football for life, although his playing career was in any case all but over.

Thomson's remarkable life came to a predictably premature end when he died from a heart attack whilst playing golf, aged just 39.

Magic Moment: *In September 1958 Don Ratcliffe lost his boot in a tackle at Hillsborough. Thomson picked it up. 'Just as I was about to take it,' smiles Ratcliffe, 'he threw it into the crowd! I had to wait for them to throw it back, because I only had one pair of boots.'*

Worst Nightmare: *In the final home game of 1952-53, with Stoke 1-2 down v Derby, Thomson shoved regular taker Frank Mountford aside to take a penalty. It was saved. Stoke lost and went down.*

STOKE RECORD	Appearances	Goals
Football League	278	6
FA Cup	24	1

No 53. **HARRY OSCROFT**
Debut: v West Brom, 14 January 1950
Farewell: v Bristol City, 7 March 1959

Harold Oscroft continued the line of goalscoring left-wingers at Stoke begun by Joe Johnson and continued by Alec Ormston.

Born in Mansfield on 10 March 1926, Oscroft began his career with Mansfield Colliery before signing for Third Division (South) Mansfield Town in February 1947. He became a local favourite and scored 39 goals in 112 League games, providing many more for his player-manager, former Stoke centre-forward Freddie Steele.

A 0-1 defeat by Tottenham in the FA Cup in January 1950 effectively ended Stoke's season. Sensing that the club was drifting, with many of the £10 teamers fading, McGrory acted to spice up his side. An injury in October looked to have put Ormston out for months, so – fingers burnt by the failures of record acquisitions McAlinden and Kiernan the previous season – McGrory settled for a lower profile signing. He persuaded Steele to part with his star player for £8,000 plus ex-Manchester City forward Verdi Godwin, who had managed only a paltry two goals for Stoke in 22 games.

Oscroft arrived at the Victoria Ground on the same day as a trial for local youngsters took place. Due to sheeting rain this was held in the gym beneath the Boothen End terrace. Among the triallists was a budding goalkeeper, Donald Lawton. 'Harry was well known for his powerful shot. He joined us for a kickabout and when he kicked the leather at me it ricocheted from a corner stanchion, struck me full in the face and laid me out for a good five minutes. I was fifteen and never made it any further in professional football!'

Oscroft proved to be McGrory's first successful signing for some time. When recovered, Ormston was switched to the right, giving Stoke twin wingers in more senses than one. Although he did not share Ormston's characteristic hump, Oscroft resembled his colleague facially, sharing a wide nose and large ears. Oscroft's prematurely balding head was accentuated by wearing his hair brylcreemed back in the style of the day. It sat atop a 5ft 6in muscular body with which he bundled past defenders.

Oscroft began scoring regularly late in 1950-51, notching four in four games at the end of March. He continued the trend until 1956-57, reaching double figures in the League each season, and top scoring in 1952-53 and also 1954-55, when he bagged 21 goals. As a winger he was at his best with the ball at his feet, beating opponents at pace. He had a knack of first cutting inside and then back to the outside before cracking in a blistering left-footed shot. His inconsistency, though, caused concern. Amongst his fellow players Oscroft's reputation was of someone prone to flashes of inspiration, but who would disappear during games. 'He tended to hide,' recalls Johnny King, 'although just when you thought Taylor would drop him, he would go and score.'

Oscroft's first goal of 1958-59, in a 1-6 collapse at Fulham, brought up his century of Stoke goals in all competitions – only the sixth player to reach this landmark. His final total left him fourth in the all-time goalscoring charts, although both John King and John Ritchie later overtook him.

In January 1959 Oscroft began to drift out of the reckoning. Now 33, he moved on to Port Vale in August, along with reserve centre-half Peter Ford and £2,000, in exchange for left-winger Dickie Cunliffe, who took his place. Like former team-mate Ken Thomson, Oscroft became tainted by the fall-out from the Tony Kaye/Bronco Layne scandal. In the final game of 1959-60 Vale defeated Swindon 6-1, with Oscroft scoring four times in the first half. When the scandal broke three years later, that game was listed as one of the many considered suspect. Whether Oscroft had any part in the fixing was never proved.

After scoring 12 goals in 51 appearances for Vale, which took his career League tally past 150, Oscroft retired to the Essex/Suffolk border where he became player-manager at Brantham Athletic, with whom he won the Suffolk Senior Cup. Oscroft later played a few games for Sutton United. He retired in 1988 and lives near Colchester.

Magic Moment: *The third goal of Oscroft's hat-trick at Lincoln in October 1954 saw him cut in from the left hand side to lash home a piledriver to finish off a sweeping breakaway move.*

Worst Nightmare: *In September 1951, with Stoke 0-2 down at home to Tottenham, Oscroft, in the absence of regular taker Frank Mountford, shot wide from the penalty spot. Stoke lost 1-6.*

STOKE RECORD	Appearances	Goals
Football League	326	102
FA Cup	23	4

No 54. **TIM COLEMAN**
Debut: v Doncaster, 17 October 1953
Farewell: v Bristol Rovers, 4 October 1958

While Oscroft provided Stoke with goals from the left wing, Neville 'Tim' Coleman contributed a steady flow from the right.

Coleman was born in Prescot, Merseyside on 29 January 1930, and joined Stoke as an amateur in 1953 from Gorleston in Norfolk, where he was completing his National Service at the local RAF base. As he had trouble obtaining permision to play, the board secured his release from service in January 1954. The club provided roughly half of the cost, with Coleman stumping up £60. He could not turn professional for a further year, on account of rules regarding those who bought themselves out of the forces.

Signed as a centre-forward, as Stoke sought a partner for Frank Bowyer, Coleman mustered five goals from nine sporadic appearances. But Frank Taylor saw that Coleman's pace and power could be best utilised out wide. The decision initially condemned Coleman to the reserves to learn his new trade, but Johnny Malkin's career-ending broken leg at Leicester in October 1956, handed Coleman his chance. He developed into a devastating right-winger – when he was in the mood. His fluctuating form produced long periods of frustration interspersed with sporadic bouts of flair.

Coleman's trademark was to lick the fingers on each hand and rub them together. 'If he did that, you knew he was going to play,' recalls Don Ratcliffe. 'He didn't seem to be trying,' adds Don Whiston. 'He wasn't particularly quick, but when he was moving he was very good, very hard to shake off the ball.'

Tallish, at 5ft 11in, Coleman's dark, long hair, untypical of the time, and engaging smile marked him out as another of Stoke's playboy 'Bad Lads'. The origin of his nickname 'Tim', however, remains a mystery, although a clue may lie in the same moniker being applied to Ernest 'Tim' Coleman, the Arsenal, Middlesbrough and England centre-forward of the 1930s.

Coleman scored twice as Stoke finally overcame Bury in a protracted FA Cup-tie in January 1955. Both goals, however, were lucky. His first, a late equaliser, saw Coleman's header hit the bar and bounce into the net via the goalkeeper's foot, while the winner was even more bizarre. Haring into the box to meet a Ratcliffe cross, Coleman tripped and fell in the sea of mud. The ball hit him on the back of the head, looping into the top corner of the net.

An example of Coleman's inconsistency came at the end of his purple patch in 1956-57. He top scored with 26 goals, including a hat-trick in a 3-1 defeat of Middlesbrough. On 23 February second placed Stoke beat Lincoln 8-0 at the Victoria Ground with Coleman scoring seven – a world record for a winger in one game. Sadly, this peak was followed by a trough in both Stoke's form and Coleman's. He failed to score in any of the remaining ten games, while City lost six in a row and finished fifth. All but one of Coleman's 26 goals came at the Victoria Ground, lending credence to suggestions that he only turned it on with a supportive crowd behind him.

In February 1959 Coleman was sold to Crewe for £1,000 – not much for a 29-year-old – to make way for winger Doug Newlands, who arrived from Burnley for £15,000. Taylor declared Newlands to be the final piece in Stoke's promotion jigsaw, although his record of just eight goals in 32 games, and an inability to gel with his fellow forwards, ensured him a free transfer to St Johnstone eight months later – another of Taylor's high-profile transfer failures.

Coleman retired in 1961. He worked at the Rolls Royce factory in Crewe before emigrating in the early 1970s. He is believed to be living in Canada or Australia.

Magic Moment: *Coleman's seventh and last goal in the 8-0 win over Lincoln saw him dive at a George Kelly cross to bury a header. Coleman received the match ball, a record for goals scored by a winger in one game – and a black eye – sustained during that dive.*

Worst Nightmare: *Coleman might have scored even more that day. He blasted his easiest chance of the game into the side-netting, while his ninth and final shot rocketed into the referee.*

STOKE RECORD	Appearances	Goals
Football League	114	46
FA Cup	12	6

No 55. **JOHNNY KING**
Debut: v Rotherham, 21 September 1953
Farewell: v Liverpool, 3 May 1961

Amid the torpor which surrounded the Victoria Ground during the 1950s, John William King's goalscoring feats stood head and shoulders above the mediocrity which surrounded him.

Born in Wrenbury, Cheshire on 9 August 1932, King's mother complained regularly when young Johnny returned home with the shoe on his natural left foot worn by hours practising with a tennis ball. He joined his local club, Crewe, in October 1949, and learnt his trade under the watchful eye of manager, and ex-Stoke skipper, Arthur Turner.

King formed a partnership with left-winger Frankie Blunstone. First Division Chelsea swooped for the pair, but King opted instead to join Stoke for £8,000 in September 1953, persuaded by the same Arthur Turner, now City's assistant manager. Many felt King should have followed Blunstone, who would win five England caps and play an integral part in Chelsea's title-winning side of 1954-55.

King's wiry body was topped by a head of light brown wavy hair. His extremely fair eyebrows gave the impression that he had none. He always took the field with his sleeves rolled tightly up above his elbows, ready for work. His magical left foot was capable of deft close control and, at 5ft 7in, King's low centre of gravity helped him to turn on a sixpence and fool lumbering defenders who struggled in his wake. He loved competing against big centre-halves. His favourite opponent was Leeds and England's Jack Charlton: 'I used to back into him, receive the ball at my feet and then spin off, leaving him for dead. I loved playing against Leeds,' he recalls.

King quickly earned the nickname 'Hovver' from his team-mates – a reference to the fact that he did not get far off the ground for headers. In fact, his chief defect was in being so one footed that his options were often reduced.

King passed double figures in all but one of his eight seasons at Stoke, finishing three times as leading scorer. After initially playing him in his natural inside-left position, Taylor hit upon the idea of deploying him at No 9. Stoke were short of a quality centre-forward to capitalise on the riches of Coleman and Oscroft on the wings. But Taylor's insistence that the ball be played forward at the earliest opportunity, in the image of his former club, Wolves, often left King isolated.

King took over penalty taking duties, bequeathed him by a much relieved Frank Mountford. King's style was to crack the ball with the outside of his left foot into the corner to the goalkeeper's right. He was invariably successful, despite never varying his method, until a miss at Blackburn late in his career brought Stoke's chairman into the dressing room moaning that his team could not even score from the penalty spot.

Although King scored consistently, Taylor struggled to find him a regular partner. To his right, King had the prolific but ageing Frank Bowyer, but to his left Bobby Cairns, Joe Hutton and Eric Lowell all failed to click. In the summer of 1955 City agreed terms with Blackpool to sign the legendary Stan Mortensen, but Morty preferred to join Hull and it was not until the arrival of one of the most colourful characters ever to don a Stoke shirt, George 'Grace' Kelly, in January 1956, that a regular partner for King emerged.

Kelly, also known as 'Spider' due to his tall lean frame, forged a dynamic partnership with King. They became known as Stoke's 'K Plan' with Kelly thriving on King's intuitive passes inside the penalty area. Stoke finished fifth in 1956-57 with the 'K Plan' in operation, and the pair scored 37 goals between them the following season as Stoke racked up 75 in the League, a total surpassed only once since. King's form won him selection for the 1956 FA tour to South Africa, against whose national side he played three times.

In March 1958 Cardiff manager Trevor Morris, planning an immediate return for his side to the First Division, signed Kelly – who had scored 37 goals in two seasons at Stoke – for £20,000, Stoke's record outgoing fee. Taylor replaced him with Wolves and England forward Dennis Wilshaw for half that fee. Although both Wilshaw and King scored regularly, their partnership failed to flourish. Perhaps they were intrinsically too similar.

In the final game of 1959-60, King grabbed the first in a 2-1 win at Bristol City, completing a century of goals in all competitions for Stoke, the seventh man to reach that landmark. Thirteen goals in his final season at the Victoria Ground left him in fourth place on the all-time goalscorers list, although he has since been overtaken by John Ritchie. Prior to the 1961-62 season, First Division Cardiff paid £12,000 for 29-year-old King. New manager Tony Waddington invested the money wisely, importing the similarly Lilliputian Jackie Mudie from Blackpool.

King failed to make the expected impact in the top flight, scoring six goals as the Bluebirds suffered relegation. Perhaps he had left it too late to venture into the highest echelon. He returned to Crewe in 1962, whereupon they won promotion for the first time. King made 178 League appearances for Crewe, scoring 43 goals, in that second spell and in 1998 was voted by fans as the most influential player ever to play for that club. He totalled nearly 500 League appearances and over 170 goals in his long career.

Magic Moment: *Stoke gave one of their best displays of the 1950s in beating Swansea 6-2 in December 1957. King scored a gem, taking a defence-splitting pass from Wilshaw on the run and netting.*

Worst Nightmare: *Presented with an open goal in the last minute of a 3-1 win over Port Vale in October 1956, King ballooned the ball towards the newly installed Victoria Ground floodlights.*

STOKE RECORD	Appearances	Goals
Football League	284	107
FA Cup	26	7
League Cup	1	–

No 56. **DON RATCLIFFE**
Debut: v Bury, 25 December 1954
Farewell: v Sheffield United, 18 September 1963

Donald Ratcliffe was a late-comer to the 'Bad Lads', but he learnt quickly from the masters of mayhem.

Born into a family of colliers in Newcastle-under-Lyme on 13 November 1934, by his own admission Ratcliffe was 'dead rough'. He dispelled his effervescent energy by scampering around waste-ground playing football and was recommended to Stoke by a local grocer, outside whose shop he played. He joined Stoke in May 1953 on £12 a week. For a 17-year-old this was big money – the same as his father earned after a lifetime at the coalface. Don recalls: 'I never had any underwear and when I first got changed at Stoke the trainer, Norman Tapken – a Geordie git he was – asked me where they were. I said I hadn't got any, and he told me I was dirty. Then, when I was cleaning my boots, he told me that I shouldn't bother cleaning them, I should concentrate on cleaning my miner's lamp as that was all I was good for. I bloody hated him.'

The impish Ratcliffe waited seven years to gain revenge on Tapken. On the day in June 1960 that the new manager, Tony Waddington, sacked Tapken in favour of the more agreeable Frank Mountford, Ratcliffe shot down to the Victoria Ground and sought out his tormentor. 'I said to him "Who's got to clean their lamp now!" He chased me all the way up the stand!'

On the pitch, irrepressible Ratcliffe was the archetypal human dynamo. Anarchic spiky brown hair stood atop his cheeky, beaming face. A fine athlete, his 5ft 8in frame appeared lightweight, but he was nevertheless a willing workhorse who flogged himself for his beloved club. Dennis Wilshaw smiles, 'If we opened the gates at the Stoke end, he'd run out of the ground.'

Nicknamed 'Ratty', his chatterbox personality made Ratcliffe the wisecracking life and soul of the Stoke dressing room. As an embryonic member of the Bad Lads, Ratcliffe was sensibly paired with the more sombre Frank Bowyer as a room-mate. On his first away trip, Ratcliffe, having dumped his kit in his room, groomed himself for a night on the tiles playing cards and quaffing ale. After watching the sprucing up ritual with amusement, Bowyer asked: 'Where do you think you're going?' 'Out' replied Ratty. 'Oh no you're not!' admonished Bowyer, locking the door, 'Go to bed.' The humbled Ratcliffe did as he was told.

Ratcliffe's dynamism concealed considerable skill. He had two good feet and loved to take on opponents for pace before getting to the by-line and looping a cross towards the penalty spot. Although a natural wide player, he played in every outfield position bar centre-half, causing Tony Waddington to once boast that Ratcliffe was the first £100,000 footballer – as he could have sold him for £10,000 in each position! The one thing Ratcliffe was not, was hard. Tommy Smith, the Liverpool curmudgeon, once approached him before kick-off: 'I hear you're fast,' said Smith. 'Yeah,' replied Ratty. 'Not with one leg you're not.' 'I kept well out of his way I can tell you,' winces Ratcliffe.

Ratcliffe found himself inextricably involved in a number of incidents which have gone down in Stoke folklore. An epic 1955 FA Cup third round tie against Bury went to a fourth replay. Desperate to get it over with, Ratcliffe saw Bury keeper Conway slip on the turf. 'I dived on top of him and he's punching me, trying to get me off him, but I wouldn't let go. Thompo heads the ball in and the referee gives a goal. I couldn't believe it. Neither could the keeper. He chased me all the way back into my half!'

John King recalls a game against Huddersfield in January 1958, with Stoke battling to hold on to a 1-1 draw. 'Every time the referee blew the whistle, Ratty kept kicking the ball into the crowd. Eventually the referee had had enough and was going to book him. I walked past them and said to the ref "You'll have to excuse him. He's very hard of hearing". The ref puts his book away, leans over to Don and says really loudly in his ear "Don't do that again". I don't know how Don kept a straight face.'

In the summer of 1961 Waddington summoned Ratcliffe to negotiate a new contract. The senior professionals at Stoke earned £40 per week. Waddo offered Ratcliffe £25 plus a £1 bonus per extra thousand for a gate over 8,000 and £5 per week for each place that City climbed above sixth. Two months later Stoke re-signed Stanley Matthews. Ratcliffe was happy to vacate his place on City's right wing. Average gates tripled to nearly 26,000 and Stoke won the Second Division title in 1962-63 having led from the start. Ratcliffe switched to the left, replacing Jimmy Adam. Whether it was his new-found financial status or the influence of the world's greatest footballer, Ratcliffe came alive after the arrival of Matthews and played his best football as Stoke romped to promotion.

Ratcliffe held the proud record of never having been dropped until September 1963, when Waddington dumped him into the reserves. Although Ratcliffe did not want to leave, Middlesbrough manager Raich Carter's offer of £27,500 was accepted. Ratcliffe's ebullient personality, however, grated with Carter and he moved on to Darlington and then Crewe before retiring in 1969. He now lives in his native Newcastle-under-Lyme.

Magic Moment: *Against Barnsley in November 1957, Ratcliffe, played a long ball down the left for George Kelly, who pulled up and*

yelled at Ratcliffe for not passing to his feet. Ratcliffe chased his own
pass, beat three defenders and lashed the ball into the roof of the net.

Worst Nightmare: *Sunderland maestro Len Shackleton stopped*
the ball, put one foot on it and beckoned Ratcliffe with his finger.
Ratcliffe and Tony Allen took the bait and dived in. Shack played a
one-two off the corner flag, leaving both men red-faced on the grass.

STOKE RECORD	Appearances	Goals
Football League	238	16
FA Cup	21	3
League Cup	5	–

No 57. **BILL ASPREY**
Debut: v Oldham, 20 March 1954
Farewell: v Leeds 23 October 1965

William Asprey served Stoke in various capacities for over fifteen
years, and yet his belligerent personality ensured that this great
club servant is never particularly fondly remembered.

Born in Wolverhampton on 11 September 1936, manager Frank
Taylor pinched Asprey from under the noses of his boyhood heroes
Wolves. He signed, initially as an amateur in 1952, turning profes-
sional on his seventeenth birthday.

Asprey's early career was interrupted by his National Service,
but he was released to shine in the youth team's progress to the FA
Youth Cup semi-finals, where City lost 1-2 to West Brom with
Asprey scoring Stoke's goal. He established himself at right-half in
the first team towards the end of 1956-57, but his adaptability
meant he appeared in eight different positions for Stoke, filling in
as emergency centre-forward more than once. He starred as Stoke
thrashed Plymouth 9-0 in December 1960 (City's biggest winning
margin) and bagged a hat-trick against Charlton the following
month. A model of consistency, he was ever present in 1958-59,
1961-62 and 1962-63, making 101 consecutive appearances, save
for the League Cup second round tie at Walsall in September 1962
in which Tony Waddington purposefully fielded a weakened side.

At 6ft 1in and 12st 4lbs, Aprey was a strong, no-nonsense sort.
He was tall for a full-back – his favoured position – where Waddo
switched him in 1960-61. Asprey formed a fine partnership with
Tony Allen and spent most of his career in the No 2 shirt. He was
a keen tackler as Allen recalls: 'He clonked 'em one I can tell you.'

Asprey, though, did not always get on with his fellow players.
He could be surly and was forthright in his opinions, making him
an outsider to the 'Bad Lads'. His dashing blond looks and winning

smile were carefully preened, earning their owner a reputation as a man who fancied himself, not necessarily willing to get stuck in to help his team-mates. Don Ratcliffe remembers: 'The only time I ever got fined was for kicking him in training after he stamped on me in a practice match. The git cost me £5!'

Along with others who had come through the ranks at Stoke – Eric Skeels, Tony Allen and Ron Andrew – Asprey formed an integral part of the 'Waddington Wall'. The manager mixed homegrown players with established top-flight defenders such as Eddie Clamp, Maurice Setters and George Kinnell to form a barricade in front of goalkeeper Lawrie Leslie. The plan involved two midfielders holding back when Stoke attacked to remain ready to deal with opposition breakaways. City were criticised for adopting an ultra-defensive formation, but the plan worked. Stoke stabilised in the First Division, allowing Waddington's youth policy to bear fruit.

Having inherited the captaincy from Eddie Stuart, Asprey played a major part in Stoke reaching their first ever major Cup final, earning a League Cup runners-up medal in 1963-64, after scoring the clincher in the semi-final win over Manchester City.

In 1965-66, following Calvin Palmer's conversion to full-back, Asprey signed for Oldham. He moved on to Port Vale in December 1967, before retiring in February 1969 to coach at Sheffield Wednesday. He also coached Coventry, Wolves, West Brom and in Rhodesia, where he became national director of football. Asprey returned to England to coach Oxford in 1978, becoming manager in 1979, but made little impact and was sacked in December 1980.

He accepted an offer in 1981 to become assistant at Stoke to Richie Barker and inherited the manager's chair on his dismissal in December 1983. Asprey turned City's season around a month later, using former boss Waddington to persuade Alan Hudson to re-sign. Stoke won eight of their next eleven games and avoided relegation on the final Saturday with a 4-0 thrashing of Wolves.

His hands tied by Stoke's calamitous finances, Asprey operated with no assistant, trainer or physiotherapist during 1984-85. Not surprisingly the season lurched through record-breaking runs of defeats, fewest goals scored, and fewest games won. By Christmas the strain had taken its toll on Asprey's health and he was forced to take time off for mental and physical exhaustion. No sooner had he returned to work than he was sacked, when supporters' protests, mainly aimed at the board, gathered momentum. Stoke only won fourteen of his 67 games in charge. He became a hotelier.

Magic Moment: *In early September 1963, as Stoke settled into First Division football for the first time in ten years, Asprey rattled a 35-yard shot past Gordon Banks in a 3-3 draw against Leicester.*

Worst Nightmare: *After Stoke's 4-0 defeat of Wolves in May 1984, Alan Hudson and four-goal hero Paul Maguire joined Asprey standing on the Boothen End. Asprey whispered to Maguire: 'I won us the game today, because I picked you.' Maguire stormed out and was handed a free transfer within an hour of the final whistle.*

STOKE RECORD	Appearances	Goals
Football League	304	23
FA Cup	19	2
League Cup	18	1

No 58. **TONY ALLEN**
Debut: v Doncaster, 14 September 1957
Farewell: v Crystal Palace, 6 September 1969

Anthony Allen very nearly signed for Port Vale, his boyhood team, rather than Stoke. Born in Stoke-on-Trent on 27 November 1939, Allen started as an inside-left and in 1954 scored a hat-trick for his 24th Boys Brigade team in the North Staffs Battalion Cup final. By his mid-teens Allen had an impressive 5ft 9in, 12st physique which, whilst playing with Stoke-on-Trent schoolboys, encouraged his conversion to centre-half.

Spotted playing in an English schools match at the Victoria Ground in 1956, Allen agreed terms with *both* Potteries clubs and travelled to Vale Park to meet manager Freddie Steele, expecting to sign. But Allen suddenly changed his mind and plumped for Stoke: 'I still don't really know why I didn't join Vale!' he smiles. The mind which influenced his decision to join Stoke belonged to reserve-team coach Tony Waddington, under whose tutelage Allen became a stylish left-back.

Within a year Allen made his debut for England Youth at Spurs in a 3-0 win over Italy, and Waddington pushed Allen's cause hard for first-team recognition with manager Frank Taylor, who was losing faith in the ageing John McCue. Allen only discovered that he was making his debut at Doncaster just before kick-off, with the seething McCue also in the dressing room and expecting to play.

Allen's distinctive shock of blond hair curled into a quiff over his right eye. His short passing was immaculate, but his main attribute was his reading of the game. Although not overly quick, Allen intuitively knew when to make his move to intercept successfully, allowing him to dispossess attackers with ease.

His stylish play marked him out and seven England Under-23 caps quickly followed, the first against Poland in September 1958. It wasn't long before he was in contention for a full England cap. Following the Munich air disaster Walter Winterbottom had to find a replacement for Manchester United's Roger Byrne, a victim of that tragedy. Allen's full England debut came just before his twentieth birthday – some feat given that Stoke were an average Second Division side. He became the first Stoke player since Neil Franklin nine years earlier to represent England.

Allen did not always have it his own way though. In a 2-4 home defeat by Blackburn, England winger Bryan Douglas taught Allen a salutary lesson in the art of wing play, skinning him at will. 'I was that ashamed I didn't get the bus home. I walked,' he recalls. That particular incident had its fringe benefits, however. 'Dennis Wilshaw spent the whole of the next training session showing me what Douglas had been doing to beat me and after that I could spot anyone who tried it a mile off.'

Allen won three full caps, against Wales, Sweden and Northern Ireland in the autumn of 1959, as Winterbottom began assembling a squad which would compete in the World Cup in Chile in 1962. But thereafer Allen lost his place to Huddersfield's Ray Wilson, who progressed to win a World Cup winners' medal in 1966.

In March 1960 Stoke's new manager, Tony Waddington, staved off a £25,000 bid for Allen's services from Manchester City. Allen then became a vital cog in the 'Waddington Wall', which enabled Stoke to establish themselves in the First Division after returning to it in 1962-63. A side effect of Stan Matthews' return to Stoke was Allen's inheriting of an unwanted habit from the ageless winger. 'Stan was always sick before every game. And I used to see him and feel it welling up inside me too. Before long I was being sick in sympathy and it stuck with me throughout my career.'

Ever present in 1960-61 and 1961-62, Allen completed a club record run of 121 consecutive League appearances, 148 in all competitions, between March 1960 and March 1963, surpassing the record set by Arthur Turner 25 years earlier. He only missed nine first-team games between his debut and the tail end of 1964-65, when he injured his knee. Allen puts this down to his temperament. A passive man, he prided himself on never losing his temper on the field, solely concentrating on countering his opponents' intentions.

Midway through 1966-67 Allen's pace began to desert him, so Waddington, knowing his value to the team, switched him to centre-half alongside Maurice Setters. The change allowed Stoke to benefit from Allen's excellent distribution and reading of the game, and prolonged his career until 1968-69, when Liverpool's £70,000 Willie Stevenson displaced him. To mark his distinguished service, Stoke awarded Allen a joint testimonial match with Eric Skeels against Derby in February 1969.

After drifting in and out of the Stoke side for eighteen months, Allen moved on to Bury for £10,000 before taking up an offer in

1972 to play for Hellenic FC in Cape Town, along with fellow Stoke player George Eastham.

Allen's first season in South Africa did not start well as Hellenic lost four of their first six games. A witch doctor was soon summoned to work his magic. 'He went around putting smut marks on all the kit with a piece of smoking rope. Then he put his hands on the match ball and muttered under his breath. It worked. We won eleven of the next twelve and won the League.'

Allen returned home, playing for Stafford Rangers whilst running a newsagency. He has suffered painful problems with his knees and in January 2001 had the first of two operations to allow him to walk without a stick. Despite his current situation, he has no regrets. 'I wouldn't change anything,' he declares. 'They could give me the same money and I'd do it all again.'

Magic Moment: *Allen rifled home his first goal in his 196th game – a right-footer into the far corner past England goalkeeper Gordon Banks during Stoke's 5-2 FA Cup win over Leicester.*

Worst Nightmare: *In an FA Cup-tie in January 1962, Allen conceded a penalty against Blackburn's Bryan Douglas. One supporter was so irate that he began legal proceedings against referee Webb.*

STOKE RECORD	Appearances	Goals
League	414 (+3 subs)	2
FA Cup	30	1
League Cup	26	1

No 59. **DENNIS WILSHAW**
Debut: v Swansea Town, 9 December 1957
Farewell: v Newcastle, 18 January 1961

Although Dennis Wilshaw grew up a Stoke fan, the club missed out on his best years as an international goalscorer of some repute.

Born in Stoke-on-Trent on 11 March 1926, the young Wilshaw idolised Stanley Matthews and spent his formative years at the Victoria Ground perched upon his father's shoulders watching his hero. But Wilshaw became one of the few talented youngsters to escape the net that Stoke City cast around the area. He was spotted by Wolves playing for his village team, Packmoor Boys Club, in a 16-0 win in which he scored ten goals. The following week Major Frank Buckley named Wilshaw in the Wolves team against West Brom in the Wartime League.

Determined to pursue his education in case his football career didn't work out, Wilshaw took a teacher training course in maths and physical education at Loughborough College from 1945 and played his entire career as a part-time professional. He spent three seasons on loan at Walsall and it took the appointment of Stan Cullis to the manager's chair at Molineux to kick-start Wilshaw's career. He made his First Division bow against Newcastle in March 1949, filling in for the injured Jimmy Mullen. Wolves won 3-0, with Wilshaw scoring all three. He went on to star in Wolves' 1954 title-winning team and featured in the floodlit games against Spartak Moscow and Honved which are etched into the memories of every football fan who lived in the 1950s.

Blessed with a prominent Roman nose, the 5ft 10in Wilshaw's main asset was pace, which got him into good positions, although Wilshaw believes instinct did the rest: 'A goalscorer is born and not made. I never thought about what I was doing when I was through on goal. If I did it probably meant that I would miss.'

Wilshaw's consistent scoring was rewarded by an England call-up against Wales in October 1953. He scored twice in a 4-1 win, went to the 1954 World Cup in Switzerland, and scored as England beat hosts Switzerland 2-0 in Berne. He went into the record books by scoring four goals on his first appearance at Wembley against Scotland in the famous 7-2 win in 1955, at that time an individual scoring record at the stadium. It has only been surpassed by Malcolm MacDonald's five against feeble Cyprus. Wilshaw won twelve caps, scoring ten goals, before losing his place to the entirely different skills of Fulham's scheming Johnny Haynes.

After 219 games and 112 goals for Wolves, in 1957-58 Wilshaw found himself no longer an automatic first choice. Speculation linked him with a move to Stoke and he received a telephone call from Frank Taylor informing him that he had permission to discuss terms. The fact that Wolves made no effort to keep him convinced Wilshaw the time was right to move on.

Stoke paid £10,000 for Wilshaw on 6 December 1957. His arrival added much needed style and firepower to the forward line. His debut resulted in a 6-2 win over Swansea, although he did not score from his unexpected left-wing position.

Wilshaw now considers the move to his boyhood team a mistake, believing he could have played First Division football for several more years. He also missed out on a championship medal with Wolves in 1957-58. Amid the chaos of the 'Bad Lads' though, Wilshaw's professionalism and dedication was refreshing, and it is no wonder that he appeared at a stroke to be one of the best players in the Stoke team.

Once George Kelly had been sold to Cardiff, Wilshaw resumed his normal inside-forward duties. He scored eighteen goals to finish as leading scorer in 1958-59 and forged a competent partnership with Johnny King, although the pair's playing styles were too similar for it to really flourish. Wilshaw scored three hat-tricks for Stoke and became club captain. Despite being 34, he was still one of the best players in the division and as such, a marked man.

Wilshaw's nickname at Stoke was 'Mr Nearly', reputedly because his first touch was not that great. This gentle joshing actually predicted the end of his career. In February 1961 he dallied in controlling a pass and received a clattering from Bill Thompson of Newcastle. Don Ratcliffe recalls with horror: 'His leg went back in a U-shape. The medics cut his sock and you could see the bone. It was the only time I have ever felt sick on the field.'

The break was serious and complicated, and Wilshaw now possesses one leg shorter than the other. Stoke's response was to release him with no compensation and no assistance in terms of a benefit match or funds for medical consultation or surgery. While recuperating, Wilshaw often popped into training to see his former colleagues. On one occasion he mentioned to Waddington that to get the club going Stoke needed the return of Stanley Matthews, currently languishing in Blackpool's reserves. Within six months Matthews was back at Stoke and the club was transformed.

Ironically, Wilshaw's work with youth players in Stoke reaped huge dividends for the club. His Stoke-on-Trent schools team, containing the likes of Denis Smith and Jackie Marsh, won the English Schools Trophy two years running, 1962 and 1963, the only occasion this has been achieved.

Magic Moment: *In January 1958 Wilshaw scored a hat-trick as Stoke beat Middlesbrough 3-1 in the FA Cup. Following a free-kick given against him, Wilshaw delayed play by walking off with the ball. Boro striker Brian Clough wrestled it out of Wilshaw's arms, but as Clough placed the ball Wilshaw kicked him up the backside!*

Worst Nightmare: *In the late 1950s Wilshaw took his Stoke Schools team to a training camp. The adolescent Alan Bloor landed a kick on Wilshaw during a session, putting him out for a month.*

STOKE RECORD	Appearances	Goals
Football League	94	41
FA Cup	14	9

Stoke celebrate the promotion-clinching 2-0 home win over Luton (May 1963)

The offical photo for 1963-64, showing the Division Two championship trophy

STOKE CITY F.C.
1963-64 Season

The twinkle-toed Matthews bemuses Huddersfield's defence on his return, aged 46

Gordon Banks punches clear at Burnley in a 0-4 defeat (April 1968)

Club record appearance holder Eric Skeels

Greenhoff scores again, but the collapse of the Butler Street stand forced his sale

Chapter Seven

~ *The Old Crocks* ~

No 60. **JIMMY O'NEILL**
Debut: v Plymouth, 20 August 1960
Farewell: v Fulham 19 October 1963

Stoke's failure to challenge for promotion yet again in 1959-60 cost manager Frank Taylor his job. The board named his assistant, Tony Waddington, as replacement, who knew drastic action was necessary. Dwindling attendances – City's gates had ducked under 10,000 for the first time since 1907-08 – ruled out any five-year plan. He had observed the positive effect of signing the experienced Dennis Wilshaw, both in terms of performance and in developing young players, and sought to repeat the experiment. Waddington signed more experienced pros, who put an emphasis on skill, and the policy was richly rewarded. His priority was to find an experienced keeper and in July he persuaded Everton to part with the first of the 'Old Crocks', James Anthony O'Neill.

The son of an accomplished professional golfer, Moses O'Neill, Jimmy was born in Dublin on 13 October 1931. His father's sporting prowess meant that young Jimmy had taken a keen interest in all sports, although football soon emerged as his favourite. He played for local club Bulfin United, and soon graduated to win schoolboy international honours, keeping a clean sheet as the Irish inflicted a rare home defeat on England at Brentford in 1948.

That performance attracted Everton manager Cliff Britton, and O'Neill signed in May 1949. By 1951 O'Neill had laid claim to the first-team jersey, displacing the legendary Ted Sagar, and starred as Everton won promotion back to the top flight in 1953-54 with the meanest defensive record in the division.

His form interested the Irish selectors, although O'Neill prefers not to remember his debut, a 0-6 thrashing by Spain. He won seventeen Irish caps, among them one for beating Austria's Wunderteam 4-0 in 1953. After 201 games in ten years at Goodison Park, 28-year-old O'Neill shrugged off interest from Bill Shankly, the new manager of Liverpool, to join Stoke for a knockdown £2,000.

O'Neill recalls some of the fringe benefits of being a professional footballer of the time. 'After five years [at Everton] I got a benefit of £750. The taxman took £250 out of it and out of the balance I got married. I then got an accrued share of the benefit when I left Everton. I got about £150 quid. They were legal payments. Not like some of the under-the-counter stuff. When I moved to Stoke, my wife Angela wanted to have a new cooker, so I mentioned to the club that we could do with one. And that was part of my transfer fee. I got a new cooker out of it.'

At just 5ft 10in, O'Neill continued the line of Stoke keepers – short on stature, but long on talent. Despite his size he was known for his safe handling and ability to deal with crosses. His long legs allowed him to leap for high balls, although they occasionally gave him problems reaching ground shots. His genial smile under close-cropped brown hair brightened Stoke's dressing room, and his acquisition proved fundamental to the stabilising of the defence. He missed just one game in each of 1960-61 and 1961-62, was ever present in the 1962-63 Second Division title-winning side, and kept 48 clean sheets in his 149 games for Stoke.

At the time it was accepted, wrongly, that the club had been founded in 1863, so on 24 April 1963 Stoke celebrated their 'centenary' by playing European giants Real Madrid. A crowd of 44,914 saw a 2-2 draw with Puskas, Alfredo Di Stefano, Gento *et al.*

Although O'Neill's green jersey was later worn by fellow veterans Harry Gregg, Harry Dowd and Lawrie Leslie, he actually lost his place to a youngster – Bobby Irvine, who arrived for £6,000 from Linfield. O'Neill moved to Darlington on a free transfer in March 1964, before joining Port Vale, Cork Celtic and Bury. He retired in 1968 to run a taxi business in Ormskirk.

Magic Moment: *Before the final game at the Victoria Ground in 1997, O'Neill asked Stan Matthews to shoot at him at the Boothen End. Matthews hit the ball past O'Neill to send the ground into raptures. O'Neill's cheeky wink revealed his intention to miss the ball.*

Worst Nightmare: *Prior to Stoke's centenary celebration v Real Madrid, O'Neill saw Puskas hit six penalties into the same corner in training. In the game, with Stoke 2-1 up, O'Neill faced Puskas from the penalty spot and dived to his right. Puskas scored to his left.*

STOKE RECORD	Appearances	Goals
Football League	130	–
FA Cup	10	–
League Cup	9	–

No 61. **JACKIE MUDIE**
Debut: v Scunthorpe, 4 March 1961
Farewell: v Arsenal, 9 October 1963

The next prominent veteran to arrive was Dennis Wilshaw's direct replacement, John Knight Mudie. Born in Dundee on 10 April 1930,

Mudie, one of seven brothers, began playing for local teams around Dundee, principally Dunkeld Amateurs, and was soon spotted by Blackpool's scouts. He signed for the Tangerines in June 1947, and emerged as a goalscoring inside-forward in the famous Blackpool side that included Ernie Taylor, George Farm and Harry Johnston. Their prolific attack became known as the three M's – Mudie, Matthews and Mortensen.

Selected by Scotland at centre-forward in October 1956 for the 2-2 draw with Wales, Mudie won seventeen consecutive caps, scoring nine goals, including a hat-trick in a 4-2 win over Spain at Hampden Park in a qualifier for the 1958 World Cup. He played in all three of Scotland's matches in Sweden and was involved in one of the most controversial incidents in Scottish World Cup history when the Yugoslavian goalkeeper, Beara, dropped a cross which bounced off Mudie's back and into the net. Swiss referee Wyssling, however, awarded a free-kick against Mudie for a foul on Beara and Scotland only drew 1-1.

Possessing a jutting chin and dark hair, the 'Mighty Midget' Mudie soon earned a reputation as a good header of the ball – despite being only 5ft 6in – a fact that he put down to playing with Stanley Matthews. 'I acquired a sixth sense over the years. I knew instinctively whether Stan was going to put over the ball to the near post or cut it back to the far post and I used to be able to beat bigger centre-halves in the air by timing and being able to hang for a split second.' In 1956-57 Mudie scored 38 goals, finishing as runner-up to John Charles in the national charts. He totalled 143 goals in 320 League games for Blackpool.

After a money-spinning FA Cup run, which saw Stoke defeat First Division West Ham 1-0 in a replay and only lose to Newcastle after Wilshaw's sickening injury, the coffers were full enough for Waddington to bid £7,500 for Mudie, nearing his 31st birthday, just before deadline day in March 1961. Mudie scored on his debut and City won three of his first four games, but slumped to finish just three places above the relegation zone.

In the summer of 1961 Waddington, wanting to invest in yet more experience, found his hands somewhat tied due to construction of the final phase of the new Boothen Stand. This housed spacious changing rooms and replaced the ageing stand that had stood since the 1890s. Mudie spent the close season playing for Toronto City in the Eastern Canadian Soccer League, alongside a number of other British players including Stanley Matthews, Danny Blanchflower and Johnny Haynes. Over the summer Mudie played a part in persuading Matthews that a return to Stoke would be in everyone's best interests and Matthews agreed, completing his return in October 1961.

Matthews was the oldest, and best, example of Waddo's policy paying off. The resurgence in form and interest in the club after the return of its prodigal son cannot be understated. Mudie, playing at No 9, spearheaded the attack with twenty goals as Stoke returned to Division One in 1962-63. Mudie loved Waddington's approach: 'He gave us all freedom to express ourselves, the playing surface was great and I enjoyed the atmosphere too. I played a lot of one-twos with Dennis [Viollet], who was a great reader of the game.'

With Stoke safely back in Division One, the 33-year-old Mudie was sold to Port Vale in November 1963 for £6,000, plus centre-half Ron Wilson. Mudie became player-manager for two years from March 1965, persuading Stan Matthews to become the club's general-manager following his retirement. But Port Vale's expulsion from the League for making illegal payments to youth players, about which the management insisted they were unaware, was too much for Mudie and Matthews to bear. They used their influence to lobby club chairmen to ensure Vale were immediately re-elected to the League, then quit the scene, reputations tarnished.

Mudie became assistant manager at Crewe in September 1967, but despite promotion he left when form collapsed early in the new season. He coached Eastwood Town, of Hanley, until February 1971, before becoming manager of Northwich Victoria. He then worked as a scout for Johannesburg Rangers of South Africa.

After football Mudie ran a successful painting and decorating business in the Potteries before his death on 2 March 1992.

Magic Moment: *Mudie scored the vital opener against Luton in May 1963 – a chip over the goalkeeper and two defenders from fifteen yards. The 2-0 win clinched the Second Division title.*

Worst Nightmare: *In the dismal 2-3 defeat by Scunthorpe earlier that month, Mudie rose to head a cross, but found himself knocked out cold by keeper Reeves' fist. Mudie 'received prolonged attention'.*

STOKE RECORD	Appearances	Goals
Football League	88	32
FA Cup	1	1
League Cup	4	–

No 62. DENNIS VIOLLET

Debut: v Bristol Rovers, 20 January 1962
Farewell: v Leicester, 29 April 1967

Dennis Sidney Viollet formed a superb partnership with Jimmy McIlroy and Jackie Mudie, which, despite an aggregate age of over

90 years between them, pulverised opposing defences as Stoke returned to the First Division.

Born in Manchester on 20 September 1933, Viollet was a child prodigy at St Margaret's Central School. He won five England schoolboys caps and signed for Matt Busby's Manchester United at fifteen. He became one of the original Busby Babes at inside-left, alongside Tommy Taylor, Bobby Charlton, Duncan Edwards *et al.* He collected two League championship medals, although why he only earned two full England caps – against Hungary in 1960 and Luxembourg in 1961 – is a mystery.

Viollet's sunken eyes, barely visible under thin dark eyebrows, drew attention to his large Roman nose. Unlike the robust Taylor, Viollet's 5ft 8in, 11st frame gave him a frail, ghoulish appearance which belied his stamina and, in particular, his skill. The most common word used to describe Viollet's play is 'ghost' – whether it be his appearance or his manner of beating defenders. As an accurate passer with a beguiling body swerve, he used his stealth and skill to turn half-chances into goals. Stanley Matthews recalls: 'Dennis was very sharp in the box and before you blinked he could have the ball in the back of the net.' The less prosaic commentator Stuart Hall rhapsodised about Viollet thus: 'A violet by a mossy stone, half-hidden from the eye. Fair as a star when only one is shining in the sky. He was just there on the spot when needed.'

A survivor of the Munich air crash, Viollet was lucky – receiving relatively minor head injuries. He converted to centre-forward due to the loss of Taylor, bagging 32 goals in 1959-60 – a club record he still holds. He totalled 178 goals in 291 games for United.

The manner of Viollet's departure from Old Trafford in January 1962 was bizarre. Animosity between the player and United chairman Gordon Pye meant Viollet was sold to Stoke without his knowledge. Tony Waddington rang him: 'Dennis, I've just signed you, can you come and sign the form.' Viollet agreed, but phoned Matt Busby to find out what was going on, receiving the reply: 'Sorry, Dennis, I forgot to mention it at training.'

The £22,000 acquisition of Viollet was viewed as a huge coup. At 28 he was actually in his prime, although the papers insisted he was another of the growing band of 'Crocks' at the Victoria Ground. Viollet signed before the 5-2 FA Cup third round replay win over Leicester and, when asked for his thoughts on such a fantastic display, he mused: 'I don't know why they need me!' His contribution sparked Stoke into life: they became the form team in the division for the rest of the season and when he bagged four goals in the last four games hopes were high for 1962-63.

But six games without a win heralded another poor start for Stoke. Viollet, combining intricately with Jackie Mudie, scored four goals against Charlton on 12 September. That win gave Stoke the impetus to embark upon an unbeaten run of eighteen games, ended by Leeds on 15 December. The atrocious winter meant that Stoke played no fixtures between Boxing Day and 2 March, although one defeat in the next thirteen games, with 23-goal Viollet at the hub of everything, ensured Stoke finished as champions.

Viollet proved popular with colleagues. He had a chirpy sense of humour and accepted with good grace the ribbing he took after the squad unlocked his best-kept secret – his middle name. Sensing his shame, the team named him 'Sid'. The banter was indicative of the team spirit which Waddington had engendered through buying players of high ability and sound temperament.

The following season, after the acquisition of inside-left George Eastham, Waddington pulled off a tactical master-stroke. He recognised that Viollet had lost a yard of pace and withdrew him into midfield where his sharp football brain could wreak havoc. Viollet quickly adapted to his new role as creator from deep, with his passing coming to the fore.

Many fans believe Viollet attained even greater heights at Stoke than at United and he was awarded a testimonial in May 1967 after 5½ years with the club. He initially retired in June 1967, but controversially decided to carry on playing with Baltimore Bays in the USA, also setting up the Dennis Viollet Dolphin Soccer camps. His decision to play on got him into trouble with Stoke and eventually cost his new club a £10,000 fee for his registration. He returned to Britain to play for Witton Albion and Linfield, and coach Preston and Crewe.

Viollet emigrated to the USA in 1974 where he coached, most notably Washington Diplomats in the doomed North American Soccer League. Following the reigns of Waddington and Eastham in the Stoke hot seat, Viollet was linked with the job, although he admitted to enjoying the American lifestyle too much to return to England. Family reasons (he had remarried) also contributed to his decision not to accept the position.

His daughter, Rachel, played for Great Britain Ladies. Viollet died on 8 March 1999 of a brain tumour. As a mark of respect, Stoke fan Graham Bridgwood campaigned for Viollet to be remembered on the site of the club's new Britannia Stadium. Some of his ashes – the remainder having been interred at Old Trafford – were scattered on the pitch in a special ceremony. A 'Dennis Viollet Avenue' was also created.

Magic Moment: *In the centenary game v Real Madrid, Viollet cut inside from the right wing, rounded Spanish full-back Vicente, and hammered the ball inside the far post to equalise Ruiz's early goal.*

Worst Nightmare: *Against Blackpool in September 1963, Viollet strained his groin. With no substitutes, he hobbled on and off for treatment before having to quit with ten minutes left. Stoke lost 1-2.*

STOKE RECORD	Appearances	Goals
Football League	181 (+1)	59
FA Cup	9	4
League Cup	16	3

No 63. **ERIC SKEELS**
Debut: v Charlton, 12 March 1960
Farewell: v Tottenham, 21 February 1976

Every successful team needs a ball-winner, whose industry allows flair players to shine. During the 1960s Stoke's 'Mr Dependability' was Eric Thomas Skeels.

Born in Eccles, near Manchester, on 27 October 1939, the unassuming Skeels trialled at inside-forward with a number of clubs, including Stockport and Birmingham. He was offered terms by Birmingham boss Arthur Turner, but Turner then left, Skeels appears to have been forgotten, and so didn't sign. The scout who had recommended him to Turner, Reg Savage, prompted Skeels to attend trials at Stoke. He did well enough and signed professional forms in November 1958. When Waddington took over he developed Skeels into a fine tackling half-back: 'I was always nippy so I could win the ball back well. Waddo saw that and turned me into a defensive player. I just took to it.'

Once Waddington had succeeded Frank Taylor, Skeels was given his chance at right-half. From September 1960 he missed just eleven games in seven seasons, establishing a reputation for consistency. During his career at the Victoria Ground he played in every outfield shirt and position, filling each with competence and care. Never flashy on the field, he won a Second Division winner's medal in 1962-63 and a League Cup runners-up medal the following season. In essence he was a defensive midfielder, although he made most of his appearances in the back four, forming a considerable brick in the 'Waddington Wall'.

'The club hadn't been doing so well,' recalls Skeels, 'and so once Waddo took over he thought that he would tighten things up and we went out with the attitude that we must not lose'. Waddington himself recalls his strategy: 'I brought nine players back behind the ball when the opponents had the ball. I played the wingers deep.' The 5ft 8in Skeels often played in the No 9 shirt, although after kicking-off he would drop back to cover in front of the defence. His consistency earned him a clutch of eminent admirers. Legendary

Manchester United manager Matt Busby thought that Skeels was 'a rare player indeed. He can play anywhere and still be happy.' Manchester City boss Joe Mercer declared: 'He's got the main attribute of any player who has made the grade – consistency.'

His team-mates remember Skeels' legendary preoccupation with avoiding mistakes. 'He always shouted "Mind your back", didn't matter whether you had a player on you, he'd tell you "Mind your back",' recalls Don Ratcliffe. 'He always played the way he was facing and if you were looking for an out ball, he would shout "Not me" if there was a player anywhere near him.'

Skeels' unprepossessing style of play was matched by his looks, although he did grow an alarming moustache in the late 1960s, when his long dark hair gave him the look of the brooding Charles Bronson. Skeels was never called 'Eric' in seventeen years at the club. He was christened 'Alfie', after his own corgi which caused havoc everywhere. Tony Allen recalls: 'that bloody dog was a rogue. He would pinch all the food on the table given half a chance.'

Against Leicester in August 1971, Skeels broke a leg in a tackle with Steve Whitworth. Skeels battled his way back to fitness in time to replace the injured Denis Smith for the League Cup semifinal second leg at West Ham. His inclusion provided an example of how Waddington listened to his senior players. Whilst staying at Selsdon Park Hotel in Croydon, Waddo overheard Banks, Dobing and Eastham discussing how sharp Skeels looked in training.

Skeels established a club record for League appearances during Stoke's run-in to the championship at the end of 1974-75, although the wartime appearances of McCue, Bowyer and Mountford mean Skeels stands fourth in terms of total games played. He had already been awarded a joint testimonial, with Tony Allen, against Derby in February 1969. At the end of 1975-76, after eighteen years service, Stoke announced that Skeels would be given a free transfer.

Skeels joined former team-mate Geoff Hurst in the NASL with Seattle Sounders before signing for Port Vale in September 1976. After becoming a publican at the Hare and Hounds in Glossop, Derbyshire, he called time on his first-class career. He still made occasional appearances for non-league Leek Town, before returning to the Potteries to keep the Noah's Ark. He now works as a porter at the Staffordshire University campus in Stoke.

Magic Moment: *In August 1962 Skeels scored the first of his rare goals. Gathering the ball on the halfway line at Derby, he advanced and let rip from 30 yards. 'It just flew in the top corner!' he recalls.*

Worst Nightmare: *Against Manchester United in December 1963, Skeels was told to mark Denis Law. Law scored four, laid on a fifth* *for David Herd, and hit the bar. Law's hat-trick arrived when Skeels was lured into a tackle by a loose ball and Law skipped away.*

STOKE RECORD	Appearances	Goals
Football League	495(+12)	7
FA Cup	41 (+2)	–
League Cup	36 (+2)	–
Other	2 (+3)	–

No 64. **EDDIE CLAMP**

Debut: v Scunthorpe, 22 September 1962
Farewell: v Bolton, 22 February 1964

Harold Edwin Clamp was the most feared enforcer in English football. Born in Coalville, Leicestershire on 14 September 1934, Clamp starred in his local village school's football team and won five England schools caps. Legend has it that, after being spotted by an eagle-eyed Wolves scout in 1949, he actually signed halfway through his paper round. Clamp turned professional in April 1952 and made his first-team debut in March 1954. Eddie, though, was not the only signing Wolves made from the Clamp household. His mother also joined the club as a laundry lady.

Clamp played 241 League and Cup games at left-half for Wolves, winning First Division championships in 1958 and 1959 and an FA Cup winner's medal in 1960. Known for his cut-throat, never-say-die attitude, at Molineux Clamp soon earned the nickname 'Chopper', an indication of his approach.

In 1958 Clamp won four England caps, including three in the World Cup in Sweden as England drew with the Soviet Union, Brazil and Austria, although Blackburn's Ronnie Clayton took his place for the play-off defeat by the Soviets.

In November 1961, as the great Wolves side of the 1950s split up, Clamp joined Arsenal for £35,000. He never settled in London and, after just 22 games, the ever alert Waddington picked him up in September 1962 for £20,000. Within days of his arrival Clamp proclaimed himself Stan Matthews' minder. Before every game he would amble over to the maestro and wink: 'It's alright Stan. I'll look after you.' He even nicknamed the 47-year-old Matthews 'Uncle'. Matthews recalls: 'I would say "I can look after myself", but if anyone had a go at me nasty during the game, Eddie would go up to them and say "If you do that again you'll end up in hospital".'

The gap-toothed Clamp had a distinctive balding head, with a clump of hair groomed Teddy Boy style and a pronounced widow's peak. He stood an imposing 6ft tall and added to his monolithic appearance by wearing his shorts high up his legs. In photographs he seems always to be smiling, but he proved a proverbial Mr Hyde once on the pitch.

In 1955 Stoke right-back George Bourne, a likely candidate for England Under 23 honours, had his leg broken by Colin Webster during a reserve game at Manchester United. Seven years later, in November 1962, this came to Clamp's attention. At half-time in the tunnel at Cardiff, for whom Webster now played, Clamp seized the 5ft 4in Webster and butted him. Webster dropped to the floor, nose bleeding, whereupon Clamp applied the boot. Don Ratcliffe, just behind him, was admonished by Clamp for not doing likewise.

Moments later, with Waddington giving his half-time pep talk, in comes the referee. Don Ratcliffe and Johnny King vividly recall the conversation: 'Mr Clamp,' said the referee, 'I understand that you have head-butted Mr Webster.' Eddie looked astonished. 'No, sir. He hit his head on that girder in the tunnel.' The bemused official left to check this version of events. Waddington, who had sunk his head into his hands, looked up. 'Eddie,' he pleaded. 'That girder is six feet off the ground. Webster's only short.'

'Eddie was mad', muses Frank Mountford, 'a good player, but mad. He never used to turn up for training and we would have to send someone to fetch him from his home in Wolverhampton. He soon realised that if he didn't turn up we would fetch him and he wouldn't have to pay to get to training.'

Although remembered for his thuggish behaviour, Clamp could play and his performances alongside Eric Skeels as the buttresses of the 'Waddington Wall' proved that Waddington had bought wisely. But Clamp could not continue his one-man rampage through the First Division without spending most of the season suspended. In October 1964 he was sold for £5,000 to Peterborough, where he made just eight appearances, before playing for Worcester City and Lower Gornal. He retired in 1970 and died on 14 December 1995.

Magic Moment: *Clamp relished responsibility. With regular taker Dennis Viollet having missed a penalty at home to Blackpool in September 1963, Clamp later strode up to blast home a second.*

Worst Nightmare: *The hardman met his nemesis when he butted Blackburn's Ronnie Clayton behind the referee's back in September 1963. But the ref was wise to Clamp, saw the incident and called him over. Clamp simply held his hand up and trotted off the field.*

STOKE RECORD	Appearances	Goals
Football League	50	2
FA Cup	5	–
League Cup	7	–

No 65. **JIMMY McILROY**
Debut: v Norwich, 9 March 1963
Farewell: v Burnley, 27 December 1965

After clinching his signature Tony Waddington eschewed the idea that James McIlroy was another of his 'Old Crocks', saying, 'I don't sign old players. I sign thoroughbreds.'

Born at Lambeg, near Lisburn, Northern Ireland on 25 October 1931, from the age of three McIlroy kicked a ball around his parents' garden with his father, Harry – a part-timer with Distillery – and his uncle, Willie – a professional with Portadown. After leaving school at fifteen Jimmy impressed for Craigavil FC and Glentoran before joining Burnley in March 1950 for £7,000. He soon cemented a reputation as one of the finest scheming inside-forwards since the War. As the 'brain' of Burnley, the 5ft 9in, 12st 2lbs McIlroy always seemed to have time on the ball, and often refused to part with it unless he could be sure of finding a colleague. He was also an instigator of inventive free-kicks which manager Alan Brown loved to develop. These often involved the ball being worked around the defensive wall for a colleague to have a clean strike on goal.

Blessed with the skill to open up a defence with an angled pass, McIlroy won 51 Northern Ireland caps, 34 consecutively, at that time a record. His neat footwork made him a crowd favourite. Ex-England manager Ron Greenwood recalls that McIlroy was 'a natural player who was rarely caught in possession. His great strength was the consistency of his service to the centre forward.' As one of the architects of Burnley's 1960 League title win, McIlroy was second to team-mate Jimmy Adamson as Footballer of the Year.

After 437 League games and 114 goals for the Clarets, McIlroy was allowed to leave for a cut-price £25,000. Waddington saw him as the final piece in Stoke's promotion jigsaw and signed him in March 1963. Many considered Burnley chairman Bob Lord insane to let McIlroy leave and the national press considered the deal 'one of the greatest football surprises of all time'. Stoke's forward line now read: Matthews, Viollet, Mudie, McIlroy and Ratcliffe.

When Stoke won six on the bounce to head the Second Division table, McIlroy's intelligent passing featured heavily. One of his first games for the club was the 'centenary' match against Real Madrid. McIlroy hit a wicked shot, aided by a deflection off Muller, to give Stoke a 2-1 lead, although Ferenc Puskas equalised from the penalty spot on the hour to complete the scoring.

McIlroy's lazy, almost laconic style, did not curry favour with all his team-mates. Don Ratcliffe, for one, did not rate him. 'He wasn't quick and he dithered. He was a good looking bloke though – a bit of a ladykiller. Once we went on a trip to Austria and he picked up two women on the first night we were there. He had to choose which one to go out with and the other wrote him this stinking letter which we all read on the plane on the way back!' Tony Allen recalls McIlroy's reputation as a lothario. 'He could walk into a room, make eye contact with a lady, not even speak to her and they would walk out together – incredible.'

McIlroy's best season was 1963-64 when he netted thirteen goals to finish as Stoke's third highest goalscorer as City re-established themselves in the top flight. He picked up a League Cup runners-up medal to boot. McIlory added four further caps at the age of 34. He had by then moved to the right side of midfield, following the arrival of Roy Vernon at the Victoria Ground in March 1965.

McIlroy's final bow for Stoke came in a 3-1 win over his former club. In January 1966 he moved into management, recruited by new Oldham chairman Ken Bates. With the Latics fighting relegation to the Fourth Division, Oldham paid Stoke £5,000 so that McIlroy could register as a player again.

McIlroy signed several former Stoke team-mates, including utility players Bill Asprey and Alan Philpott, central defender George Kinnell, and winger Keith Bebbington. However, McIlroy did not handle the pressure of management and resigned after a 0-4 hammering by Luton in the opening game of 1968-69. He returned to Stoke as assistant manager to Waddington, before moving on to Bolton as coach and assistant to Nat Lofthouse. McIlroy had an eighteen-day spell in charge after Lofthouse's departure, but resigned on principle after being told by the board to sell players.

Having written his own newspaper column whilst a player, McIlroy became a journalist with the weekly *Burnley Express*, using that outlet to bemoan the lack of quality and skill in modern football. McIlroy also owned a gentleman's outfitters in Burnley. He retired early to play golf and attend art school.

Magic Moment: *McIlroy's first-time pass through a sea of mud at the Victoria Ground released Stan Matthews for the clinching goal against Luton in the 1962-63 promotion campaign.*

Worst Nightmare: *McIlroy's Stoke career could not have begun in worse fashion. City took a 0-6 thrashing at Norwich on his debut which led to a picture of McIlroy and Matthews on the front cover of the* Sentinel *under the banner headline 'Forget it Stoke'.*

STOKE RECORD	Appearances	Goals
Football League	96 (+2)	16
FA Cup	7	3
League Cup	11	–

No 66. **PETER DOBING**
Debut: v Tottenham, 24 August 1963
Farewell: v Leicester, 28 October 1973

Peter Dobing was the pipe-smoking gent of English football. Born in Manchester on 1 December 1938, the son of a Rugby League professional, Dobing was a natural athlete. At first he chose to play as an amateur, which allowed him to turn out for different clubs. This nearly backfired. Having signed for both Manchester United and Blackburn, he was selected by each club for the same 'A' team game against the other. Dobing extricated himself from the sorry mess by declining to play at all.

Dobing signed professionally for Blackburn in December 1955. He scored 89 goals in 179 games for Rovers, forming a lethal left-wing partnership with England's Bryan Douglas which in 1957-58 helped Rovers win promotion back to the First Division after an absence of ten years. Following a £37,500 move to Manchester City in July 1961, Dobing's inside-forward play led to seven England Under-23 caps. He scored 31 goals in 82 League games for the Light Blues, although he failed to settle and, after City's relegation in May 1963, decided to move on.

Following Stoke's euphoric promotion, Tony Waddington knew the squad needed strengthening and, sensing that Dobing was ripe for the picking, offered a then club record £37,500 for his services. In 1963-64 Stoke established themselves back in the top flight with Dobing scoring sixteen League goals, only two fewer than leading scorer John Ritchie. A broken leg against West Brom in January 1965 curtailed that season.

Recovering at home allowed Dobing time to pursue his beloved leisure pursuits. He fished for trout in the River Tern and occasionally roamed the fields from his Market Drayton home, making up the numbers in shooting parties. Although he admitted to a secret ambition to become a poacher when he retired from football, he later retracted: 'I'd never actually kill anything. That's something I could just not do.'

Sartorially elegant in a three-piece suit and a hat, Dobing was inseparable from his pipe, lighting it to wind down after matches. 'You get far more satisfaction out of a pipe. I used to smoke cigarettes but now I never touch them.' He became something of a trendsetter in Stoke's dressing room, with team-mates Greenhoff, Ritchie and Stevenson, and trainer Frank Mountford, taking up pipe smoking. Unfortunately for Dobing, his disciples often availed themselves of his tobacco too.

Despite looking every inch the country gentleman, with blond hair, combed across from a left-side parting, steely blue eyes and with a beguiling, shy smile, Dobing proved he was a modern foot-baller, adapting to a physical and defensive pattern of play which developed under Waddington.

Although a success at Stoke, Dobing enjoyed a love-hate rela-tionship with the Boothen End. Their suspicions were raised by his wage demands, which saw him refuse to re-sign early in 1965-66, although he finally accepted the terms on offer after three weeks on the transfer list. Dobing finally won the fans over with a superb dis-play against Leeds and England defender Jack Charlton at the Victoria Ground in 1967. Dobing ran rings round Charlton, and his hat-trick goal saw him race 40 yards with Charlton in his wake before cutting in and swerving a shot beyond Gary Sprake.

A man of few words, he was not averse to being forthright. 'We've never been one of the better supported clubs. I don't know why, but it may be because pottery workers are not highly paid and want something for their money. For 108 years Stoke have won nothing, so its imperative we change that.' On one occasion, tired of daft questions put to him by a sports reporter, Dobing turned the tables by asking the hack his views on 'dialectical materialism'.

Following the signing of Jimmy Greenhoff, Waddington eased Dobing back into midfield, where his passing skills could be utilised to good effect, particularly in tandem with George Eastham. The pair improved the flow of Stoke's attacking play as the team shook off its defensive reputation of the previous decade. Dobing's form saw him mentioned in dispatches by the national press as an out-sider for the 1970 England World Cup squad, although his age eventually counted against him.

Dobing also had a natural hard streak that earned him a bad disciplinary record. In an era reputed for its hard-man defenders, Dobing, though slight in build, could dish out stick with the best. In October 1970 he earned himself a then English record ban of nine weeks for exceeding disciplinary points. The punishment was aca-demic, as he was out of the game, breaking his leg in a crunching tackle with Ipswich's Mick Mills.

After recovering from the break, Dobing captained Stoke to the League Cup final, scoring three goals en route. On the Monday before the final he pulled a thigh muscle and almost lost his place. Though still restricted in his movement on the day, Dobing was determined to play, especially after having tasted defeat with Blackburn at Wembley in the 1960 FA Cup final.

Eventually the injuries took their toll and, having made 564 career League appearances, Dobing retired to became a pottery worker in Longton, while still playing for local non-league club Parkway. He now lives in Stafford, from where he runs a company selling crockery wholesale to hotels and restaurants.

Magic Moment: *As captain of the first Stoke side ever to win a major trophy, Dobing lifted the League Cup presented to him by UEFA President Gustav Wiederkehr.*

Worst Nightmare: *In August 1967 Dobing quit. Waddington said: 'Dobing asked for certain demands today when we were discussing a new contract. These demands were against the regulations of the FA so he promptly asked for his cards and we gave them to him.'*

STOKE RECORD	Appearances	Goals
Football League	303 (+4)	82
FA Cup	22	3
League Cup	39 (+1)	9
Other	8	1

No 67. **CALVIN PALMER**
Debut: v Sheffield United, 18 September 1963
Farewell: v Southampton, 3 February 1968

Compared to the acerbic Calvin Ian Palmer, Peter Dobing was a sheep in wolf's clothing. Palmer was born in Skegness, Lincolnshire on 21 October 1940. He began his career with Skegness Town but was spotted by First Division Nottingham Forest, signing in March 1958. He established himself in Andy Beattie's side as a tough tackling firebrand in midfield and made 90 League appearances, scoring fourteen goals, and appearing in seven different positions. His enthusiastic displays earned him recognition as a reserve for the England Under-23 side in 1962.

On the prowl for new players as Stoke suffered five successive defeats early in 1963-64, Waddo was so impressed by Palmer's display in a 1-0 Forest win at the Victoria Ground that he sought out Beattie after the game and brokered a deal. Palmer cost £30,000.

Signed to bring young blood to an ageing midfield, Palmer was the long-term replacement for Eddie Clamp. Palmer proved to be less transparently violent, although his irrepressible personality was often reflected in 'over-exuberance'. Blessed with boundless energy, he regularly tackled back in his own penalty area, then hared upfield to try to play his part in the resulting breakaway. Described as 'the finest attacking wing-half I have seen for a long time', by journalist Ronald Crowther, Palmer had an impressive goal ratio for a midfielder, averaging one every five games. The 5ft 10in, 11½st Palmer had film star looks, with blond hair, neatly parted on the right-hand side and large sideboards. Musing on what Palmer might do at the end of his career, George Morley, writing in Stoke's programme in May 1966, stated: 'I can't see management ever being exciting enough for Calvin. He might take up racing to beat Jim Clarke or paratroop into Vietnam.'

Palmer's excesses also manifested themselves behind the scenes. At the end of 1965-66 the club prepared for a summer trip to the United States to compete in a tournament under the name of 'Cleveland Stokers'. Playing five-a-side in the gym under the Boothen End, the combative ex-Manchester United centre-half Maurice Setters barged Palmer into the wall. Palmer's short fuse sparked fisticuffs. The pair were separated by Tony Waddington, who barred them both from travelling to America. Setters later apologised to Waddington for the incident, but Palmer would do no such thing. Setters travelled after all, playing against the likes of Dundee United and ADO, of Holland, while Palmer kicked his heels in disgrace in England.

Palmer was often called upon to bridge the gaps in Stoke's thin squad. He scored as a centre-forward at Tottenham in December 1963, and from 1965-66 was converted to right-back, displacing Bill Asprey, in another of Waddington's tactical changes that paid off. Despite his more defensive role, Palmer retained his goal ratio, racing forward to fire cannonball shots. England manager Alf Ramsey was known to be impressed and newspapers speculated about an England call up in December 1966.

Palmer made few friends when publicly criticising the Stoke crowd for failing to show sufficient support. He tabled a transfer request in December 1966 and, although it was granted, it took him twelve months to find a club. In the meantime, Palmer starred in Stoke's remarkable 4-3 win over West Ham – having been informed that his family had been involved in a car crash. He filled in at centre-back for the injured Alan Bloor as Stoke came back from 0-3 down to win 4-3, the last occasion when any Stoke side achieved this feat.

His legs beginning to go, in February 1968 Palmer finally found a club willing to take him when Alan Brown took over for a second spell at Sunderland. Palmer cost £70,000 and signed off from Stoke by scoring the winner at the Dell in a 2-1 victory. His sale paid for new equipment for the club's treatment room, which made the facilities at the Victoria Ground second to none in the country.

His year at Roker Park was marked by friction with management and, despite being only 28, he could find no other English club willing to take him. He spent a happier two years in Cape Town before returning to England to assist former Stoke team-mate Dennis Viollet at Crewe in 1971.

Palmer's redoubtable spirit did not prevent him bearing a grudge, as a number of his opponents discovered. Like others, he also found Stoke City's attitude to its former players difficult to accept, declaring that he would have nothing more to do with the club after he ended up living in a DHSS hostel in Skegness.

Magic Moment: *On 7 January 1967, during a 2-1 victory over Everton, Palmer ghosted up from right-back, coolly controlled Alan Martin's waist-high cross and fired the ball home from fifteen yards.*

Worst Nightmare: *In the second leg of the 1963-64 League Cup final Palmer was carried off with a leg injury with the score 1-1. Down to ten men, City conceded two goals. Palmer returned to the fray but City could only pull back one goal, from George Kinnell.*

Stoke record	Appearances	Goals
Football League	165	24
FA Cup	12	–
League Cup	19	3

No 68. HARRY BURROWS
Debut: v Wolves, 20 March 1965
Farewell: v Norwich, 28 April 1973

In 1965 Stoke's major weakness was the left flank of their attack. The transfer deadline signings of Henry 'Harry' Burrows and former Everton skipper Roy Vernon rectified the problem.

Born in Haydock, Merseyside on 17 March 1941, the young Harry attracted interest from First Division clubs, including Burnley, Liverpool and Aston Villa. He turned down an offer from Wolves – making him one of the few players ever to say 'No' to Stan Cullis – instead turning his thoughts to an engineering apprenticeship with the British Coal Board. Persuaded by manager Joe Mercer to sign part-time for FA Cup holders Aston Villa in March 1958, having successfully deputised for legend Peter McParland, Burrows became a fixture in a successful Villa side.

In 1959-60 Burrows helped Villa regain top-flight status at their first attempt, and also win the inaugural League Cup in 1961, scoring in the 3-2 defeat of Rotherham in the final. Villa fans nicknamed him 'Blast', after Mercer, suspecting his pace could pose problems down the left, converted him into an out and out winger. Burrows won an England Under-23 cap against Greece and finished as Villa's leading scorer in both 1961-62 and 1962-63, totalling 73 goals in 181 games, although the departure of the talismanic Mercer in 1964 ended a golden period in Villa's history.

The signings of new boss Dick Taylor all earned higher basic wages than the existing Villa staff, which caused friction. 'I had just got married,' recalls Burrows, 'and I asked for £5 on my basic

wage, which wasn't that much, but he refused. I went onto a monthly contract and asked for a transfer at Christmas. They offered me
full terms then, but it was too late.' Burrows was one of a number
of stars, Tony Hateley was another, to leave, and within five years
Villa were languishing in Division Three.

Burrows was a highly prized asset and his transfer to Stoke for
£27,000 on deadline day March 1965 was seen as a coup for Tony
Waddington. It also marked a departure from his previous policy of
preferring experienced older heads. Burrows turned 24 on the day
he signed and scored on his debut.

Burrows' first acquaintance with Stoke could not have contrasted more with his acrimonious departure from Villa. 'I did so well
that Waddo got me into his office after just eleven games and
ripped up my contract in front of me – I wondered what he was
doing! He then said he was giving me a £5 a week rise. I loved him
for that.' Waddington's peculiar motivational methods did not end
there. On another occasion he and Chairman Albert Henshall tried
to put an end to a bad run early in 1970-71 by bringing champagne
into the dressing room before Stoke went out to face Leeds.

The thunderous shot in the 5ft 7in Burrows' left foot ensured he
soon became a favourite with Stoke fans, who named him 'cannonball'. Opposing full-backs, wise to his tricks, would force Burrows
inside and as a consequence he grew stronger on his right foot.

1966-67 began well for Stoke and, boasting the meanest defensive record in the division, at Christmas they stood third behind
Manchester United and defending champions Liverpool. 'We made
a lot of what we did up ourselves as we went along. We just knew
football,' Burrows remembers.

The improved form could have been partly attributable to
Waddington's pre-season fitness regime. Stoke utilised the services
of British 10,000 metre champion Roy Fowler for stamina work.
This involved running in the hills around Stoke, while sprint champion Derek Ibbotson took the players for speed work on the track.
Sadly, City's inconsistency, particularly away from home where
they drew two and lost nine after Boxing Day, denied them a serious championship challenge.

Burrows twice finished as City's joint top League scorer, match-
ing Dobing's fifteen goals in 1967-68 and Ritchie's fourteen in 1969-
70. In 1969 he scored the third as Stoke took a 3-0 half-time lead in
the Nou Camp in a friendly with European Cup-Winners' Cup holders Barcelona. David Herd, a free transfer signing from Manchester
United, netted the other two. Barca hit back with two goals in the
second half, but City clung on in front of 65,000 Catalan fans.

A quiet man on and off the field, Burrows was happy to let his
feet do the talking. By the time Waddington finally moulded a suc-

cessful side, in the early 1970s, Burrows was past his peak – although he featured in all four FA Cup semi-final games against Arsenal in 1970-71 and 1971-72, the latter season as a substitute.

An injury sustained whilst going for an equalising goal against Liverpool in April 1971 kept Burrows out for the remainder of the season. Complications set in, a cyst developed, and Burrows spent nine months out following cartilage surgery. His rapport with the adoring Butler Street paddock fans led to a tearful farewell: 'They would sing *"I'd walk a hundred miles for one of your goals, Harry!"* to the tune of Mame, and when I left they had a big flag with my name on it and sent me a card.'

Released on a free transfer in the summer of 1973, Burrows joined Plymouth and helped them to win promotion to the Second Division. But his knee was still giving him trouble and convinced Burrows that it was time to call it a day.

On his retirement Harry returned to North Staffordshire and ran a carpet business, a pub and a Post Office, while still finding time to turn out for charity games.

Magic Moment: *The third of Burrows' hat-trick confirmed Stoke's annihilation of his former club, Aston Villa, 6-1 in December 1966.*

Worst Nightmare: *Burrows took Stoke's penalties. He liked to hit the ball hard to one side. Said Harry: 'The one time I changed my mind, against Ipswich [in 1969] – because I had already taken one and couldn't decide which side to go – I missed it by pushing the ball wide.' He only missed twice in his career. This one cost Stoke a win.*

STOKE RECORD	Appearances	Goals
Football League	239 (+6)	68
FA Cup	19 (+2)	5
League Cup	12 (+1)	3
Other	5	–

No 69. **GEORGE EASTHAM O.B.E.**
Debut: v Nottingham Forest, 20 August 1966
Farewell: v West Ham, 29 September 1963

All modern day professional footballers owe a debt of thanks to George Edward Eastham. Born in Blackpool on 23 September 1936, Eastham came from a footballing family. His uncles George and Harry both played professionally, but the star of the family was his father, George Snr, who won an England cap as an inside-forward against Holland in 1935. Known as 'Diddler' in the press due to his dazzling ball skills, the young George's predominant memory of his father remains the moment the string-tie broke on his shorts in mid-dribble – the adoring son still insists that his dad shuffled past six defenders, despite his shorts determinedly progressing towards terra firma.

Eastham Jnr began playing at Ards in Northern Ireland where his father had become player-manager, confusing local journalists who had two George Easthams in the 1954-55 team. In March 1955 he took the eye for the Irish League in a 5-2 defeat of a Football League side that included Tommy Taylor, Jimmy Armfield and Johnny Haynes. What he saw convinced Newcastle's chief scout Bill McCracken, and Eastham signed for £9,000 in May 1956.

Eastham became a shrewd schemer and distributor of the ball who could mastermind a game. He played 124 League games for the Toon, scoring 29 goals, before hitting the headlines by taking a stand against Newcastle's repeated refusal to allow him to leave. The frustrated Eastham decided to take a job outside football with family friend and cork-making millionaire Ernie Clay. Newcastle tried to put a stop to this too, claiming the right to dictate what he could and could not do. Ironically, the Newcastle manager was one of the 1950 Bogota rebels, Charlie Mitten who, hypocritically given his personal history, branded Eastham 'the guy with the biggest head, shortest arms and deepest pockets in the business'.

Cliff Lloyd, secretary of the PFA (Professional Footballers Association), portrayed Eastham as a martyr, determined to assert his right to earn a living. Despite Mitten's ultimatum: 'If you won't play for us you won't play for anyone,' Newcastle caved in, allowing Eastham to join Arsenal in November 1960 for £47,500.

Eastham, believing he was owed substantial sums by Newcastle for the period he had been in limbo, and encouraged by Lloyd and Jimmy Hill, the PFA's chairman, continued the crusade to quash the 'retain and transfer' system in court. Gerald Gardiner QC, likened the system to feudal life in the Middle Ages. The judgment, delivered by Justice Wilberforce on 4 July 1963, declared the existing contracts of professional footballers a 'restraint of trade' and paved the way for the lifting of the maximum wage, which had been restricted to £20 per week. Top players immediately commanded three or four times that, with Fulham and England's Johnny Haynes becoming the first £100 per week footballer.

In six years Eastham played 207 League games, scored 47 goals, became Arsenal captain, and won nineteen caps under England manager Alf Ramsey. When making his England debut against Brazil at Wembley in 1963, the Easthams became the first father and son to win England caps. Though selected in Ramsey's 1966 World Cup squad, allocated shirt No 22, Eastham played no part in the finals.

After Waddington – searching for a headline-grabbing signing following England's World Cup triumph – failed to lure Blackpool's Alan Ball or Blackburn's Mike England, he had better luck with Eastham, who joined Stoke in August 1966 for £30,000. It ended a four-year wait for Waddington, whose initial approach had been when Eastham was out of favour under Arsenal manager Billy Wright during 1962-63.

Although nearing 30, Eastham proved to be one of Waddo's most astute older signings. His calm experience in the late 1960s reflected well on the emerging youngsters, such as Terry Conroy, John Mahoney and John Ritchie. George puts his calmness under pressure down to having inherited 'the complete lack of butterflies on the big occasion from my father'. His acquisition allowed Dennis Viollet to move deeper into midfield, and the pair linked well with intelligent diagonal passing. Trevor Brooking remembers Eastham as 'a very neat short-passing player – ten or fifteen-yard passes were his speciality – and he always put exactly the right weight on the ball'.

Possessing the classic looks of a 1950s footballer, Eastham had blond wavy hair, combed across, much like Calvin Palmer and Peter Dobing's, in a neat cut. At 5ft 7in, and 9½st, he relied on his fragile passing skills. He had a genial personality, which belied his steely opposition to Newcastle's intransigence, and led to him being universally known as 'Gentleman George'.

By 1969 Eastham was developing his own coaching ideas and spending six months of the year coaching in South Africa. He played for Hellenic, managed by his father, with whom he won the South African Championship, Cup, and Player of the Year trophies. The spur for Eastham's return from exile came when the FA announced a refereeing clampdown early in 1970-71, aimed at allowing creative players to express themselves, free from scything tackles. Waddington got straight on the phone to contact Eastham, telling him: 'You've got to come back. It's made for you.' The renaissant Eastham now revelled in the time and space afforded him, with defenders having to curb their aggressive instincts. His form was such that he wryly sighed: 'I wish I was ten years longer.'

Eastham's one major deficiency was his goalscoring tally, which was never as high as it should have been. It was particularly poor at Stoke, where he scored just five goals in nearly eight years. The last of these, however, was the winner in the 1972 League Cup final. At the age of 35, Eastham still holds the record as the oldest player to score a Cup final winning goal at Wembley.

To complete a perfect year, Eastham finished third in the 1972 Footballer of the Year Awards, behind club colleague Gordon Banks. After being awarded the O.B.E. for Services to Football in the Queen's birthday honours list, he once again concentrated on coaching, only appearing occasionally for Stoke. He played his last game at the age of 37 years and six days.

Eastham took over the hot seat when Waddington left the club in January 1977. With no alternative but to turn to youth, relegation was almost inevitable. Ninth in November, prior to the collapse of the Butler Street stand roof, Stoke lost at Villa Park on Monday 16 May and fourteen years of top flight football were over. Eastham failed to arrest the decline, although in reality he stood no chance. He was given none of the money from the sale of City's stars to invest in new recruits and was far too nice to motivate players who had seen the club plummet so quickly. He lasted just under a year in the job, resigning in January 1977.

Eastham emigrated permanently to South Africa. Opposed to Apartheid, he concentrated on coaching black youngsters. He also set up his own sports wholesale business called Hat Trick.

Magic Moment: *When Peter Bonetti parried Jimmy Greenhoff's volley in the 1972 League Cup final, Eastham reacted fastest to beat Peter Dobing to the rebound to slot home the winning goal.*

Worst Nightmare: *Relegated to Division Two, Eastham's Stoke – with four new signings – lost 1-2 at promoted Mansfield. The nightmare sparked trouble on the terraces which Eastham denounced.*

STOKE RECORD	Appearances	Goals
Football League	184(+10)	4
FA Cup	22 (+1)	–
League Cup	17 (+2)	1
Others	1 (+1)	–

By 1969, Waddo's blend of experience and youth had produced a formidable team

The League Cup-winning squad display the club's first major trophy

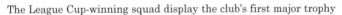

The impish Terry Conroy dazzled on Stoke's right wing throughout the 1970s

The pipe-smoking gentleman of British football – Peter Dobing

Chapter Eight

~ *Glory Hunters* ~

No 70. **GORDON BANKS O.B.E.**
Debut: v Chelsea, 22 April 1967
Farewell: v Liverpool, 21 October 1972

Association Football has produced a galaxy of stars, but few can claim a place in the soccer stratosphere. Gordon Banks is one.

Born in Tinsley, Sheffield on 30 December 1937, Banks was dropped by Sheffield Boys after a 'poor performance' in a Yorkshire Schools cup-tie. After being told to forget football by his parents, Banks only returned to the game by chance, when his works team, Millspaugh, asked him to make up the numbers one Saturday.

Spotted by Chesterfield, he signed in September 1955 and, after just 26 games, was snapped up by Leicester manager Matt Gillies for £6,000 in May 1959, although the stunned Banks admitted he did not know what colour shirts the Foxes played in. He played in 293 League games for Leicester and won his first England cap in April 1963 against Scotland, becoming a regular as Alf Ramsey's team won the 1966 World Cup.

Banks entered football in the era of Ted Ditchburn and Bert Trautmann, and wore either simple woollen gloves or none at all. He would often be seen nervously blowing on his hands, only to pull off a flying save moments later. Trevor Brooking believes 'Banks was probably the man who took goalkeeping into the modern age. He was the man who made goalkeeping glamorous.' Alf Ramsey noted that Banks' 'dedication, his masterly skill, his enthusiasm no matter what the occasion, his loyalty and great sense of sportsmanship are qualities which cannot be overpraised.' Renowned for his meticulous application in training, Banks put his legendary cool down to his personal code of conduct – the three C's: composure, control and concentration. He possessed a dossier-like mind, storing the strengths and weaknesses of his opponents.

Leeds' Mick Jones recalls how disheartening facing Banks could be: 'I was clear, coming in on the edge of the box. Gordon came dashing out and just as I'm setting myself up to slip the ball past him he suddenly starts going slowly backwards. Shoot past him? Chip over him? Take it on? I finished up falling over the ball.' It wasn't just his fellow professionals who thought highly of him. Liverpool's Kop reserved a special place for Banks in their heart. Whenever he visited Anfield the Kop would rise as one to acclaim him before, typically, singing with gusto: 'Clemence for England!'

Remarkably, Leicester were blessed with a second sublimely gifted goalkeeper in teenaged Peter Shilton. In 1967 Gillies told Banks that he was second choice and therefore available for transfer. Waddington stole in and nicked Banks from under the noses of Liverpool and West Ham for £52,000. The signing marked the culmination of Waddington's transfer policy. For years he had brought in quality players in the twilight of their careers. Now established amongst the country's elite, Stoke could compete for internationals, in their prime, and in Waddington the club possessed a manager with the charisma to convince such stars to come. Banks scuppered press rumours that he was another of Waddington's 'Old Crocks' by announcing on his first day: 'I've not come here to retire you know, I've come here to win something.'

What happened over the next five years established Banks as quite simply the greatest goalkeeper of all time. At the height of his powers he made that wonder save from Pele in Guadalajara, Mexico. Banks recalls: 'I didn't think it was special until I saw it on TV later, but I suppose I should've realised from the look on his face.' Pele shouted 'Goal – at that moment I hated him, but when I cooled down I had to applaud him with my heart.' Banks' heroics earned him an O.B.E. He went on to earn a then record 73 England caps for a goalkeeper, which included 36 while at Stoke – making Banks the club's most capped player.

With the 'Banks of England', as he had become known, in goal, Stoke pushed for honours for the first time in 25 years. Against West Ham in extra-time of the second leg of the 1972 League Cup semi-final, Banks yelled for Mike Pejic to leave the ball. Attempting to deceive the oncoming Harry Redknapp, Pejic waited until the last minute to allow the ball to run under his foot. Banks panicked and brought Redknapp down with a rugby tackle.

Taking the penalty was Geoff Hurst, who had not missed one for four years. Hurst opted for power and cracked his shot almost down the middle. Banks, already diving to his right, flung up both arms to fist the ball over the bar. It was estimated that the save put £100,000 into Stoke's coffers, taking into account the replay Banks had earned, the final, and subsequent European competition.

The next vital penalty Banks faced did not end happily. Against Arsenal in Stoke's first FA Cup semi-final for 72 years, City led 2-1 with four minutes of extra-time played. Peter Storey's scuffed kick passed low to Banks' left, but his weight was on his right and he could not recover. The experience traumatised Banks who felt he had been fouled in the build up to the penalty: 'I couldn't do or say anything. I felt so numb I just sat in the bath for a long, long time.'

The 'nearly men' of Stoke City finally won their first ever major trophy, the League Cup, in March 1972. With Stoke 2-1 up and only three minutes remaining, Banks saved Mike Bernard's bacon after his rash back-pass fell to Chelsea's Chris Garland. Bernard recalls: 'My heart was in my mouth. He only had Gordon to beat. I was going to be the man who threw away victory at Wembley. But dear old Banksy blocked the shot. He saved the day. He's the greatest.' Banks was voted 1972 Footballer of the Year, and at Stoke's next home game he was applauded onto the pitch by both teams, earning a standing ovation from all four sides of the ground.

But Banks' later years were punctuated by outbursts which cost his team dear – a marked change from the famous ice-cold temperament. Banks had been 'rested' by England manager Ramsey, in order to blood his nemesis Peter Shilton, and Banks was worried.

On 22 October 1972, perhaps preoccupied with events at Anfield of the previous day, Banks crashed his car when, in overtaking a crawling lorry, he swerved off the road to avoid an oncoming van. The crash made headlines and a shocked nation learned that after surgery Banks had lost the sight in his right eye. Although he made numerous comeback attempts, he announced his retirement in August 1973. His testimonial, in October, saw his XI, including the likes of Eusebio and Bobby Charlton, lose 1-2 against Manchester United in front of over 20,000 at the Victoria Ground.

His deputy at Stoke, England Under-21 keeper John Farmer, was something of a poet. He penned these lines about his thoughts on the end of Banks' career and the resurgence of his own.

The mystery that was in my mind / Is sinking slow
And my hands that once were frozen / Are thawing fast:
It's shame on me that my day

Has been long coming, But yet it's been so hard for me
To gauge the proper distance:
The velvet touch that now is close / Within my grasp
Is indeed most well befitting / To your chimes of glory

Banks took charge of Stoke's youth set-up, but after just a season in the job he tried to revive his playing career in America, in the over-hyped NASL. When he found himself atop a sleek white horse wearing a Roy Rogers cowboy outfit waiting to ride onto the pitch before his first appearance for Fort Lauderdale Strikers, he wondered 'What the hell am I doing here?' On his return to England a career opened up as an after-dinner speaker. He coached at Port Vale, then became general manager at Telford, and launched his own corporate entertainment company.

In May 2001 Banks was named Stoke's club President, succeeding Stanley Matthews, and in August 2001 was voted by listeners to Radio 5 Live the greatest goalkeeper in footballing history – ten per cent ahead of Peter Schmeichel.

Magic Moment: *Banks' penalty save in the League Cup semi-final at Upton Park, punching away a blaster from Geoff Hurst, allowed Stoke to reach their first Wembley final.*

Worst Nightmare: *A red mist at Anfield led to the car crash that ended Banks' career. The referee penalised Banks for taking too many steps. Liverpool netted the free-kick and Banks went berserk.*

STOKE RECORD	Appearances	Goals
Football League	194	–
FA Cup	27	–
League Cup	19	–
Other	6	–

No 71. **JOHN RITCHIE**
Debut: v Walsall, 25 September 1962
Final Farewell: v Ipswich, 24 September 1974

In September 1961 Tony Waddington took a telephone call from another manager who bemoaned the fact that, having found a non-league player who interested him, his club could only afford £2,000 of the £2,500 asking price. At the end of that conversation, Waddo rang round several colleagues to ask about John Henry Ritchie. He learned of a big, strong striker who had scored 40 goals the previous season. Waddington rang Kettering to settle the deal immediately. Ritchie actually took a pay drop to join Stoke as he had been working in a local shoe factory and playing part-time.

Born in Kettering on 12 July 1941, Ritchie made only sporadic appearances while Viollet and Mudie held sway in the first team. Three months into 1963-64 he was given his chance in place of the injured Viollet. Ritchie grabbed it with both hands and scored twice in a 4-3 win over Bolton. That sparked a scoring streak of fourteen goals in nine games, breaking Jack Peart's 1910 club record for scoring in consecutive matches, although only six of Ritchie's were League games. The run was rounded off in a 4-4 draw against Sheffield Wednesday by Ritchie's first hat-trick. He also set a record for the formative League Cup of ten goals in a campaign, which has only been beaten twice. Ritchie's efforts propelled Stoke to their first ever Cup final, although he failed to add to his total in either leg of the final as Stoke lost 3-4 to Leicester.

Standing 6ft 1in and weighing 12st 4lbs, it did not take long for the Boothen End to christen Ritchie 'Big' John. One of a dying breed of big, direct and fast centre forwards in the mould of Steele, Lawton and Lofthouse, Ritchie used his burly frame to good effect, shrugging off defenders with ease.

He twice scored four in a game – against Sheffield Wednesday in April 1965 and Northampton in February 1966 (it took 34 years for another Stoke player to bag four goals in 90 minutes). Rated as one of the most exciting strikers the club had seen, Ritchie scored 30 and 29 goals respectively in his first full seasons. Imagine the shock when in November 1966 he was sold to Sheffield Wednesday for £80,000. His departure, all the more surprising as Stoke had pocketed £30,000 from the sale of reserve forward John Woodward to Aston Villa not a month earlier, set a new club record for an out-going transfer fee. Waddington later admitted it was a mistake.

Hillsborough was not so kind to Ritchie. As Wednesday's record signing, he scored 35 goals in 89 appearances, but suffered a season of drought in 1968-69. New boss Danny Williams decided that Ritchie was past his best and Waddington took the chance to recti-fy his error by buying him back for £28,000. In fact, Waddington had wanted to make a splash by signing West Ham's Martin Peters or Cardiff's John Toshack. Neither deal came off, but the return of Ritchie exited the Potteries' fans.

Ritchie returned as Jimmy Greenhoff arrived. The pair struck up an understanding which bordered on telepathic, being famously described in one match report thus: 'You could have fired a can-nonball at Ritchie and he would have nodded it down to Greenhoff's feet.' Their partnership was the focus of Stoke's flowing football which graced the First Division in the early 1970s. Although their on-field relationship blossomed, off the pitch Ritchie, taciturn and bluff, rarely warmed to his more fun-loving team-mates. Greenhoff recalls 'I was always glad when John scored on a Saturday. It meant that he would come into the dressing room on Monday with a cheery 'Good Morning'. If he didn't score he'd never say anything. He could be a grumpy sod.'

As well as pace and power, for a big man Ritchie developed good skill on the ball, typified by the second of his brace against Arsenal in a 5-0 victory in September 1970. He gathered a loose ball, beat three Arsenal defenders and drove left-footed past Bob Wilson. The goal won Match of the Day's 'Goal of the Season'.

Although Ritchie damaged cartilage ligaments against Everton in November 1970, he battled back to fitness after surgery. Before an FA Cup-tie at Ipswich, Ritchie, having been injured for three months, tried to persuade Waddington to play him. 'We had to turn down his offer,' remembers Waddington, 'but it was typical of the spirit in the dressing room.' When he did return, Ritchie produced one of his finest performances. Against Hull in an FA Cup quarter-final, Stoke found themselves 0-2 down after 35 minutes in a blizzard. Ritchie scored twice as City won 3-2 to reach their first semifinal in 72 years. He also scored the second goal as Stoke went 2-0 up in the semi against Arsenal, latching onto Charlie George's backpass and rounding Bob Wilson. Alas, Arsenal equalised with an injury-time penalty.

Ritchie finished as Stoke's leading scorer in 1970-71, 1971-72 and 1973-74. In the summer of 1973 Stoke toured the Antipodes. In an 8-0 win over Otago of New Zealand Ritchie scored all eight. Now a 32-year-old veteran, in February 1974 he was the subject of a £30,000 bid from Preston manager Bobby Charlton, but Ritchie turned down the move.

Along with many others, Ritchie enjoyed the social aspect of being a Stoke player. During the debate of the early 1970s over the issue of playing football on Sundays he famously commented: 'Of course I'm against Sunday soccer. It'll spoil my Saturday nights!' City did try Sunday football, circumventing the Sunday trading laws by allowing free entrance to the ground with every copy of the team-sheet purchased. The experiment proved a success. In January 1974 over 32,000 saw Stoke defeat Chelsea 1-0, thanks to Geoff Hurst's late penalty.

Increasingly injury prone, Ritchie had his leg broken by a heavy Kevin Beattie challenge in September 1974. The complex double fracture ended his career and arguably cost Stoke the chance of a League title. City lacked goals at crucial times which an experienced poacher like Ritchie could have given them. Ritchie's retirement left him five short of Freddie Steele's League goals record, although the first of his brace in a 5-2 win against Birmingham in November 1973 had allowed Ritchie to break Steele's overall club goalscoring record in all competitions which had stood since 1949.

Ritchie recovered sufficiently to play part-time for Stafford Rangers, while concentrating on setting up a pottery business, which thrives to this day. A proud man, he still feels that the club have not been respectful towards him since his departure. The final straw came when his son, Dave, was sold by Alan Ball to Stockport for £10,000 in March 1990. Ritchie severed all ties with the club.

Magic Moment: *In March 1974, after a press row with Saints' Peter Osgood, who criticised Ritchie's heading ability, Ritchie completed his hat-trick against Southampton by dribbling around the keeper, stopping the ball on the line, and kneeling to head it in.*

Worst Nightmare: *In September 1972, substitute Ritchie was sent off after nine seconds in Kaiserslautern for aiming a punch at Idriz Hosic. Stoke lost 0-4 to slump out of Europe at the first hurdle.*

STOKE RECORD	Appearances	Goals
Football League	261 (+8)	135
FA Cup	27	15
League Cup	37 (+1)	18
Other	12 (+1)	8

No 72. **JIMMY GREENHOFF**
Debut: v Wolves, 9 August 1969
Farewell: v Leeds, 10 November 1976

James Greenhoff is perhaps the only player who can challenge Stoke fans' idolisation of Stanley Matthews.

Born in Barnsley on 19 June 1946, Greenhoff grew up as part of a sporting family. His father, also James, played part-time for Lincoln, while younger brother, Brian, also became a professional with Leeds and Manchester United.

After playing in the Barnsley Schools side which won the English Schools Trophy in 1961, Greenhoff had to buy himself out of his final year at Holgate Grammar School, paying a £10 fee for his release from full-time education. He became an apprentice at Elland Road in June 1961 and his early duties included fetching packets of Embassy cigarettes for his boyhood idol, John Charles.

Taken under the wing of Leeds youth coach, ex-Luton centre-half Sid Owen, Greenhoff developed into a quality inside-forward, deft of touch with grace and flair. Leeds' new manager Don Revie blooded Greenhoff gradually, but he was a regular in the promotion side of 1963-64 and helped win the 1968 League Cup. With Peter Lorimer often preferred, due to his goalscoring, Greenhoff was desperate for first-team football and in August 1968 joined Second Division Birmingham for £70,000. Bizarrely, the transfer took place in the midst of a Cup final. Greenhoff played in the 1-0 home leg of the Inter-Cities Fairs Cup final against Ferencvaros, but was sold before the 0-0 draw which sealed Leeds' first European trophy.

Leeds won the League the following season. Greenhoff admits he was naïve in signing for Birmingham – the first club to make an offer for him. Although he won an England Under-23 cap against Wales, he did not settle at St Andrew's. After bagging four goals against Fulham in October 1968, he was summoned to manager Stan Cullis's office where he was told he was not scoring enough! Greenhoff swore never to play for Cullis again. Waddington offered £100,000, making Greenhoff Stoke's then record signing. Everton manager Harry Catterick showed belated interest but Greenhoff stuck to his word, although the 'what might have been' must have drifted through his mind as Everton won the League the following season – a second consecutive title medal he had missed out on.

Greenhoff's signing proved to be one of Waddington's shrewdest. Acting as the linkman between the midfield and striker John Ritchie, Greenhoff brought a new dimension to Stoke's play with his passing and interchanges, feeding off Ritchie's knockdowns to spread the ball to the wide players, initially Terry Conroy and Peter Dobing, and latterly Sean Haslegrave, Jimmy Robertson and Geoff Salmons.

Greenhoff had a mane of golden hair and a distinctive crouched style when on the ball, evenly distributing his weight and allowing him a sharp turn to surprise defenders. He was also one of the best volleyers of his, and arguably any other, generation: 'I practiced volleying every day. One of the most important elements is your body shape and I learned from Sid Owen that you control the ball better if your body is balanced correctly with hands and arms out in the direction you want it to go.' Greenhoff could also receive the ball under pressure and turn to spread play, taking opposing players out of the game. Terry Conroy recalls: 'Waddo purred about Jimmy every day in training. He wanted the other players to model themselves on him.'

Waddington's footballing philosophy was simple: 'If you can play football it doesn't matter what I say. Just go out and play.' It motivated Greenhoff to produce his best form. 'All I wanted to do was entertain the wonderful fans. Make them go away thinking "God, that was brilliant". They were a big part of my game. So warm.' In February 1971 Greenhoff scored the only goal as Stoke defeated Huddersfield in the second replay of an FA Cup fourth-round tie. In an act which set the tone for Stoke fans' deification of Greenhoff, before the next home game an adoring fan ran on to the pitch, knelt down and kissed the spot on Greenhoff's right boot which smote the winner.

In the 1972 FA Cup semi-final, Greenhoff saw Arsenal forward John Radford, in goal as replacement for the injured Wilson, make a fantastic save from his shot low to the bottom left corner. That save earned earned the Gunners a 1-1 draw. The replay still rankles: 'We were beaten by the refereeing and we needed someone to shake us up, but none of us had been there before and no one had the experience to get a hold of us on the field and force us to concentrate.' Stoke lost 1-2 to a debatable penalty and a goal from the outrageously offside Radford.

Stoke's fine goalscoring record in 1972-73, with Greenhoff top scoring with sixteen, qualified them for the Watney Cup, a pre-season tournament for the top two goalscoring sides in each division from the previous season. Stoke defeated Hull 2-0 in the final at the Victoria Ground, with Greenhoff netting both and, as new skipper, lifting the trophy, presented by Bobby Charlton.

But it was with the arrival of Alan Hudson that Greenhoff really started to shine. The pair combined to propel Stoke into a serious title challenge in 1974-75. Greenhoff broke his nose in a 3-0 win at Birmingham, after scoring twice, and missed two games, both of which Stoke lost. City's horrendous injury list eventually took its toll and the title was lost to Derby. To add insult to injury UEFA, who had previously set such stall by their 'one club one city' rule, tore up the regulations to permit both Everton and Liverpool to enter, and Stoke missed out on another European campaign.

Greenhoff's form meant new England boss Don Revie – who had sold him to Birmingham and retained his doubts about him – succumbed to a press campaign and picked him in the squad to play Wales in March 1976. Greenhoff was withdrawn from the squad by his club, along with Hudson, to play at Derby in a re-arranged League fixture. Greenhoff, however, remains phlegmatic about the age-old club versus country dispute which deprived him of international honours. 'I had always been brought up to believe that club football was my bread and butter and Don [Revie] had the guts to select me after selling me at Leeds. I thought my chance would still come.' He was never selected for England again.

In January 1976 high winds brought down the wooden roof of the ageing Butler Street stand. Greenhoff was the first casualty of the financial crisis brought about by the board's failure to properly insure the stand. 'I got a phone call. It was my brother Brian and he said "What's this about you coming to United?" It was quite a shock and I stormed off to find Waddo to see what it was all about. I found him in the tunnel crying his eyes out. I took one look at him and burst into tears too.'

At the next day's board meeting, manager and player refused to accept the deal. Alex Humphreys, the director in charge of finances, and responsible for insuring the stand, challenged Greenhoff: 'To be honest, we think you're past it anyway, Jimmy.' 'I turned to Waddo,' Greenhoff recalls, 'and said "Sorry boss. I'll be signing for United tomorrow". They needed me to go.' The £120,000 fee proved scant consolation to the Stoke faithful, who reacted angrily when news broke of their idol's departure.

Greenhoff's sale ranks alongside that of Matthews to Blackpool as the most controversial, damaging transfers in the club's history. City were ninth, United in the bottom four. Come May, Stoke had been relegated and the Reds had won the FA Cup with Greenhoff scoring the winner when he unwittingly deflected Macari's shot past Ray Clemence. 'I tried so hard to get out of the way,' he smiles. 'I thought of Alex Humphreys that day.'

Whenever able to, Greenhoff returned to watch his former teammates at the Victoria Ground. As soon as the eagle-eyed Boothen

Enders spotted him in the players' seats the chants of 'Greenhoff, Greenhoff' would go up. 'It got so as it upset the players on the park and I didn't like it. The club began to give me tickets at the very back of the Stoke End stand so no one would recognise me. I had to stop coming then.'

Greenhoff never scaled the same heights at Old Trafford and was released in December 1980. He moved on to Crewe, Toronto Blizzards and Port Vale. He became player-manager at Rochdale in December 1983, but in truth proved too nice to be a manager and resigned after four months. He scored 146 goals in his career.

He set up an insurance company, which went under, taking Jimmy's life-savings with it. He now works for a pharmaceutical company. He goes through the routine of donning his kit every day, although it is no longer boots, shorts and shirt, but overshoes, gown and gloves to prepare nasal sprays and anti-histamine cures.

Magic Moment: *At Birmingham in December 1974 Greenhoff scored a gem. On the right of the penalty box, back to goal, he chested the ball up and over his shoulder and swivelled to volley it into the far corner. The strike was voted ATV's Goal of the Season.*

Worst Nightmare: *In the 1970-71 FA Cup semi-final, with Stoke 2-0 up, Greenhoff left Peter Simpson for dead, going one-on-one with keeper Bob Wilson. The ball bobbled and Greenhoff ballooned the chance over the bar. At 0-3, Arsenal would not have recovered.*

Stoke record	Appearances	Goals
Football League	274	76
FA Cup	27	11
League Cup	28	9
Other	14	7

No 73. **ALAN BLOOR**
Debut: v Brighton, 18 September 1961
Farewell: v Blyth Spartans, 6 February 1978

If Ritchie and Greenhoff forged the rapier edge to Stoke's attacking sword, then Alan Bloor was the bastion of Stoke's imposing, home-grown defensive shield.

Bloor was born in Stoke-on-Trent on 16 March 1943. He played for Stoke schoolboys and captained England Youth against Scotland in February 1960. In 1961 he skippered the Stoke youth side to the semi-finals of the FA Youth Cup, where they lost 2-5 on aggregate to Everton. He signed professional forms on his seventeenth birthday, although Waddo, not wanting to rush him, made

Bloor wait for a regular centre-back berth, allowing the experienced Maurice Setters, Eddie Stuart and George Kinnell to secure Stoke's place in Division One.

After the sale of Setters to Coventry, Bloor's emergence helped spark a new era for Stoke, as Waddington's policy of bringing on local youths began to bear fruit. One of Bloor's assignments was to mark Denis Law in January 1965 in the FA Cup fourth round. He announced his arrival as a tough no-nonsense stopper by keeping Law quiet, even finding time in the interceding League game to steal forward to score.

A hulking 13st, the 6ft 1in Bloor used his physique to outmuscle opponents. He was a voracious tackler and quite capable of using a judicious kick to ensure forwards with big reputations appreciated his presence. Managers as eminent as Matt Busby, Ron Greenwood and Bill Shankly described him as one of the players they feared most. His glowering, dark looks added to his brooding demeanour and led to his nickname of 'Bluto', in honour of the ruffian foe of the cartoon character Popeye.

Bloor formed a bludgeoning pairing with another Queensbury Road School product, Denis Smith. Both were aggressive, destructive and played with a passion which exemplified the club throughout the late 1960s and early 70s. They played together 189 times. Bloor's consistency led to his name being whispered as a possible England successor to Jack Charlton in the aftermath of the 1970 World Cup. A calf injury cost him what chance he had of being available for an experimental line-up to play East Germany in November 1970 and Roy McFarland of Derby emerged as Ramsey's man. In fact, Bloor's physical approach led to numerous injuries and, needless to say, many appearances when he was only half-fit. According to midfielder Mike Bernard, Bloor could hardly walk before the 1971 FA Cup second replay against Huddersfield at Old Trafford. Bloor creaked onto the pitch and marked the prolific Frank Worthington out of the game as Stoke won 1-0 on the way to the FA Cup semi-final.

The quietly destructive Bloor proudly paraded the club's first major trophy, the 1972 League Cup, around Wembley to the strains of City's Cup final song.

We'll be with you, be with you, be with you
   Every step along the way
We'll be with you, be with you, be with you
   By your side we'll always stay
   City, City, tell the lads in red and white
   Everything will be alright
   City, City, you're the pride of all of us today

Written by Tony Hatch and Jackie Trent, who also wrote the themes for TV soaps Crossroads and Neighbours, the track reached No 34 in the charts.

Late in his career Bloor was crippled by a back injury which kept him out for almost the whole of 1974-75. He was never quite the same afterwards and, after struggling to make five appearances in 1977-78, he returned to the starting line-up for what was supposed to be a cosy FA Cup-tie against non-League Blyth Spartans. Stoke's humiliating 2-3 home defeat prompted the board into swift action. In came a new manager, Alan Durban from Shrewsbury. That spelled the end of Bloor's career as Durban handed him a free transfer. Bloor's 478 appearances leave him standing fifth in the club's all-time appearance chart.

Bloor joined Port Vale as player and youth team coach. From September 1979, following the sacking of Dennis Butler, he had an unhappy four-month spell as manager. Bloor became a carpet salesman, giving rise to the bizarre chant of 'Alan Bloor's Carpet Factory', which could occasionally be heard on the Boothen End in quiet moments as the club wallowed following his departure.

Magic Moment: *In Stoke's 5-0 hammering of Arsenal in September 1970, Bloor supported Jackie Marsh's breakaway. Marsh's shot was saved, but the ball fell for Bloor who volleyed goal number five.*

Worst Nightmare: *In April 1968, Bloor refused to be substituted after twisting his neck. At a corner he lost Jack Charlton, who headed Leeds level at 2-2. Dobing's hat-trick spared Bloor's blushes.*

STOKE RECORD	Appearances	Goals
Football League	384 (+4)	17
FA Cup	38	–
League Cup	37	1
Other	15	1

No 74. **DENIS SMITH**
Debut: v Arsenal, 14 September 1968
Farewell: v West Brom, 20 May 1982

Denis Smith epitomised the spirit and passion of the successful Stoke sides of the early 1970s.

Born at Meir, Stoke-on-Trent on 19 November 1947, Smith attended Queensbury Road School, with whom he won the Stoke Schools Trophy, and he also played for Stoke-on-Trent Schoolboys. During his teenage years Smith established a pattern that would shape the rest of his career by breaking his left leg twice in typically committed tackles. Persuaded by his parents to remain at school until the age of eighteen, Smith eventually signed for Stoke in September 1966.

Held back by Waddo until nearly 21, Smith established himself in Stoke's first team alongside Alan Bloor at the end of 1968-69. Their partnership at the heart of Stoke's homegrown back four became the rock upon which the success of the 1970s was built. At this early stage of his career, Smith was paid a fine tribute by Tom Finney, who believed 'he could develop into another Neil Franklin'.

At 5ft 11in and 12st of solid muscle, the voracious tackling of Smith gave him a reputation as a hard man prepared to charge through a brick wall in the cause of Stoke City. He would launch himself at opponents, determined to win the ball or stop his man at all costs. Ron Davies, the Southampton striker, declared in ironic understatement: 'The lad is a very hard nut to crack.' When Geoff Hurst joined Stoke from West Ham he declared he did so as he did not want to play against Smith and take penalties against Gordon Banks. Smith's commitment saw him idolised by the Stoke fans who would unsettle opposing forwards by singing 'Denis is gonna get you', although his combative style meant that he ceaselessly nursed one injury or another. Smith broke his leg five times during his career, with one fracture contributing to Stoke missing out on championship glory in 1974-75. He boasts an unwanted entry in the *Guinness Book of Records* as the world's most injured footballer.

The blond Smith had twinkling blue eyes and a nose which bore the brunt of his style of play, being broken four times. His breathy voice and shy temperament belied his on-field image, although his conduct around the club meant that he was often invited to attend functions on behalf of the club.

One episode spoke volumes for Smith's commitment. Ruled out of City's FA Cup quarter-final against Manchester United in March 1972, on account of a back injury, Smith returned home needing his wife's help even to get out of his car. On returning to the ground, the 49,091 crowd meant Smith had to park half a mile away. As he got out of the car he felt something click in his back, but thought no more of it as he entered the dressing room to wish his team-mates luck, parting from his wife with a cheery 'See you in the stand'. The next she saw of him was on the field. His back felt much better and Waddo dashed off to ask the referee to accept a late change to the team-sheet. Smith produced one of the best performances of his career, subduing Brian Kidd and stealing forward to head the vital equaliser. Stoke won 2-1.

Indeed Smith often used his height at free-kicks and corners to grab vital goals, the most important of which came in the FA Cup semi-final of 1971. With Stoke on top and putting Arsenal under pressure at a corner, Smith stuck his leg out to block Peter Storey's clearance at the near post and the ball ricocheted into the roof of the net before keeper Bob Wilson could blink.

Smith's weakness was speed on the turn, which caused a rumpus when new keeper Peter Shilton arrived. Shilton liked defenders to push up quickly to leave twenty yards of space for him to patrol and insisted Stoke play this way. This brought instant criticism from Alan Hudson, who realised Smith would be exposed for pace if City employed such tactics. Hudson goes so far as to believe that Stoke would have won the title had Waddington not signed the England goalkeeper.

Smith never won an England cap. This is remarkable, not least because he played through the Don Revie era when caps flew around ten-a-penny. Smith's one representative honour arrived when he played for the Football League as a substitute against the Irish League at Norwich on 23 September 1970, although he had to be satisfied with twenty minutes at full-back.

In January 1976, after Jimmy Greenhoff's sale to Manchester United, Smith took over as club captain. Following relegation he formed another good partnership, this time with Mike Doyle, a £50,000 signing from Manchester City, which helped Stoke win promotion in 1978-79. Smith's dedication was never better shown than when he injured himself against Luton in April 1979. Smith found that his calf hung like a flap, but after being stitched up by club doctor Sandy Clubb, who expected Smith to be out for a month, he played at Wrexham five days later. His appearance spurred Stoke on to a vital win, although the wound opened up again.

A pre-season cartilage injury forced Smith to miss the whole of 1980-81. He spent the time coaching the reserves, whetting his appetite for a future career in management. After a spell on loan at York, Smith was handed a free transfer and in May 1982 was appointed player-manager. His York side won the Fourth Division title in 1983-84 with a then record 101 points.

Having cut his managerial teeth, in June 1987 Smith moved to Sunderland, who had been humiliatingly relegated to the Third Division for the first time in their history. Smith led them to promotion in his first season. In 1990 the Rokerites were back in the top flight – despite losing in the play-off final – on account of a financial scandal that engulfed the victors, Swindon. Relegated a year later, Sunderland struggled in Division Two and in December 1991 Smith was sacked.

He was the Stoke board's first choice after the Alan Ball debacle left the club in its lowest ever League position – fourteenth in the Third Division in 1991, but Smith held back knowing that he would only alienate the fans who still idolised him if things went wrong.

Instead he chose to join Bristol City, and then Oxford, who he guided to promotion to the new Division One in 1995-96. His stock high, Smith replaced Ray Harford at West Brom, but lack of progress meant he lost his job some three years later.

In February 2000 he returned to Oxford, but second time round the magic had gone. He was subsequently seen house-hunting in the Stoke area. Perhaps he is preparing for his summons should Gudjon Thordarson fail to deliver.

Magic Moment: *Smith netted a far-post header to complete Stoke's comeback to beat Leeds 3-2 in February 1974. Jack Charlton then wrecked Leeds' dressing room in frustration. The result ended Leeds' record 29-game unbeaten run from the start of the season.*

Worst Nightmare: *Smith was read the last rites whilst in North Staffordshire Royal Infirmary, such was the seriousness of a blood disorder picked up through a wound received on the pitch.*

STOKE RECORD	Appearances	Goals
Football League	406 (+1)	29
FA Cup	29	4
League Cup	33	5
Other	19	4

No 75. **JACKIE MARSH**
Debut: v Arsenal, 19 August 1967
Farewell: v Blackburn, 31 March 1979

John H Marsh was the life and soul of the Stoke dressing room throughout the glory days of the early 1970s.

Born in Stoke-on-Trent on 31 May 1948, he was the star of the Stoke Boys team as a youth and realised his schoolboy ambition when he played for Stoke City. He was handed his debut by Waddo on the opening day of 1967-68 at Arsenal, but to calm his nerves the manager kept his line-up to himself: not even the announcer at Highbury was given the name of Stoke's No 2. The following season Marsh made the right-back berth his own, allowing the unsettled Calvin Palmer to move on to Sunderland.

A combative right-back, Marsh had good control and a fair turn of speed for a small chunky player. Named 'Jo' by his team-mates, he specialised in hard low crosses on the run, which allowed forwards to flick on to others or volley towards goal. Jimmy Greenhoff recalls: 'Jackie was so skilful. I am sure if he had played for Man United he would have played for England. He was a defender who played like a midfielder.'

Marsh loved to attack at full throttle, but although pacy he did not have a particularly athletic build. He stood 5ft 8in and weighed 12st. His square head sat atop rounded shoulders and noticeable beer belly. His long black hair hung straggily about his face in the fashion of the day. He was one of the many Stoke players, including Alan Hudson and Geoff Salmons, who liked a beer or ten. Despite declaring himself to be a fitness fanatic, Marsh still found time to exercise his elbow at various nightspots.

During City's run to the 1972 League Cup final, Marsh took care of the team's mascot – a red and white striped knitted chimpanzee which sat atop the kit basket in every dressing room Southport in round two onwards. The chimp was donated by Margaret Crowe, wife of vice-chairman Gordon Crowe, but was never named as the players felt that this would be unlucky.

The chimp worked its magic. Marsh recalls his proudest moment: 'When the whistle went I glanced up at the new Wembley electronic scoreboard and it said 'Chelsea 1, Stoke 2' and I thought "That's my hometown club". I was moved to tears.'

Marsh became an even better player after picking up good habits from the likes of Smith, Bloor and Greenhoff. He remained, though, a passionate performer prone to rash tackles and silly mistakes on the pitch. And he was just as loose a cannon off it. On one occasion he ran off with one of the Golden Goal girls who sold the half-time draw tickets, causing a minor scandal.

He is still haunted by the part he played in one of the blackest days in Stoke's history – the 2-3 home defeat by Northern Premier League Blyth Spartans in the FA Cup in 1978. 'We daren't show our faces around town. It was OK though because no fans turned up at any of our games for the next three weeks anyway!'

Given a free transfer in 1979, Marsh played for Los Angeles Aztecs in the NASL and then joined Terry Conroy at Bulova in Hong Kong. Marsh returned to England to play for Northwich Victoria before retiring in 1984. Like so many of his peers, Marsh still lives in the area and is often to be found hosting executive boxes on a matchday at the Britannia Stadium. He has, though, now fallen on harder times and has spent much time out of work. His situation is typical of many ex-footballers of his, and previous generations, who played for the love of the game but received very little in return, unlike his modern day counterparts.

Jackie Marsh stands eighth in the all-time appearance chart.

Magic Moment: *In the League Cup final, Marsh recognised that Conroy's elation at scoring had got the better of him; he was shuffling about as in a dream. Marsh stormed over, fist clenched and teeth gritted, and told him in no uncertain terms to snap out of it.*

Worst Nightmare: *Marsh was spotted grovelling on his knees during the League Cup final. He was looking for his contact lenses.*

STOKE RECORD	Appearances	Goals
Football League	346 (+9)	2
FA Cup	33	–
League Cup	34	–
Other	18	1

No 76. **MIKE PEJIC**
Debut: v West Ham, 8 April 1969
Farewell: v Manchester City, 5 February 1977

The real hard man of Stoke's rugged defence was Michael Pejic.

Born in Chesterton, Staffordshire on 25 January 1950, Pejic supported Stoke from an early age. As a star-struck youngster he once turned to his father, a Yugoslavian immigrant farmer, on the terraces at half-time, and predicted: 'Dad, one day I'll be running down these wings.' In his teenage years Pejic developed into a pacy left-winger, playing for Newcastle schools. He went straight into City's reserves after signing professional forms in 1967.

Tony Waddington took the decision to turn Pejic into a pacy left-back, and Pejic learnt his trade from Northern Irish international full-back Alex Elder, who he displaced in September 1969. Blessed with a sweet left foot, which produced deep, curling crosses, Pejic was a strong athlete with chunky legs supported by enormous calves. He also sported a mullet haircut which preceded Chris Waddle's by some ten years. He liked to roam upfield and ping crosses to the far post in the direction of John Ritchie and later Ian Moores. Pejic's goals were rare but tended to be spectacular. He scored from 25 yards against Coventry in September 1972 and against Leeds in a 3-2 win in February 1974.

Compactly built at 5ft 8in, Pejic was a ferocious tackler who enjoyed nothing more than to let his opposing winger know he was around with a scything tackle. He was a fitness fanatic who, unlike many of his team-mates, applied discipline to his life outside the Victoria Ground. He was something of a loner, who loved the countryside and kept a farm near Leek. Despite his unsociable nature his ability and commitment once he crossed the white line was not in doubt. Whatever he did, he had to be a winner.

Pejic's gutsy displays won him eight Under-23 caps before he graduated to the full England squad in April 1974 in an experimental team containing six new caps to play Portugal. He was lucky in that several clubs withdrew players from the squad. But Pejic won three further caps, against Wales, Northern Ireland and

Scotland, under the caretaker stewardship of Joe Mercer. Pejic's display at Hampden Park is remembered for his air kick, which cost England a second and decisive goal, scored by Peter Lorimer. Pejic lost his England place to Alec Lindsay of Liverpool.

The downside of Pejic's belligerence was his frequent visits to the FA to receive suspensions. He earned a five-week ban which left him kicking his heels for the whole of March 1972, although as it applied only to League games he was free to play in the League Cup final. The following season he got himself sent off for two yellow cards against Leeds, and the following year's corresponding fixture saw him booked within a minute of the kick-off. In January 1976, he then conducted a running battle with Manchester City wideman Dennis Tueart, and was sent off for head-butting the England player.

Pejic's luck with injury could not continue indefinitely, and in February 1975 he broke his leg in a clash with Wolves' Steve Kindon. The timing could not have been worse. Stoke were pushing for the title, but then suffered a mounting injury toll that included leg breaks for Pejic, Smith, Robertson and Bloor.

After the wooden roof of the Butler Street stand collapsed in January 1976, Pejic enterprisingly arrived in his Land Rover to collect the debris to be used as firewood on his farm. He sensed the difficulties now facing the club and added to City's woes by seeking a transfer. Within a month he had been sold to Everton for £135,000. In December 1978 Pejic suffered another leg break, this time against Leeds. Displaced by John Bailey, in September 1979 Pejic moved to Aston Villa, although persistent groin and pelvic injuries eventually forced him to retire in 1981.

Pejic succumbed to the managerial bug and coached Leek, Northwich Victoria, Port Vale, and a Kuwait team, before becoming manager at Chester in the summer of 1994. Chester won just three games under his charge and Pejic was sacked in January 1995.

He resurfaced at the Victoria Ground in September 1996 as first-team coach under Lou Macari, and his reputation for physical training kept Stoke's players on their toes. The club's demise following the relocation to the Britannia Stadium saw Pejic unceremoniously sacked during the three-month reign of Chris Kamara. Kicking out Pejic was widely condemned.

Magic Moment: *Pejic began the famous comeback against Leeds in February 1974 by rifling home Alan Hudson's short free-kick from twenty yards past the startled David Harvey.*

Worst Nightmare: *Pejic was actually booed by his own fans in the Boothen paddock after scything down Southampton's Terry Paine.*

STOKE RECORD	Appearances	Goals
Football League	274	6
FA Cup	23	–
League Cup	28	2
Other	15	1

No 77. **JOHN MAHONEY**
Debut: v Sunderland, 18 March 1967
Farewell: v Aston Villa, 16 May 1977

In the mid-1970s Stoke possessed an international midfield quartet, one member of which was John 'Josh' Francis Mahoney.

Born on 20 September 1946, Mahoney grew up in Manchester, where his father played Rugby League for Oldham. Josh began playing with non-league Ashton United before signing for Crewe in March 1966. With Liverpool also showing interest, former Stoke player John King recommended that Waddington sign Mahoney, which he did for £19,500 in March 1967.

A rough diamond at first, Mahoney regularly lost possession by over-elaborate dribbling. Waddo taught him to pass, then move to collect the return ball, and transformed Mahoney into a quality midfielder. Owing to competition for places, in February 1972 he was sought by Millwall for £50,000, but he declined. 'I decided I wanted to stay and fight for my place, but we were waiting for the train to Stoke after going to Gordon Banks' 'This is your Life' programme and Millwall manager Benny Fenton pops out from behind a pillar all cockney-like and tries to persuade me to sign. I told him I didn't want to come to London.' Mahoney's patience was rewarded by a substitute appearance in the 1972 League Cup final.

Sensing that Mahoney had matured into the kind of player he wanted him to be, Waddington sold his major rival for a place in Stoke's midfield, Mike Bernard, to Everton for £140,000 in May 1972. Waddo thought Bernard lacked big-match temperament. Now Mahoney was a guaranteed starter. Bernard's sale financed the arrivals of Ipswich midfielder Jimmy Robertson, for £80,000, and Geoff Hurst of West Ham and England for £70,000.

A fearsome sight with long flowing dark hair and dark staring eyes, the moustachioed Mahoney had an enormous appetite for work. 'I used to run from one eighteen-yard box to the other. Huddy played free, and Geoff Salmons as a winger, I hung latch a bit to win the ball back and give it to either of them.' Mahoney loved to shoot from distance, particularly after cutting in from either wing, and could be relied upon to contribute five or six goals a season.

Although born of Welsh parents, Mahoney had not been considered Welsh until journalist Peter Jackson discovered the fact while talking to Mahoney's cousin. A possibly desperate Welsh FA official uncovered his birth certificate and a fine international career was born. Mahoney won his first senior cap against England in October 1967. He won 31 caps whilst at Stoke and totalled 51 appearances for Wales. His international colleague Terry Yorath recalls: 'John was passionate. He loved football and playing for Wales. He was creative in the centre of the park and wanted to win.'

Waddington believed that Mahoney matured into a 'world-class craftsman'. His best seasons coincided with Alan Hudson's arrival. The pair rated amongst the best in the country, alongside Derby's Bruce Rioch and Archie Gemmill, and Queen's Park Rangers' Gerry Francis and Don Masson. In 1974-75 a strong Stoke side entered the final three games knowing that three wins would land the title, but two draws and a defeat left Stoke fifth.

Another victim of the Butler Street debacle, Mahoney joined Middlesbrough for £90,000 in July 1977. 'I didn't want to leave but when I looked at the fixture list and Stoke had Mansfield on the opening day, but Middlesbrough had Liverpool, I knew I had to go.'

Mahoney moved on to Swansea with whom he perched on top of the League three months into their first season in Division One. On St David's Day 1983, Mahoney came off worse in a crunching tackle, ending his career and leaving him with a permanent limp.

As manager, Mahoney took Bangor City into the 1985-86 Cup-Winner's Cup, losing by a respectable 0-3 on aggregate to Atletico Madrid. He then spent three years in charge of the newly reformed Newport club, after County's demotion from the Football League in 1987. He has also coached the Welsh semi-professional side and Carmarthen. Since 1999 he has suffered with rheumatoid arthritis and has undergone a long and arduous rehabilitation.

Magic Moment: *On the first day of 1974-75, Mahoney opened Stoke's account against Leeds. It was Brian Clough's first game in charge of the champions. Mahoney block-tackled Billy Bremner and beat David Harvey from 25 yards.*

Worst Nightmare: *In the last minute of the 1971 FA Cup semi-final, Mahoney dived to tip McLintock's header away. Peter Storey equalised from the spot. 'It was just instinct,' Mahoney remembers. 'Just think. If he had missed the penalty I would have been a hero.'*

STOKE RECORD	Appearances	Goals
Football League	270(+12)	25
FA Cup	16 (+1)	1
League Cup	21 (+2)	1
Other	11	1

No 78. **TERRY CONROY**
Debut: v Leicester, 6 September 1967
Farewell: v Luton, 16 April 1979

One of the most popular players ever to don a Stoke shirt, Gerard Anthony Francis Conroy laid the considerable ghost of Stanley Matthews by turning in a decade's worth of dazzling performances in the No 7 shirt.

Born in Dublin on 2 October 1946, the eighth of ten children, Conroy was known as Terry from birth as his Uncle Gerard also lived in the same house. Determined to make a career in football, Conroy played for Home Farm, with whom he won four Eire youth caps, before joining Northern Irish club Glentoran, where he stood more chance of being spotted. Sure enough, in a friendly with Stoke he caught the eye of Tony Waddington. Initially Conroy turned down Stoke's offer as he wanted to finish his printer's apprenticeship, but after completing it he crossed the Irish Sea in March 1967 to sign for £10,000. Waddo gave Conroy his first start in September 1967 and he scored the winner in a 3-2 defeat of Leicester. In 1968-69 Conroy won a regular spot, finishing as second top scorer with nine goals.

He was at his best on the right wing, where his pace and accurate crossing established him as one of the most effective wide-men in the League. The 5ft 9in Conroy's distinctive running style, with socks rolled down to his ankles, exposing milky white, slim legs, coupled with his flowing auburn locks and huge sideburns, made him an obvious target for opposition fans and players alike. His pallor gave Waddington much cause for concern. 'He would send me into hospital for check-ups all the time,' Conroy recalls. 'He thought I was anaemic and gave me Guinness and steak to build me up.'

His prowess soon earned international recognition. He debuted for the Republic of Ireland in Prague in October 1969, 24 hours after playing in a League match for Stoke. Conroy went on to win 27 caps over eight years, earning a dubious claim to fame when Franz Beckenbauer saw fit to crock the impish Conroy with a crude tackle from behind as Ireland lost narrowly to West Germany in Berlin in 1970.

His ability to make something out of nothing endeared him to the Stoke faithful, who sang 'Terry, Terry Conroy, Terry Conroy on the wing, wing'. *Daily Express* journalist Derek Potter recalls: 'This red-haired ghost impressed me at Anfield where he was bundled over the touchline by a massive Liverpool defender. Terry got up, took the return pass and after battling down the line he eventually flicked the ball past Tommy Lawrence with the outside of his right foot. Terry, bless him, had made his sortie from the left flank. That is flair.' Malcolm Allison added: 'Every defence in the First Division is looking out for this lad – he is now a marked man.'

Conroy's injury tally over the coming seasons confirmed this. He suffered from a series of cartilage injuries which kept him out of the side for long spells – indeed in only three of his twelve seasons with Stoke did he exceed 30 appearances. He underwent four separate cartilage operations and made successful comebacks from each one. He possessed tremendous stamina, had a good shot in both feet, and regularly weighed in with goals. Indeed, Conroy was more than happy to fill in as a support striker whenever necessary. In January and February 1971 he was directly responsible for each of Stoke's eight goals, scoring five, making two and having a shot deflected in for an own-goal.

Conroy's most memorable goal came in the televised 5-0 hammering of Arsenal in September 1970. He collected the ball on the right, played a one-two with Peter Dobing, and hit a first-timer from the edge of the box into the top corner. The goal finished third in the BBC's Goal of the Season competition behind John Ritchie's effort earlier in the same game. Always in the thick of the action, Conroy added to the drama of Stoke reaching their first ever major final by accidentally kicking West Ham goalkeeper Bobby Ferguson on the head in the semi-final replay, forcing him off the field for repairs. Conroy then rocketed home the goal – past the patched up Ferguson – which took Stoke to Wembley.

Conroy then scored the first of Stoke's two goals which defeated Chelsea in the final – a header from eight yards after Bonetti parried from Denis Smith. Conroy remembers: 'When I saw the ball in the back of the net I immediately looked at the referee. Then at the linesman ... then at the referee again ... then I realised I had actually scored.' Conroy's distinctive goal celebration, running behind the goal with both arms raised vertically, was suggested to him by *Sentinel* photographer Huston Spratt.

In 1975, after spending over a year recovering from yet more surgery, Conroy stormed back into the side, filling in for injury victim John Ritchie. He scored ten goals in eleven starts and five substitute appearances as Stoke chased the League championship. He recalls: 'We could give anyone a footballing lesson and often took the lead at Anfield and the like, but power teams could wear us down.' Stoke eventually finished fifth.

Conroy also acted as the squad's unofficial social secretary, which meant numerous visits to the races – his other passion. 'Players need escape from football at times and I find I can relax and forget about my worries when I go racing.' His genial manner and wise-cracking sense of humour made him a popular presence in the dressing room and he is at the hub of reunions still.

Freed by manager Alan Durban in July 1979, Conroy played for Bulova in Hong Kong for six months before rejoining Waddington at Crewe. He hung up his boots in 1981 to start his own insurance business before, belatedly, being employed by Stoke to run match-day hospitality at the Britannia Stadium. Universally known as 'TC', Conroy is now the perfect role model for Stoke City to follow.

Magic Moment: *Conroy starred in the video of the League Cup final with his rendition of 'We'll be with you', Stoke's cup final song, in the Wembley bath after the match.*

Worst Nightmare: *Arriving in Czechoslovakia to make his debut for Ireland, Conroy found himself barred from entry. The FA of Ireland had forgotten to apply for a visa.*

STOKE RECORD	Appearances	Goals
Football League	244(+27)	49
FA Cup	25	11
League Cup	22 (+3)	5
Other	12 (+1)	2

No 79. **ALAN DODD**
Debut: v Sheffield United, 4 November 1972
Final Farewell: v West Ham, 14 May 1985

Perhaps the most underrated member of Stoke's championship challenging side, Alan Dodd boasted an extravagant array of skills, but lacked the vital ingredient of a killer instinct.

Born in Stoke-on-Trent on 20 September 1953, Dodd grew up addicted to football. 'Even if I ran an errand to the shops I used to take a ball with me. I always had a ball at my feet.' He progressed through the Stoke-on-Trent Schoolboys team and chose Stoke ahead of a clutch of other interested clubs, dreaming of playing for his boyhood team. Signed by chief scout Cliff Birks, Dodd settled into the reserve team at centre-half, but in 1972 made his first-team debut in midfield due to City's prolonged injury crisis. Early in 1973-74 Alan Bloor's injury handed Dodd an extended run. He oozed class in the air and on the ground, was naturally two-footed and had a running ability more akin to an athlete than a footballer. Atop his skinny frame, the 6ft Dodd sported bushy brown hair, worn long in a style similar to Mike Pejic's. He had a thin nose and often wore stubble on his chin and cheeks.

On Bloor's return Waddington could hardly drop his able stand in, so he played Dodd at right-back or in midfield. Now a first-choice player, his versatility seemed to count against him. 'At the time it didn't bother me,' he recalls. 'I was just happy to play, but later I felt I was not doing myself justice. I had always been a natural centre-half and was much happier there.' Dodd eventually wore all Stoke's outfield shirts bar No 9, but it took another injury to Bloor to allow Dodd to become Smith's regular partner.

His performances for Stoke as they pushed for the title in 1974-75, propelled Dodd into the international arena. He made the step up easily, making six appearances in the England Under 23-team. Dodd was denied a full cap only by Sunderland's Dave Watson and Derby's Colin Todd. Crucially, his temperament was placid and he lacked that extra swagger or self-belief to make it to the next level. He seemed constantly to have his head in the clouds and was often thought of as dozy by his team-mates. This manifested itself on the field as occasional lapses in concentration resulted in misplaced back-passes that gave away goals.

From 10 January 1976 to 29 April 1978 Dodd made 102 consecutive League starts (113 in all competitions), making him the most recent of only five men to pass the century mark for Stoke (ignoring substitute appearances). Despite this record, Dodd found himself displaced from the side by new signing Mike Doyle, a £50,000 arrival from Manchester City in the summer of 1978. New Stoke manager Alan Durban reasoned that success in the Second Division required a physically solid central defence, and the pairing of Smith and Doyle marshalled Stoke's defence so well that City conceded only 31 League goals all season. Dodd was not over-enamoured by Durban's tactical changes: 'It took the fun out of the game for me. We only spoke about the opposition, not how we were going to play ourselves. Long term, Stoke lost a lot of supporters because the football we played was not pretty to watch – or to play in.'

Feeling undervalued, Dodd refused a new contract in August 1979 and was transfer listed. He eventually settled his differences and forced his way back into the side, performing so well that Stoke's fans voted him Player of the Year.

As a result of Smith's pre-season injury, Dodd began 1980-81 partnering Doyle. As Durban had predicted, the pair did not function and he was forced to convert striker Brendan O'Callaghan to centre-back in order to stem the flow of goals conceded. Dodd reverted to midfield – an older head amidst Stoke's bubbly youngsters such as Adrian Heath and Paul Bracewell.

Dodd was granted a testimonial in April 1982 against Port Vale. A poor crowd of 3,729 saw Stoke win 3-2 thanks to Lee Chapman's hat-trick. That November Dodd moved to Wolves for just £40,000, yet he was only 29. 'I was surprised that I went so cheaply, but I was relieved to go. I couldn't see a future at Stoke under Richie Barker, but it was the most upsetting day of my footballing life when I left. Every time I drove to Wolves I kept thinking I should drop off at the Victoria Ground. I never wanted to leave.' Dodd returned to Stoke on a monthly contract in January 1985, although his pace had gone and he was regularly exposed by the speed of First Division attackers.

Prompted by journalist Peter Keeling, Dodd moved to Sweden, playing for Elfsborg, GAIS Gothenburg, and Landskrona over a six-year period. Interspersed between the Scandinavian seasons he returned home to play for Port Vale and also Cork City in Ireland. He eventually returned to Staffordshire with non-league Rocester.

Aged 39, he retired from football to run a property rental company in Stoke-on-Trent, replacing the thrill of playing football with the challenge of running marathons. 'It had always been my ambition to run a marathon and I decided to take the plunge when I retired.' In his first race, Dodd finished in a respectable two hours and 49 minutes, raising money for the Children of Bosnia appeal in the process. He now runs half-marathons and cross-country races for Staffordshire.

A lover of heavy metal music, particularly Led Zeppelin and Deep Purple, Dodd still regularly attends gigs, although these days his tastes, perhaps influenced by his daughter Laura, have mellowed to include the more melodic David Gray.

Magic Moment: *In November 1976, in his 151st game for Stoke, Dodd scored his first goal – a far-post header in a 1-1 draw at Leeds.*

Worst Nightmare: *With Stoke needing a win at Villa Park to avoid the drop in May 1977, Dodd shoved centre-forward Andy Gray in the back. That early penalty condemned Stoke to relegation.*

STOKE RECORD	Appearances	Goals
Football League	365 (+8)	3
FA Cup	16	–
League Cup	24	1
Other	4	–

No 80. **ALAN HUDSON**
Debut: v Liverpool, 19 January 1974
Final Farewell: v Crystal Palace, 28 September 1985

Without doubt one of the most gifted players of his generation, Alan Anthony Hudson was the catalyst which transformed Stoke into championship challengers during the halcyon period of the 1970s.

Born within walking distance of Stamford Bridge on 21 June 1951, Hudson signed for Chelsea on leaving school in 1967. The original Chelsea Boys – Hudson, Webb, Osgood, Cooke, Baldwin and Hutchinson – were the Princes of the King's Road. Their infamous drinking antics included nights on the tiles with stars such as Elton John and arm-wrestling matches with actor Richard Harris. Fashion photographer Terry O'Neill recalls: 'Chelsea was like the cast of a film. Chopper was like Lee Marvin, Cookey was James Dean. Huddy was the young Robert Mitchum.'

Hudson played a major part in Chelsea's progress to the FA Cup final in 1970, although he was injured and missed the big day. He finished second in the Footballer of the Year awards, just one vote behind Leeds' skipper Billy Bremner, remarkable for a 19-year-old in his first full season. He returned to full fitness to play in the following season's European Cup-Winners' Cup final triumph.

By all accounts Hudson did not get on with Chelsea manager Dave Sexton, and was outspoken in his criticism of him. Transfer listed after he and Peter Osgood had a training ground row with Sexton, Hudson was persuaded by the silver tongued Waddington to swap the bright lights of London for the smoke-laden Potteries. In Waddington Hudson found a man he could admire. He cost a Stoke record £240,000 in January 1974 and might have been joined at the Victoria Ground by Osgood, who shook hands with Waddo on a deal, but chose to sign for Southampton instead. Saints ended that season relegated.

Hudson's debut against Liverpool was breathtaking. Former Wolves manager Stan Cullis, commentating on radio, declared it as the finest he had ever seen. Allowed free rein by Waddington, Hudson combined brilliantly with Jimmy Greenhoff, sparking a run of only two defeats in nineteen games to the end of the season. 'Alan always wanted the ball,' Greenhoff recalls. 'Whether he was free or had players surrounding him. In that sense he was like me. We both wanted it all the time.' Blessed with an uncanny ability to pass with pinpoint accuracy, Hudson seemed to skim across the muddy Victoria Ground pitch. Waddington dubbed Stoke's style of football the 'Working Man's Ballet', a title which Hudson borrowed for his 1997 autobiography.

Trevor Brooking remembers: 'He appeared to possess what I can only describe as a revolving kneecap which allowed him to turn in the tightest of situations, keeping the ball on his right foot all the time. To be so one-footed would be considered a weakness by some, but he would jink past a defender on both sides, using either the inside or outside of his right foot.'

Despite the Potteries' initial appearance as the antithesis of the glamorous King's Road, the heavy drinking Hudson soon discovered Stoke's answer to the bright lights, a nightclub in Hanley called The Place, which Stoke's players ritually visited on Monday nights. Greenhoff recalls: 'We were all good friends, but I couldn't keep up with him off the park. Huddy wanted to go out until four or five in the morning!' In Geoff Salmons, a £160,000 signing from Sheffield United in July 1974, Hudson found a bosom pal who could keep pace. Ever the playboy, Hudson even opened his own club, Hudson's, in Newcastle-under-Lyme.

Hudson was in his element. In his first two years he missed only one game out of 162 and his insouciant approach allowed Stoke to set a club record 23 undefeated home games from December 1973 to December 1974. In August 1975 Hudson scored one of his all too rare goals as Stoke beat Arsenal 1-0 at Highbury. The build-up of the two coaches bears interesting comparison. Waddington simply left his players to chat and study the racing form, while Don Howe filled his team's heads with tactics on a blackboard. All the more remarkable was the drinking session which had taken place at the Markham Arms and La Val Bonne in Soho the night before, which left Hudson taking the field dazed and Geoff Salmons unable to tie his own boots. On 1 September Hudson received a telegram from the errant George Best simply stating 'You are still the best player in the country by a mile. Ram it down their throats on the pitch.'

The Stoke fans agreed. 'Alan Hudson walks on water' read one banner while the Boothen sang

Land of Smoke and glory
Home of Stoke City
Higher, higher and higher
On to victory

After Stoke beat Liverpool 2-0 in March 1975, putting them into pole position for the championship with only four games remaining, Bill Shankly strode into Stoke's dressing room and shook Hudson's hand saying, 'I never thought I'd see anyone play as well as Peter Doherty [his boyhood hero] but you surpassed him today.' Hudson remembers: 'I didn't get on with one or two in the Stoke dressing room so I just looked at them and said "Told You".'

After captaining England Under-23s on tour in 1974, Hudson belatedly earned a full cap for a friendly against West Germany. Hudson starred in a 2-0 win and also played in the 5-0 home thrashing of Cyprus in which Malcolm MacDonald of Newcastle scored all five. Yet the outspoken Hudson clashed with England manager Revie over his famous dossiers on opposing players, which were considered essential reading by Revie. With the pressure on England to win by a hatful in the return game in Cyprus, Hudson was dropped. England only won 1-0 and failed to qualify for the 1976 European Championships. It took heavy media pressure to get Hudson selected again. This time, in March 1976, a rearranged League game at Derby saw Stoke withdraw Hudson from the England squad. Hudson broke his leg at the Baseball Ground and was never picked for his country again.

After the roof fell in on the Butler Street stand, Hudson was vocal in his disapproval of the board. He finally fell out with Waddo early in 1976-77 over being forced to play whilst not fully recovered from an injury and was sold to Arsenal in December 1976 for just £225,000 – a loss, although it set a new outgoing transfer record.

Hudson earned a loser's medal in the 1978 FA Cup final but his form failed to reach the same heights as at Stoke. In 1979 he moved to the USA with Seattle Sounders. Four years later he rejoined Chelsea on a non-contract basis. He did not make the first team and languished in the reserves as Stoke's new manager Bill Asprey sought the advice of Tony Waddington on how to approach the task of rescuing Stoke from relegation. Hudson returned to the Victoria Ground, at Waddington's suggestion, for £22,500 in January 1984.

Hudson recalls: 'I went into the gym the following morning and said "Look. If we're going to go down we'll go down by playing the game properly".' George Berry smiles: 'Everything went through Alan Hudson. Huddy was fantastic at getting time on the ball and space to play in. He made people play around him and because of that we believed in ourselves.'

Stoke picked up 33 points in seventeen games and clinched survival with a 4-0 win over Wolves on the final day of the season. But in 1984-85 Stoke slumped humiliatingly into Division Two on the back of statistically the worst season in English professional football. Hudson's personal season reflected the club's. He suffered hamstring and groin problems and, frustrated, lost his cool against Sunderland in February 1985 and was sent off for the first and only time in his career.

That summer Hudson applied for the vacant manager's job and agreed terms with chairman Frank Edwards, whose untimely death left the club in limbo. The Stoke board, under new chairman Sandy Clubb, did opt for a player-manager, but instead of Hudson it proved to be former England skipper Mick Mills. Hudson was made captain for the 1985-86 season, however a recurring knee injury forced him to retire in September.

Having hung up his boots, Hudson worked as an opinionated columnist for the local evening paper, the *Sentinel,* whose editor of ten or so years, Sean Dooley, described working with Hudson as like 'playing basketball with a hand grenade'.

After cheating death in a road accident, Hudson currently draws disability benefit, but still passes typically dismissive comments about the game. When asked what he felt about the differences between football today and in the 1970s, he replied: 'I never played for the money, not like they do today. I played for the love of it.'

Magic Moment: *In February 1975 Hudson inspired Stoke's 4-0 win over Man City. He scored the second, playing a one-two with Ian Moores, beating three players, and shooting past Keith MacRae.*

Worst Nightmare: *One of Hudson's drinking sessions possibly cost Stoke a lucrative run in Europe. He crashed his car after a night out with Tony Waddington and Geoff Hurst and was still in shock with a damaged hand when Stoke drew 1-1 with Ajax in the UEFA Cup.*

STOKE RECORD	Appearances	Goals
Football League	141 (+1)	9
FA Cup	7	–
League Cup	8	–
Other	2	–

One of Stoke's greatest servants, Denis Smith, the most injured man in football

Jackie Marsh, voracious tackler and socialiser

Garth Crooks celebrates with Adrian Heath at Middlesbrough (February 1980)

'Big Bren' flashes home a trade-mark header against Burnley

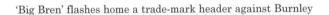

Peter Beagrie hands over a cheque to encourage local kids to play football

The Second Division champions 1992-93

Chapter Nine

~ *Homegrown Heroes* ~

No 81. **GARTH CROOKS**
Debut: v Coventry, 10 April 1976
Farewell: v West Brom, 3 May 1980

With the glory days well and truly over, Stoke sought to rebuild using the tried and tested method of bringing through local talent. Throughout the 1970s the likes of Sean Haslegrave, Terry Lees and Kevin Sheldon found their path to the first team blocked by established stars and expensive purchases. Now Stoke needed its youth-products more than ever. The first to emerge, Garth Anthony Crooks, established himself in the first team mainly due to the selling of players to fund repairs to the Butler Street stand.

Born in Stoke-on-Trent on 10 March 1958, Crooks grew up in Butler Street itself, adjoining the Victoria Ground. Football was consequently always in his thoughts, although the apocryphal story of him being signed by Waddington after kicking a ball against the manager's window are denied. As an only son with four sisters, he sought refuge from them on Stoke's matchdays, waiting for the gates to open before dashing in to watch the closing minutes. One of his formative experiences was to watch his hero, Pele, play at the Victoria Ground for Santos in 1969. His heart was with Stoke once chief scout Cliff Birks gave him an early fourteenth birthday present – a ticket to the 1972 League Cup final. Henceforth Birks became the only man that the cocky youngster called 'Sir', even after he signed professional forms in March 1976.

As one of the first black stars of modern times, with West Brom's 'Three Degrees' – Cyrille Regis, Laurie Cunningham and Brendan Batson – Crooks emerged into a climate of racial hatred around many grounds in Britain. But these pioneers paved the way for the explosion of talented blacks who populated the League from the early 1980s. Crooks suffered terrace taunts and a hail of bananas, but took it all with a sizeable pinch of salt. His answer was to ram the taunts back down people's throats with his performances.

Still raw, Crooks finished top scorer in his first full season – albeit with only six goals – as Stoke failed to avoid relegation. Blessed with lightning pace, particularly over the first ten yards or so, Crooks frightened defenders, and Division Two proved to be just the stage for his talent to blossom. Strongly built at 5ft 8½in and 11st 2lbs, he liked to cap his devastating runs with a whiplash shot from his left foot. A natural predator around the six-yard box,

Crooks possessed an athletic litheness which allowed him to twist and turn to reach balls, or get in shots, which would have been beyond less nimble strikers.

Despite the team struggling under George Eastham in 1977-78, Crooks bagged eighteen goals. His treble against Blackburn in March 1978 made him the youngest ever scorer of a Stoke hat-trick, although that record subsequently passed to Lee Chapman. Crooks' streak of form led to an England Under-21 call up. He made his debut in a 5-0 demolition of Bulgaria, scoring a hat-trick, including a penalty and a rare header. He won three further Under-21 caps, but never made the full England side.

The arrival of £150,000 Paul Randall in December 1978 saw a change of role for Crooks. He now played wide on the left, supplying his former partner Brendan O'Callaghan and new boy Randall. Never one to conceal his thoughts, Crooks openly criticised manager Alan Durban's decision and his form suffered in consequence. Stoke stuttered to home defeats by Sunderland and Blackburn, and Crooks was the one to step down. The pithy Durban stayed true to his big money signing. Knowing, however, that Crooks was the best goalpoacher at the club, Durban restored his partnership with O'Callaghan in time for the promotion decider at Notts County which Stoke won 1-0.

Back in the big time, Crooks made hay and was clearly the star of a workaday Stoke side. By the time he had netted his match-winning hat-trick against West Brom in December, he was openly courting transfer speculation. Tension increased between himself and Durban, to the point that the manager dropped Crooks from the team to play at Leeds in April, despite Stoke being threatened by relegation. Crooks demanded a transfer. Durban, determined to stamp his authority, ensured Crooks knew that he would be sold when the time was right – for the club.

With Stoke's First Division assured, Crooks was sold to Tottenham in the summer of 1980 for £650,000, at that time Stoke's record outgoing transfer. Crooks partnered Steve Archibald in a Spurs attack which won consecutive FA Cups, with Crooks scoring in the epic 3-2 replay victory over Manchester City in 1981. One banner at the civic reception joked: 'Maggie isn't the only one with Crooks at No 11.' Crooks became something of a celebrity, being black, cool and into popular culture. Setting a precedent for his career after football, he once presented Top of the Pops and hid his disappointment at missing out on Ron Greenwood's squad for the 1982 World Cup in Spain by working as a BBC reporter.

He also played for Manchester United (on loan), West Brom and Charlton before a series of back injuries forced him to retire in November 1990. Always ready to voice an opinion, in 1988 Crooks became Chairman of the Professional Footballers' Association. He has since moved into television and radio broadcasting, co-hosting a regular Saturday afternoon show on Greater London Radio and acting as a roving reporter for the BBC's Match of the Day.

Magic Moment: *The only time Crooks ever became tongue-tied was when face to face with his idol, Mohammed Ali, in Birmingham. Ali, prompted by Stoke's commercial director Dudley Kernick, said in his drawl, 'So you play for Stoke City?' Crooks' jaw dropped.*

Worst Nightmare: *In September 1979, Crooks took a penalty at Old Trafford. With the score 0-2 and 50,000 United fans whistling, Crooks bottled it, tamely striking the ball at keeper Gary Bailey.*

STOKE RECORD	Appearances	Goals
Football League	141 (+6)	48
FA Cup	3 (+2)	1
League Cup	10 (+2)	4

No 82. **BRENDAN O'CALLAGHAN**
Debut: v Hull, 8 March 1978
Farewell: v Sunderland, 2 February 1985

No other player has made an impact in a Stoke shirt quite as quickly as Brendan Richard O'Callaghan. Born in Bradford of Irish parents on 23 July 1955, after playing for Bradford Boys and Yorkshire schools, O'Callaghan was spotted by Doncaster as a 17-year-old. But the offer to turn professional in July 1973 left him in something of a quandary, as he had been accepted by Loughborough College to undertake a PE teaching diploma.

O'Callaghan chose to sign, deferring college for a year in case the football did not work out. Promoted to Doncaster's first team after six months in the reserves, he formed a keen partnership with Peter Kitchen and finished as top scorer in 1975-76 with 28 goals. By the time that tally had risen to 77 goals from 212 games, scouts were flocking to Belle Vue. Alan Durban, Stoke's new manager, had tried to sign O'Callaghan whilst in charge at Shrewsbury, but had more luck this time. On 1 March 1978 he got his man – his first signing for Stoke – for £40,000.

The following Wednesday O'Callaghan warmed the bench as City struggled to break down Hull. Goalless with just twelve minutes left, Stoke won a corner. The Boothen End clamoured for the new signing. Durban took the cue, turned to O'Callaghan and half-jokingly told him to 'Get me a goal'. The instant reply, equally joking, came: 'No problem'. O'Callaghan rose to meet the flag-kick and netted a header with his first touch in Stoke colours. He had been on the field for just ten seconds. It made him and Durban heroes.

Stoke had lacked a big centre-forward since the demise of John Ritchie in 1974, and O'Callaghan proved to be the perfect foil for the speedy Garth Crooks. Tall at 6ft 2½in and weighing over 13st, 'Big Bren', as he became known, worked as a willing target man, shielding the ball and acting as a link between the midfield and Crooks. O'Callaghan matched Crooks' scoring rate too, finishing as leading scorer with sixteen as Stoke won promotion in 1978-79. 'Every time we attacked I felt I could score. I had always been confident about getting goals and with the chances our midfield made, particularly Sammy Irvine, I had plenty to convert.'

His thick walrus moustache and solid physique marked him out as a throwback to a bygone era and, in an age of fly-by-night stars, O'Callaghan proved to be a staunch servant of the club. Courteous and thoughtful, he was always well presented in a club blazer when on duty. Indeed, this kind of dedication ran through O'Callaghan's approach to his game. Always one of the first to arrive, O'Callaghan prepared assiduously by warming up in the gym, having readied his boots the day before. His methodical approach allowed him to make the most of his modest ability while other, potentially more talented players, fell by the wayside.

In May 1979 he was selected by the Republic of Ireland and made his debut against West Germany in Dublin. His opportunities were restricted by competition from Frank Stapleton, Ireland's all-time leading scorer, but O'Callaghan won seven caps including one against Brazil in May 1982, although the Irish lost 0-7.

With the arrival at Stoke of Paul Maguire, O'Callaghan posed a new threat. He would occupy the near post at corners, while dead-ball specialist Maguire floated the ball onto his head. Stoke scored any number of goals with players arriving late to latch onto Bren's flicks. When George Berry arrived the pair caused mayhem for opponents: 'It got so that the Boothen End would cheer when we got a corner as they thought it was as good as a goal. It was almost impossible to defend,' recalls O'Callaghan.

As Stoke floundered at the start of 1980-81, Durban converted O'Callaghan – who had lost his place to young Lee Chapman – to centre-half, filling in for the injured Denis Smith. O'Callaghan took to the switch quickly. 'I thought to myself "What don't I like when I'm playing against a centre-half", and then tried to put it into practice. The main thing was to stay on your feet and not to let the ball drop over your head. I couldn't believe how easy it was.' His partnership with Mike Doyle allowed City to climb to mid-table.

Despite his straight image Big Bren loved a laugh. Dutchman Loek Ursem, Stoke's first foreign signing, owned a pristine, canary yellow Vauxhall. Whilst recovering from a torn ankle ligament, O'Callaghan, and fellow prankster Peter Fox, filled a bucket with manure used to fertilise the pitch, diluted it, and painted Ursem's car. The fuming Ursem espied what appeared to be O'Callaghan's metallic green Rover on the other side of the car park and daubed it in the same foul mixture, only to discover that the car in fact belonged to club secretary Mike Potts. Ursem now had two cars to clean.

Manager Richie Barker's announcement during the summer of 1983 that he intended adopting the long ball tactics so successful for Graham Taylor's Watford, forced O'Callaghan to put in for a transfer. But Barker's tenure came to an end just before Christmas. His successor, Bill Asprey, tempted Alan Hudson to return and Stoke managed to clamber clear of the relegation places. Happily, O'Callaghan chose to stay and he played a major part in the great escape.

In February 1985 it became clear that O'Callaghan's days were numbered. He missed out on a move to Luton due to an injury, but joined Oldham Athletic for £30,000 later that month. During the first game of 1985-86, O'Callaghan injured his leg. The problem was later diagnosed as an adductor muscle strain, which flared to such an extent that doctors talked of him being wheelchair ridden. Typically O'Callaghan battled through it, although the injury ended his career at the age of just 29.

Unlike many players of the era, O'Callaghan was well insured and the PFA helped him take a degree in Business Administration at the University of Dublin. Having been the PFA representative whilst at Stoke, he worked in 1989 as a Community Development Officer at the Victoria Ground. This was not best suited to his talents and O'Callaghan became area manager for Save the Children, running 23 branches in the north-west Midlands.

Magic Moment: *Against Liverpool in April 1984, Stoke were 2-0 up against the champions elect. O'Callaghan stood on the ball, beckoning the Reds to come and get it. This insensed Graeme Souness so much that on the final whistle he smashed a window with his fist.*

Worst Nightmare: *O'Callaghan was substituted only once as a Stoke player. Manager Richie Barker pulled him off against Fourth Division Peterborough in a 0-0 draw in the League Cup.*

STOKE RECORD	Appearances	Goals
Football League	255(+10)	44
FA Cup	10	–
League Cup	19	3

No 83. **PETER FOX**
Debut: v Wrexham, 16 December 1978
Farewell: v Burnley, 8 May 1993

Peter David Fox continued the long line of Stoke goalkeepers small in stature, but big in bravery and ability.

Born in Scunthorpe on 5 July 1957, Fox became the youngest player ever to play for Sheffield Wednesday, aged fifteen years and eight months, in a 2-0 win over Orient. Unfortunately he broke his toe that day and lost his place to another young keeper, Chris Turner. Following the arrival of Jack Charlton at Hillsborough in October 1977, Fox found himself on the sidelines. Charlton liked big keepers, whose kicks could penetrate deep into the opposition half. After playing on loan at Barnsley in December 1977, the alert Alan Durban snapped up Fox for £15,000 in the summer of 1978.

After a season in the reserves – who challenged hard for the Central League title – Fox took over from Roger Jones as No 1 in April 1980 as Stoke battled to stay in the First Division. He kept clean sheets in the final two games, which City won to stay up.

Small for a goalkeeper at only 5ft 10in, the compact and agile Fox, who modelled himself on Peter Shilton, commanded his area. He believed that his defenders benefited from good communication which would fill them with confidence. His thinking was simple: 'Some keepers like to make an impression by making a straightforward save look good but I would aim to not have to make any saves at all.' However, when forwards did break through, they faced a fine shot stopper, particularly good in one-on-ones, rushing out to spread himself and block with any part of his body.

Fox rates his luckiest break as 'changing next to Denis Smith. He guided me with advice on football and life. He would do so many extra-curricular dos and functions – so I followed suit.' Fox worked tirelessly for the club off the field and won the admiration of supporters. One of these good deeds landed Fox in trouble while Stoke were on tour in Trinidad and Tobago. In a swimming pool, whilst teaching young kids how to dive, he launched himself in an elaborate penguin dive and cracked his head on the bottom, knocking himself out. He awoke in the local hospital, having been fished out by his team-mates, to find his hospital bed surrounded by lizards and ants. He swiftly discharged himself.

In 1981 Fox was mooted in the national press as a possible England squad keeper, behind Clemence and Shilton, although after one of his less impressive displays, at Middlesbrough, manager Richie Barker mused: 'People tell me he's a good goalkeeper but every time the ball goes in the box I close my eyes. If he keeps on missing crosses like that he won't be playing a lot longer.'

Ever present in 1980-81 and 1983-84, Fox was voted Player of the Year in 1980-81, 1981-82 and 1989-90, in which year he saved four consecutive penalties. Fox prepared diligently before each game and took to the field carrying an early version of the now familiar goalkeeper's bag which he carefully placed into the back of his net. Its contents were nothing special. Spare gloves, a peaked hat, a spare stud and a tie-up, but they bear the hallmarks of the dedicated professional.

Fox had to withstand back injuries and the challenge of rivals – Eric McManus, Mark Harrison and Scott Barrett – to regain his place. After being sent off for handling outside the penalty box against Luton in September 1982, Fox considered quitting as he felt he had been branded a cheat. Brendan O'Callaghan remembers seeking out Fox at half-time: 'He was in the physio room crying his heart out. He took it really badly.' His failure to regain his place, on account of spectacular performances by stand-in Mark Harrison, caused Fox to demand a transfer. This was rejected in December 1982. When Harrison broke his jaw against Norwich, Fox won his place back.

In late 1984 a back injury, which led to a disc being removed, kept him out for six months. The injury nearly cost Fox his career when he was just entering his prime. Of his return in May 1985 Fox recalls: 'After all I'd been through to get back to full fitness, to run out and see the packed Boothen End give me an ovation – I can't explain what that means to a player. Supporters will never understand how much they can build you up and knock you down.' In the 23rd minute of his comeback against Chelsea, in a save reminiscent of Banks' from Pele, Fox pulled off a twisting dive to scoop Kerry Dixon's bullet header off the line.

Fox was granted a testimonial in 1989, which Stoke lost 2-4 to Colin Harvey's Everton. After the game Fox returned to the pitch to a standing ovation from an embarrassingly poor attendance of 3,767.

Alan Ball made Fox club captain in early 1990, in succession to George Berry, but after twelve years as first-choice keeper Fox lost his place under new manager Lou Macari, with Jason Kearton and Ronnie Sinclair preferred. Both, however, were cup-tied, allowing Fox to claim a winners medal as Stoke beat Stockport 1-0 in the Autoglass Trophy final at Wembley in May 1992.

Fox spent the autumn of 1992 on loan to Linfield. He was stuck on 399 League appearances for Stoke – as he had been for a year. Recalled, Fox reached the 400 mark in a 2-1 win over Leyton Orient in October 1992, deputising for the injured Sinclair. In March 1993 Fox joined Wrexham on loan, although before he could appear in the first team he found himself recalled to play in the last few

games of City's promotion campaign, after on-loan keeper Bruce
Grobbelaar was recalled to Liverpool. The final game of the season,
against Burnley, ensured Fox qualified for a championship medal –
a fitting end to his career at the Victoria Ground. Fox broke the
appearance record for a Stoke goalkeeper by a distance, displaying
an uncommon loyalty in these days of serial signing-on fee seekers.

Released on a free transfer, Fox joined Alan Ball as player-coach
at Exeter City in July 1993. Fox was passed over in favour of Terry
Cooper when Ball received the elbow, but became player-manager
after Cooper's sacking in June 1995. Voted Exeter's Player of the
Year in 1993-94, he passed the 650 career appearance mark in
1996, an ever present that season at the age of 38. He then retired
to become full-time manager.

Sacked towards the end of 1999-2000 as Exeter struggled to
avoid the drop to the Vauxhall Conference, he was replaced by Noel
Blake. Fox now coaches goalkeepers at Huddersfield – under former Stoke manager Lou Macari – and Notts County.

Magic Moment: *Fox made a vital double save from Plymouth's
Warren Joyce as Stoke clinched the Second Division championship
with a 1-0 win in April 1993.*

Worst Nightmare: *Against Leeds in April 1989, Fox was chipped
by debutant Gordon Strachan from a free-kick taken whilst he was
still organising the wall. The goal stood, giving Leeds a 3-2 win.*

STOKE RECORD	Appearances	Goals
Football League	409	–
FA Cup	24	–
League Cup	31	–
Others	14	–

No 84. **ADRIAN HEATH**
Debut: v Northampton, 3 October 1978
Final Farewell: v Stockport, 16 May 1992

Another player to emerge off the production line of local talent,
Adrian Paul Heath began visiting the Victoria Ground to watch his
heroes at the age of four with his father. Born in Stoke-on-Trent on
11 January 1961, Heath emerged through the Lads and Dads
League, which still operates in the Potteries area, in which games
are organised by dads and played by lads. He joined Stoke as an
associate schoolboy at the age of fourteen, becoming professional at
seventeen. Taken under the wing of player-coach Howard Kendall,
Heath's zestful performances helped the reserves finish second in

the Central League in 1978-79, with Heath winning Stoke's Young Player of the Year Award. When Stoke's youth team played in the annual Haarlem tournament in Holland in the summer of 1980, Heath's dynamism led to him being named as Player of the Tournament.

Known as 'Inchy', due to his short 5ft 6in, 10st frame, Heath had long light brown hair and a beaming smile on a fresh youthful face. Even many years later Heath still looks incredibly young. Once Kendall had departed to manage Blackburn, Heath announced his arrival in the First Division with a series of mature performances, scampering down the right wing to deliver crosses. Initially a direct replacement for Kendall, Heath's goalscoring flair from midfield soon became apparent. He bagged both goals in vital 1-0 wins in the last two games of 1979-80 to ensure Stoke's First Division safety and began 1981-82 in a more advanced position, partnering the bustling giant Lee Chapman in attack.

Heath pipped Chapman and Paul Bracewell to international recognition, making his England Under-21 debut in Romania on 14 October 1980 – in a very forgettable 0-4 defeat. He did, however, notch two goals in the return game as England won 3-0. He earned eight caps, plus an England B appearance, but these served to whet his appetite for success and desire to play for an ambitious, big-name club – despite previously having stated that he only wanted to play for his boyhood team.

In August 1980, fresh from signing a new two-year contract, Heath rocked Stoke with a transfer request. 'I want success,' he said. 'In the two years I have been involved in the first team we've never even looked like we could actually win anything.' His comments brought him a one week suspension. Heath's form fell away amidst rumours that his former mentor Kendall, now manager of Everton, was interested in his protégé. New manager Richie Barker was persuaded to let the pint-sized striker go to Everton for £700,000 (a record outgoing transfer fee) in January 1982.

As a replacement, Richie Barker lined up Swedish international midfielder Robert Prytz. But despite parading the £80,000 Prytz to the media, clad in a Stoke shirt, work permit problems scuppered the deal.

Heath's arrival sparked Everton into life and he won an FA Cup winners' medal in 1984 and two League championships in 1984-85 and 1986-87. He moved on to Espanol in Spain, Aston Villa and Manchester City before, in March 1992, Stoke manager Lou Macari added Heath's experience to his squad for the push for promotion from Division Three. After returning on a free transfer, Heath played ten games. Stoke lost to Stockport in the play-off semi-finals before gaining revenge in the Autoglass Trophy final in May.

Heath left on another free transfer to Burnley, then Sheffield United, before returning to Turf Moor, this time as manager. When he failed to carry Burnley into the play-offs he was sacked, so he joined former Everton colleague Peter Reid at Sunderland, becoming first-team coach.

Wherever he has roamed Heath always jumps at any opportunity to see his beloved Stoke play. He returned to play in the pre-match festivities at the last match at the Victoria Ground and admitted to being 'a bit emotional' at seeing his old stamping ground bid farewell.

Magic Moment: *Against Coventry in November 1979, Heath back-headed past a bewildered Les Sealey to set up Stoke's first away win of their first season back in the First Division.*

Worst Nightmare: *A naïve young Heath once told a Radio Stoke reporter: 'It's a great job. We come in at 10am, train in the mornings and then have lunch and get home about 2.30.' When manager Alan Durban heard this, Heath found himself sweeping the corridors.*

STOKE RECORD	Appearances	Goals
Football League	99 (+2)	16
FA Cup	4	1
League Cup	9	–
Autoglass Trophy	3	–

No 85. **PAUL BRACEWELL**
Debut: v Wolves, 22 March 1980
Farewell: v Tottenham, 14 May 1983

Another of Stoke's homegrown products to emerge from the youth ranks, Paul William Bracewell also achieved enduring success away from the Victoria Ground.

Born at Heswall, on the Wirral, on 19 July 1962, Bracewell grew up in Church Athern in Shropshire. Phil Stokes, the coach of his youth team, Edgmond Rangers, recommended him to Stoke and Bracewell became captain of Stoke's youth side. Due to midfielder Sammy Irvine's car accident, Bracewell made his first-team debut before his eighteenth birthday. He took his chance and developed into a skilful midfielder who specialised in winning the ball and distributing it. The crowd appreciated having local lads in the side and took to Bracewell, Heath and Lee Chapman.

Described by reporter Stuart Hall as 'pure rapture', Bracewell was noted for passing with both feet and fans argued about which was his natural foot. Bracewell puts this ability down to hours of hard work and practice. 'We used to do gym work, bench presses and the like on Mondays, Tuesdays and Wednesdays, and that helped build up my leg muscles. I think being able to pass with both feet is part of the job of a professional footballer and I pride myself that no one could tell that my natural foot was my right.' To prove the point, Bracewell broke into the team as a left-sided midfielder.

Although a gifted passer, by his own admission Bracewell did not score many goals. However, those he did score lingered long in the memory. A raking right-footer from sixteen yards earned a vital 1-0 win against Aston Villa at the tail end of the 1981-82 season, as Stoke battled against relegation.

Stoke began 1982-83 in a whirlwind with the midfield earning press plaudits. Bracewell was the engine of that international midfield quartet, alongside Northern Ireland's Sammy McIlroy. The pair also roomed together: 'Sammy was a model professional with boundless enthusiasm,' remembers Bracewell. 'He loved to play football and was always very positive, something which I took from him. I don't like negative thinkers.' In December 1982 Bracewell appeared as a substitute for England Under-21s in a 0-1 defeat by Greece. He eventually won thirteen Under-21 caps, two at Stoke. Having enjoyed his best season and been made captain, Bracewell hoped for a wage rise. Manager Richie Barker responded: 'You win more games and you'll earn more bonus.'

As with Heath, Bracewell's lack of progress at Stoke provoked a transfer request, and he followed Alan Durban to Roker Park for £250,000 in the summer of 1983. With his departure Stoke had sold nearly half a team of home-grown produce, whilst pocketing more than £2 million in transfer fees. Had the club shown more ambition and moved mountains to keep that talent, who knows how good a side Stoke might have produced. Instead, fingers burnt by the Butler Street stand fiasco, the board opted to cash in while they could. The club could not sustain this policy indefinitely, particularly after the departure of Cliff Birks, the club's chief scout. The supply of local of talent dried up and soon City's financial lifeline had been extinguished by their own misjudgment.

In 1984 Bracewell joined Everton for £425,000 and won two League championships plus the European Cup-Winners' Cup. He also played in four losing FA Cup finals, the last with Sunderland in 1992. Bracewell's integral role in Everton's midfield, alongside Peter Reid, Kevin Sheedy and Trevor Steven, saw him finally win full international recognition. He won three caps and seemed set to be named in Bobby Robson's 1986 World Cup squad. But a broken leg received against Newcastle on New Year's Day cost him his chance. X-rays proved inconclusive and it took a trip to America for surgery to finally cure the injury.

Bracewell rejoined Sunderland before moving on to Newcastle and then back to Roker Park for a third time to become player-coach to Peter Reid. He then joined Fulham in a similar role under Kevin Keegan. Despite continuing injury problems, when he finally hung up his boots he had made 587 career League appearances. Promoted to manager at Craven Cottage after Keegan's departure to become national coach in early 1999, Bracewell was sacked by Fulham owner Mohammed Al Fayed at the end of 1999-2000 – paying the price for failure to win promotion to the Premiership with a blank cheque-book.

A short spell as manager followed at Halifax, where, somewhat strangely, he was assisted by former Stoke manager Richie Barker – the architect of Stoke's long-ball game. This led former team-mates to wryly observe that Bracewell had sold out.

Magic Moment: *Bracewell's first Stoke goal finally arrived via a cracking left-foot drive from the edge of the area to level the scores at 2-2 against Wolves in a titanic FA Cup third-round tie.*

Worst Nightmare: *On Stoke's pre-season tour to the Caribbean, Bracewell lost his immigration form on departure from Barbados airport. Rather than owning up he hid near the departure gate. The team were allowed to fly once he had been cleared through customs.*

STOKE RECORD	Appearances	Goals
Football League	123 (+6)	5
FA Cup	6	1
League Cup	6	–

No 86. **SAMMY McILROY M.B.E.**
Debut: v Sunderland, 10 February 1982
Farewell: v Coventry, 17 May 1985

One of the finest British midfielders of the time, Samuel Baxter McIlroy brought experience to manage Stoke's exciting youngsters.

Born in Belfast on 2 August 1954, McIlroy became the last player to be signed by Sir Matt Busby for Manchester United. He made his first-team debut at seventeen and quickly established himself as one of the best passers of the ball in the First Division. He won the FA Cup in 1977 and in ten seasons at Old Trafford made 342 League appearances, scoring 57 goals.

Stoke paid a club record £350,000 for his services on 2 February 1982. The move paid quick dividends as McIlroy scored a breathtaking goal on his debut in a vital 2-0 win at Sunderland. His addition strengthened Stoke's midfield to the point that the 1982-83 quartet of McIlroy, Chamberlain, Bracewell and Thomas were considered as good as any in the country.

A shy, but genial man, on the pitch he orchestrated tactics from the centre of midfield, scurrying around with his fair hair streaming behind him. He would often poke the ball between an opponent's legs to create space and time in which to make a pass. He captained Stoke after the departure of Paul Bracewell in 1983 but played little part in the club's off-field activities, preferring to get away as quickly as possible for his Manchester home.

A fixture in the strong Northern Ireland side of the early 1980s – featuring Pat Jennings, Norman Whiteside, and Mal Donaghy – McIlroy won 88 caps, the third highest total behind Jennings and Donaghy. He was ever-present in Northern Ireland's World Cup final campaigns of 1982 and 1986.

Alongside Alan Hudson, McIlroy masterminded Stoke's escape from relegation in 1983-84 but, beginning to lose his pace, he could not prevent City subsiding in 1984-85, setting new records for a 42-game season of fewest wins (3), fewest goals scored (17), most home defeats (15) and overall defeats (31). Despite his growing limitations, in the absence of any other suitable candidates McIlroy was voted Player of the Year.

In an attempt to seek a financial injection, the club had backed an £8m deal with ASDA, hailed as the 'Saviour of Stoke City', to turn the capacious car park behind the Boothen End into a supermarket. Planning permission was refused and the deal fell through. It had been hoped that 400 jobs would be brought to a decaying area of Stoke-on-Trent. Instead the decay spread to Stoke City.

Handed a free transfer in the summer of 1985, Stoke's record signing of three years earlier was now worth nothing, even though he was only 30 – surely a serious error on the club's behalf. Supporters remain divided over his merits, with many feeling that he never performed well against Manchester United when he had something to prove, and did not really do enough to justify the record fee paid to secure his services.

McIlroy joined First Division Manchester City, then FC Ogryte in Sweden (on loan), Bury and FC Moedling of Austria. He became player-coach at Preston North End before taking his first managerial post at Northwich Victoria in 1991. He also managed Ashton United before joining Macclesfield Town in 1992.

At Moss Rose, McIlroy won the Vauxhall Conference in successive seasons, the second of which in 1997 earned elevation to the Football League, now that the ground had been brought up to standard. The Silkmen won promotion at the first attempt, but relegation duly followed, although McIlroy's team knocked Stoke out of the Worthington Cup, 3-2 on aggregate, in August 1998.

McIlroy was often touted as a possible Stoke manager, as City suffered numerous managerial shuffles in the late 1990s. He was interviewed for the job in the summer of 1997, but the board preferred to offer the job to first-team coach Chic Bates. McIlroy's achievements at Moss Rose saw him succeed Lawrie McMenemy as manager of the Northern Ireland team in 1999.

Magic Moment: *Against Liverpool in April 1984, McIlroy tricked England right-back Phil Neal by running into him to earn a free-kick for obstruction. He then whipped across the left-wing free-kick for Colin Russell to flick home a header to put Stoke 1-0 ahead.*

Worst Nightmare: *At the Victoria Ground in March 1983, McIlroy shrugged off three defenders to net the winner against Nottingham Forest, only to discover that the referee had awarded him a penalty for an earlier foul – which McIlroy then skied over the bar.*

STOKE RECORD	Appearances	Goals
Football League	132 (+1)	14
FA Cup	6	–
League Cup	5	–

No 87. **MICKEY THOMAS**
Debut: v Arsenal, 28 August 1982
Final Farewell: v Reading, 11 May 1991

In August 1982, following awful pre-season results, Richie Barker declared: 'I really want to improve the image of Stoke City Football Club and lose the "boring" tag associated with it.' Two signings secured on the Thursday before the curtain raiser did exactly that.

Born in Mochdre, North Wales on 7 July 1954, the irrepressible Michael Reginald Thomas signed for Wrexham as a 16-year-old junior. He went on to score 33 goals in 230 League games and won a Third Division championship medal in 1978.

By then an established Welsh international – having previously won two Under-21 caps – he was bought by Manchester United boss Dave Sexton for £350,000 in November 1978. Thomas became a popular character at Old Trafford but his cheeky wink to camera, which appeared in the title sequence to the BBC's Match of the Day, is said to have so upset one of the directors' wives that Thomas was put up for sale. He played for Everton and Brighton, but failed to find the pick-me-up his career had been seeking. Thomas's wife found it hard to settle so far from home. In a rare moment of bravado, the normally prudent Richie Barker risked £200,000 on Thomas in August 1982 – the player's fourth move inside four years.

The impish Thomas sported black curly hair and a permanently cheeky smile. At just 5ft 6in he was a bundle of energy that never stopped running on the pitch – or talking off it. Always hyperactive, Thomas caused Barker all sorts of problems: 'He was a scoundrel,' Barker austerely recalls, 'but he could be up all night in London, sleep in the Chelsea bootroom, drive up to Stoke for quarter to ten and still lead the cross-country in training.' Famously described by Barker as 'irresponsible on the field and irresponsible off it', Thomas found himself interminably in trouble of one kind or another. Caught *in flagrante delicto* with a young lady in his car, Thomas suffered the indignation of having the intimate details revealed in the national press, although he openly admitted: 'She didn't wear the football gear – it used to be me!'

Thomas took wing at Stoke and revelled in the fluid play which propelled City towards Europe. He finished 1982-83 as leading scorer with thirteen goals. Stoke fans revered his style and commitment – exemplified by his attempt to play on during a 4-4 draw with Luton with a badly gashed leg. His dismay at having to be substituted endeared him to the Boothen End and, unsurprisingly, Thomas won the Player of the Year poll hands down.

Renowned for being almost comically superstitious, Thomas had a protracted pre-match routine which involved putting on and taking off his boots three times. Once on the pitch, he never ceased winding up opponents. When playing for Wales in 1978 he conducted a personal vendetta against the entire Turkish midfield, never known to be the most sympathetic opposition. On arrival in Turkey for the return a year later, Thomas recalls that the Welsh were greeted by headlines: 'Mickey Thomas is here!' 'Mike England [the Welsh manager] went ballistic. He got me into his room at the hotel after Byron Stevenson had been sent off in the match and we had lost 0-1 and shouted "You started all the trouble, kicking all their players"!'

Before the start of 1983-84, Barker made Sammy McIlroy club captain in preference to Thomas, who began to feel disillusioned with life at Stoke. Barker's conversion to the long-ball game added insult to injury and Thomas was vocal in his criticism: 'We'd been hammering teams the previous season and Barker wanted us to play the sort of football Watford were playing. When he said it down at the training ground, Sammy McIlroy came over to me and said "We won't be here long". Suddenly everybody wanted to leave. And they did. So I went too.'

Thomas joined Chelsea in January 1984 for a bargain £75,000, while his nemesis at Stoke, Richie Barker, soon made his way out of the Victoria Ground. He did so in his club sponsored Toyota Crown car, which the club bizarrely allowed him to keep. Thomas helped Chelsea win the Second Division title in 1983-84, before joining West Brom, Derby (on loan), Wichita Wings in the USA, Shrewsbury and Leeds, while reaching a total of 51 Welsh caps.

Alan Ball made arguably his shrewdest move as manager when he brought Thomas back to Stoke on loan at the end of 1989-90, as City hurtled towards Division Three. Thomas jumped at the chance to sign permanently at the start of the new season at the age of 36. He won Player of the Year by a mile once again, despite struggling with the physical demands of two games a week. Thomas, though, did not have a particularly high opinion of Ball: 'Alan Ball was my hero as a kid. I loved Alan Ball, but as a manager some of the things he did were very wrong. I think he bought bad and some of the players he brought in weren't quality.' Thomas played his final game for Stoke aged 36 years and 308 days.

Handed a free transfer by caretaker-manager Graham Paddon, new boss Lou Macari refused to reverse the decision, despite the protestations of Thomas and most of the adoring Stoke faithful. Instead Thomas returned to Wrexham, where he famously rattled in the free-kick which knocked champions Arsenal out of the 1992 FA Cup, at a time when Wrexham propped up the entire Football League. His head now shorn of his famous locks, Thomas's next adventure was to spend time at Her Majesty's Pleasure for his part in a money counterfeiting ring.

Thomas managed Welsh League side Portmadog for a year from 1996, but management was not for him. One of the great characters of the last 25 years, Thomas came from a generation for whom playing football was everything. Come 3pm every Saturday he gave his considerable all on a football field. Unfortunately for Stoke, his kind have proved few and far between in recent years. In July 1997 Wolves hosted a benefit match for Thomas with Wrexham.

Magic Moment: *Thomas trapped a clearance on his left thigh and half-volleyed home left-footed from 30 yards past Bruce Grobbelaar as Stoke drew 1-1 with Liverpool in October 1982.*

Worst Nightmare: *In the Milk Cup second round second leg at Peterborough, Thomas conducted a running war with Ray Hankin, who was booked after just 30 seconds and later sent off. Thomas received his own marching orders after aiming a kick at Ivor Linton.*

STOKE RECORD	Appearances	Goals
Football League	97 (+6)	21
FA Cup	6	–
League Cup	9 (+1)	1
Freight Rover Trophy	1	–

No 88. **MARK CHAMBERLAIN**
Debut: v Arsenal, 28 August 1982
Farewell: v Middlesbrough, 10 September 1985

The other signing to arrive at the Victoria Ground just before 1982-83 kicked off was winger Mark Valentine Chamberlain.

He was born in Stoke-on-Trent on 19 November 1961, and joined Port Vale as a junior in 1977. He made 110 appearances as a right-winger at Vale Park, playing alongside his brother Neville, a centre-forward. On Friday, 13 August 1982 Stoke visited Vale Park for a pre-season friendly. It proved lucky. Stoke won 1-0 to put an end to their atrocious pre-season preparations which had seen them installed as bookies' favourites for relegation. The following week Barker signed Chamberlain and goalkeeper Mark Harrison in a joint deal worth £181,000.

Barker asked Chamberlain where he wanted to play – down the right or in the middle. Chamberlain responded that he preferred the wing. He had a dazzling debut, running rings round Arsenal's England left-back Kenny Sansom. He took the First Division by storm and by November had won his first England cap as a substitute against Luxembourg. Mark scored the quickest England debut goal just three minutes after coming on, with a flying header in a 9-0 win. The goal was included in an FA coaching manual as illustrating the classic downward header. Chamberlain sniggers: 'It actually came off my nose. I can't believe they still use it.'

Chamberlain's slim, athletic build made him seem taller than his 5ft 9in height. His dribbling style was upright with chest puffed out, his stride languid, with the ball being almost toe-ended by his right foot. A favourite trick saw Chamberlain wave his left foot over the ball and wiggle his hips before dabbing it past the defender with the outside of the right. A good sprinter, he believed he could outpace any opponent. This led to problems as he began to take on too many players and lose the ball rather than releasing it early.

George Berry, misty eyed, recalls: 'The football we played was breathtaking.' In the seesaw 4-4 draw with Luton in September 1982, Chamberlain, with his back to goal, span on a sixpence to get in a cross which Berry converted. 'I just knew he would get the ball across', remembers Berry. 'I had seen him do the same thing so many times in training.'

Chamberlain's sensational form was halted by a series of hamstring pulls which reduced his speed. It did not help that, by being naturally fit, he failed to prepare for games properly, leaving his muscles easily over-stretched. With Chamberlain's effectiveness curtailed, Stoke suffered a late season slump, notably after the departure of the experienced Dave Watson to play in the NASL.

Manager Richie Barker's insistence on playing the long ball all but ended Chamberlain's usefulness. 'Richie's decision is effectively why the club are in the position they are today,' he believes. 'There have been other factors, of course, but he bypassed an international midfield who all left the club.' In desperation Barker tried to hang on to his job by playing a nine-man defence. 'We spent the whole week before our visit to Liverpool preparing how we were going to defend. We all said "Yes, Richie, but how are we going to score?" But he wasn't worried about that.'

The arrival of Alan Hudson resurrected Chamberlain's career. Hudson's passes released Chamberlain in full flight, with the fullback already on the half-turn, unbalanced and ripe for the picking. Stoke's form in the second half of the season saw Bobby Robson recall Chamberlain to the England set up via the Under-21s. Chamberlain scored in the 3-1 Under-21 European Championship semi-final victory over Italy. Robson's response was to tell the player that he needed to improve his left foot.

Selected for England's 1984 summer tour of South America, Chamberlain played in England's win over Brazil in the Maracana – a game remembered for John Barnes' wonder goal – with Robson actually playing two wingers. On the flight home Chamberlain, and his fellow black internationals Barnes and Viv Anderson, had to endure a group of racist English fans who had somehow found their way onto the team's plane. They harangued the FA chairman: 'You prefer Sambos to us,' they screamed. The phlegmatic Chamberlain did not react: 'I didn't pay any attention to any taunts. It didn't bother me.'

Chamberlain famously would rarely give a straight answer to anything and often used the third person when talking about himself. Although often considered lazy because of his languid style, he had a steely determination. One day, while accepting a lift home from Stoke's commercial director Dudley Kernick, Chamberlain took him on a detour to see his old school in Burslem. On arrival they saw a group of youngsters running a cross-country race. Mark leaped out of the car and remonstrated with the stragglers who seemed to be about to give up. 'I used to be up there with the leading group. Not back here with you lot. Now get going,' he bawled. Not surprisingly, the stragglers did not have much catching up to do. Those at the front had turned around and high-tailed it back to meet their hero.

Midway through 1984-85 Chamberlain began to float his wish to move on. After Stoke's humiliating relegation he refused to sign a new contract and signed for Sheffield Wednesday. The fee, settled at tribunal, was a measly £300,000 for a player who a year before had been an established England international.

Chamberlain moved on to Portsmouth and Brighton before joining his former Stoke team-mate Peter Fox at Exeter in 1995, where he was converted to right-back. In September 1996 Chamberlain passed 500 career appearances before retiring. He is currently the last Stoke player to represent England.

After spending some time working in sales, and hating every moment, Chamberlain was tempted back into the game as Director of Football of Fareham Town in the Dr Martens League. He assumed managerial responsibility at Christmas 2000 and inspired a team which had collected just eight points to finish with 48. 'I thought I would be able to live without footy but now I'm back I can't get enough of it.' Chamberlain also coaches at Southampton's youth academy and works with special needs kids.

Magic Moment: *At Birmingham, Chamberlain scored a sensational goal when he beat five players in a run from the halfway line and cracked the ball into the top corner from 20 yards.*

Worst Nightmare: *At Tottenham in October 1984, Chamberlain's slack pass fell to John Chiedozie, who scored No 2. Spurs won 4-0.*

STOKE RECORD	Appearances	Goals
Football League	110 (+2)	17
FA Cup	4	1
League Cup	9	–

No 89. **GEORGE BERRY**
Debut: v Arsenal, 28 August 1982
Farewell: v Newcastle, 16 April 1990

George Frederick Berry was the darling of the Boothen End for the latter part of the depressing 1980s.

Born in Rostrup, West Germany, on 19 November 1957, the son of a serviceman of Jamaican origin, the Berry family moved to Blackpool while he was young. George played in a youth team two years above the nephew of former Liverpool striker Alun Evans. Evans spotted Berry and recommended him to Wolves for a trial. When they offered him terms, Berry could not leave school quickly enough and signed the day after completing his 'O' levels in 1973. He fought his way into the Wolves first team and under John Barnwell won a League Cup winner's medal in the 1-0 defeat of Nottingham Forest in 1980.

Berry's 6ft, 13st 4lbs physique brought him to the attention of Welsh manager Mike Smith. Berry qualified to play for the principality thanks to his mother's side of the family. 'They were rugby people and thought football was a bit of a nancy's game, but they all came to watch.' Berry became only the second black player to represent Wales, making his debut against his country of birth, West Germany, in 1979. He won three further caps whilst at Molineux, but Wolves' relegation in 1982 saw a wholesale clearout of players. The unwanted Berry signed for Stoke on a free transfer, tempted by the opportunity of joining Barnwell's former assistant, Richie Barker, City's newly appointed manager.

A superb header of the ball, Berry compensated for his lack of natural skill with his determination and commitment. He took the young Mark Chamberlain under his wing and nursed the winger's brittle confidence after he took knocks or suffered racial taunts. Berry himself had known racism whilst at Molineux. He had once taken matters into his own hands when a Wolves fan abused him as he left the field after a 0-3 FA Cup home defeat by Watford. 'I just lost it and jumped into the crowd and started beating him up. We had to go down to the Police Station and I got a bollocking from the Chief Inspector, but it all got hushed up.'

Berry became part of the near-post corner routine with Paul Maguire and Brendan O'Callaghan which caused havoc amongst opposing defences. Indeed, Berry claimed that his bushy Afro hair-cut, which brought him so much stick, was in fact a tactic. Its expanse made it impossible for defenders to see past him until the ball had been flicked on. His form for Stoke thrust him back into the international limelight and he picked up a fifth Welsh cap against England in February 1983.

Barker's dismissal in December 1983, with Stoke propping up Division One, also saw Berry banished to train with the youth team, as caretaker Bill Asprey sought to restore defensive stability to a team which had conceded 33 goals in its first seventeen games. Berry received no explanation for this public humiliation and the pair never spoke again. Typical of the man, Berry battled back into the side after a loan spell at Doncaster and a spell of inactivity when he trained alone in Portugal.

In the aftermath of Stoke's dire relegation season of 1984-85, under new manager Mick Mills, Berry was appointed captain. Now shorn of his trademark haircut, but sporting a thick beard instead, he formed a resolute central defensive partnership with Steve Bould which carried Stoke to within a whisker of the 1986-87 play-offs.

During the time Mills was rebuilding, George's special relationship with Stoke fans deepened. Although wholehearted and committed, Berry was prone to occasional clangers. Peter Fox recalls: 'George used to think he was Beckenbauer.' In March 1987 an over-confident pass across the back four found Brighton's Kevin Wilson who scored after just 28 seconds, leaving Stoke chasing the game against the bottom club. Despite his fallibility George was always the first to get stuck in to try to redeem himself. With Berry there was always something going on. Against Huddersfield, for example, he ran into a goalpost whilst attempting to convert a cross. To add insult to injury, Graham Shaw poked the ball home only for Berry, prone on the goal-line to be given offside.

Berry loved public engagements. In 1989 he competed in a 'Milkathon' for Radio Stoke's 'Send a Cow to Uganda' appeal and milked his own cow, Daisy, dry of 2½ gallons to great acclaim. His dressing room antics were legendary. Brendan O'Callaghan recalls 'He came to an away game in a really crumpled shirt and borrowed Winnie, the kit woman's, iron and managed to burn a big hole right across his right breast. To cap it all, he decided to wear the shirt and put Tippex on his left tit to disguise the hole.'

Astonishingly Mick Mills appointed Berry as penalty taker after Graham Shaw and Keith Bertschin had both missed from the spot. 'Everybody fell about laughing when I handed George the job,' said Mills, but Berry's confidence encouraged him to be an excellent taker. He missed only once. So loved was George that he was even given his own evening show on a local radio station in which he was asked to play his favourite soul music.

His eight years' service was rewarded with a testimonial in August 1990 against Port Vale, which Stoke won 1-0. Substituted after 30 minutes, Berry kissed the turf to rapturous applause and spent the second half standing on his beloved Boothen End. Freed that summer, Berry joined Peterborough, Preston and Aldershot before becoming commercial manager at Stafford Rangers.

Berry currently works for the PFA's Commercial Department in Manchester and is proud still to be the President of the Stoke City Southern Supporters Club.

Magic Moment: *Berry was at Wembley in 1992 to see his successor, Vince Overson, lift the Autoglass Trophy. Stoke fans spotted him in the crowd and chanted 'Ooh Georgie Berry!' George admits he cried.*

Worst Nightmare: *Berry declared after a 2-0 home victory over Millwall in September 1986 that he would wear his new bright red trousers until Stoke lost. City won just two of the next eight games.*

STOKE RECORD	Appearances	Goals
Football League	229 (+8)	27
FA Cup	13	1
League Cup	10	–
Full Members Cup	9	2

No 90. **STEVE BOULD**
Debut: v Middlesbrough, 26 September 1981
Farewell: v Shrewsbury, 2 May 1988

As one of the finest players produced by Stoke City in the modern era, Stephen Andrew Bould has had a glittering career. It is a mark of the fall of the club that all of his success has been achieved away from his beloved Stoke.

Born in Stoke-on-Trent 16 November 1962, Bould emerged through the Lads and Dads League. It was there that, when young Steve's team lost 1-10, his father threatened to make him wear a dress if it ever happened again. A natural sportsman, Bould took part in English volleyball trials and hoped to continue playing that sport after he signed professional terms with Stoke in November 1980. The club said no.

Despite standing 6ft 2in tall, Bould began life in Stoke's first team as a right-back. Toughened up by being loaned to Torquay in the autumn of 1982, he returned to Stoke, only to suffer a barrage of terrace criticism during Stoke's horrendous start to the 1983-84 season. He found it hard to play on the flank due to his high centre of gravity, and his passing wasn't good enough to play one-twos to extricate himself from being caught on the touchline. Despite this tough introduction, he grew in stature and his improved perform-ances earned the fans' respect to such an extent that they voted him Player of the Year.

After the chaos of 1984-85, Bould became the mainstay of Mick Mills' attempts at stabilising the club. Mills knew a full-back when he saw one – and the lanky Bould certainly did not fit the bill. Mills moved Bould to centre-half after the transfer of the pedestrian Paul Dyson to West Brom for £60,000, and signed Lee Dixon from Bury for £50,000 in the summer of 1986 to fill the gap vacated by Bould. With supporters deserting the club in droves, there were fears that Stoke might enter the kind of free-fall which had recently befallen fellow founder members of the League, Wolves and Burnley.

Mills' shrewd move allowed Bould to mature into the best cen-tre-half in the Second Division and he attracted the attention of a number of managers, including Arsenal's George Graham. Late in 1986-87, with Bould in prime form, a back injury that required sur-gery removed him from the team. Stoke's form slumped. The side had fought its way into the play-off places, but without Bould the defence leaked seventeen goals in twelve games, winning only four, to miss out on the chance of promotion.

Like Bould, Lee Dixon had also been closely monitored by Graham, and in February 1988 Dixon joined Arsenal for £300,000. At the end of that season Graham took a risk on Bould's dodgy back

and tempted him to Highbury. Stoke offered Bould a five-year contract to stay, but he made it clear that he wanted to win things. 'I
wanted to play in the First Division. Stoke struck me as a club lacking that spark of ambition to make it there.' Bould was valued by
Stoke at more than £2 million, so the fee, set by tribunal, of just
£390,000 was greeted with disbelief. The furious Mills fumed: 'Time
will tell how good a player Bould is.'

Mills was proved right. Bould became a fixture in the most successful back four in Arsenal's history, alongside Dixon, Adams and
left-back Nigel Winterburn. He won three League titles, the FA and
League Cup double in 1992-93, and the FA Cup again to complete
the more traditional double in 1997-98. He somehow failed to win
more than two England caps.

After eleven seasons at Highbury, Bould moved to Sunderland
in the summer of 1999, but a toe injury put paid to his career and
he announced his retirement in September 2000. He has often stated his desire to manage his boyhood team and was connected with
the job after Lou Macari vacated the post in 1997.

Without doubt Bould was the last 'great' player to be produced
by the club. That he emerged over twenty years ago is a sad indict-
ment of how Stoke City FC have languished without any significant
planning for future success on the pitch. Until the club returns to
its roots and develops local talent – as has happened throughout
Stoke's illustrious past – no sustained progress can be made.

Magic Moment: *At Millwall in January 1986 Bould's challenge
sent striker Tony Cascarino into the crowd, over the top of the home
dugout. Bould got a red card, but ensured Stoke won 3-2. Millwall
boss George Graham signed him when he became Arsenal manager.*

Worst Nightmare: *Bould scored a classic own-goal against West
Ham in March 1983, lobbing Peter Fox from 40 yards. It was voted
own-goal of the season by Jimmy Greaves on 'Saint and Greavesie'.*

STOKE RECORD	Appearances	Goals
Football League	179 (+4)	6
FA Cup	10	–
League Cup	13	1
Full Members Cup	5	–

Vince Overson in typically dominant mood

Mark Stein staggers under the weight of his Player of the Season awards (1993)

Larus Sigurdsson

Captain of the 1995-96 play-off team, Icelandic international Larus Sigurdsson

Try keeping them away. A team of Golden Oldies before the last game at the Vic

Graham Kavanagh (in stripes), who scored Stoke's last goal at the Victoria Ground

Kav shapes up for another long-distance attempt

Chapter Ten

~ *The Ice Age* ~

No 91. **PETER BEAGRIE**
Debut: v Ipswich, 27 August 1988
Farewell: v Sheffield United, 21 October 1989

As happened with many fading giants, such as Burnley, Wolves and Preston, who fell from grace in the 1980s, manager Mick Mills turned Stoke City into a selling club – buying players on the cheap, turning them into saleable assets and realising their value simply to keep the club afloat. This hand to mouth existence would have been unthinkable only a decade before. Lee Dixon realised a profit of £250,000 in February 1988, while Steve Bould's £390,000 fee, although miserly, was soon being spent.

Born in Middlesbrough on 28 November 1965, Peter Beagrie began his career with non-league Guisborough before signing for his hometown club in September 1983. Sheffield United boss Billy McEwan paid £35,000 for Beagrie in August 1986 and while at Bramall Lane Beagrie won two England 'B' and two Under-21 caps. Widely acclaimed as the most talented player outside the First Division, Mills took advantage of the Blades' relegation to the Third Division by splashing out £215,000 on Beagrie in June 1988.

At just 5ft 8in and 9st 10lbs, the whippet-like Beagrie had a low centre of gravity which allowed him to twist and turn to his heart's content. His skills flummoxed defenders who simply could not cope with his favourite trick. Beagrie would line up his full-back, cut inside and then make to cross. As the defender lunged to block, Beagrie would perform an adroit 'Cruyff turn' and speed off down the wing. As defences became alert to this party trick, he attracted two or even three markers, but still left defenders non-plussed as he scampered to the by-line to cross, or cut inside to shoot with either foot. The fans loved it. Beagrie's skill had midfielder Chris Kamara, a £27,500 arrival from Swindon in 1988, effusing: 'He is the best winger in the country – better even than John Barnes.'

Unfortunately the moustachioed Beagrie not only confused opponents, but often his team-mates. Mills found Beagrie's insistence on beating his defender all ends up before releasing the ball infuriating. Colleagues could not time their forward runs and Beagrie's centres either found them tightly marked or offside. It took Mills until Christmas to acquire a big striker to make the best use of Beagrie's crosses, journeyman Dave Bamber, who singularly failed to convert the myriad of chances provided by Beagrie.

Although essentially a provider, Beagrie could score spectacular goals himself. Against Barnsley in the FA Cup, he completed a Stoke fightback from 1-3 down by sidestepping two defenders and lashing a left-footed shot high into the net. The Boothen End loved Beagrie's goals because he celebrated in his own inimitable way – a cartwheel leading into a springing back-flip, ending with a clenched fist salute.

1988-89 saw the start of a nationwide craze for bearing inflatable items to football matches. Banana-mania spread amongst Manchester City fans and Grimsby supporters sported Harry Haddocks. Stoke club shop manager Paul Gerkin plumped for Pink Panthers. Stoke fans took them to their hearts. The craze led to the team taking the field to Henry Mancini's theme tune to the Peter Sellers films of the same name, and one Stoke fan attending away games dressed as the fuchsia feline.

Following City's record poor start to the 1989-90 season – eleven League games without a win – speculation linked Beagrie with a multi-million pound move. Though Tottenham, Manchester United, Liverpool, Chelsea and Queen's Park Rangers were all interested, he eventually joined Everton in November for a club record outgoing transfer fee of £750,000. His departure effectively signalled Stoke's resignation to relegation. Mills put on a brave face by arguing that Beagrie's late release of the ball confused Stoke's attacking pattern. The real answer was that none of Stoke's side possessed the ability to live with Beagrie. City plummeted to the foot of the table, scoring just 35 goals, the second lowest in the entire League.

After four years with the Toffees, Beagrie moved to Manchester City for £1.1 million, and then to Bradford City in July 1997 for £200,000. At Valley Parade, Beagrie enjoyed an Indian summer, scoring twelve goals to assist the Bantams to win promotion to the Premiership in 1999. New manager Chris Hutchings turned to his own signings to try to rescue the Bantams as they sank like a stone in 2000-01. Beagrie joined Second Division Wigan on loan in February 2001, before joining Scunthorpe in the summer of 2001, just before his 33rd birthday.

Magic Moment: *In October 1988 Beagrie beat five Bournemouth players in a dribble from the edge of Stoke's penalty area before scoring left-footed from 20 yards – and unleashing his trademark back-flip celebration on the Victoria Ground public for the first time.*

Worst Nightmare: *Beagrie side-footed a penalty wide, condemning Stoke to defeat by Fourth Division Leyton Orient in the Littlewoods Cup in October 1988 – this after having hit a penalty over the bar at the close of normal time which would have sent Stoke through.*

STOKE RECORD	Appearances	Goals
Football League	54	8
FA Cup	3	1
League Cup	4	–

No 92. **JOHN BUTLER**

Debut: v Manchester City, 26 December 1988
Farewell: v Luton, 7 May 1995

While Stoke plummeted in the late 1980s and early 90s, the one player to perform consistently well was John Edward Butler.

Born in Liverpool on 7 February 1962, Butler played non-league football for Burscough and Prescot Cables before signing for Wigan, newly promoted to Division Three, in January 1981. Butler performed consistently for the Latics and made 302 appearances, playing in every position, including once as a stand-in goalkeeper.

With Stoke manager Mick Mills seeking to replace the departed Lee Dixon, he began to trawl the lower divisions. One of his first ports of call was Springfield Park, from where he had plucked midfielder Tony Kelly three years earlier. Mills secured Butler's signature for £75,000 in December 1988 and Butler debuted alongside fellow new boy, striker Dave Bamber, who arrived from Watford for £190,000. With Stoke needing a boost to push for the play-offs, Mills touted the dual signings as 'the missing link' – although many mused that Bamber looked and played more like Piltdown Man.

When it came to full-backs Mills, having been an international in the position, was a better judge. Butler missed just two games in the next two years. Steady and dependable, his consistency meant that he was not an obvious hero, but *Sentinel* reporter Ian Bayley recalls: 'It is almost impossible to remember him having a bad game.' Butler's almost anonymous appearance, 5ft 10½in tall with mousy hair, belied a cheeky personality and rugged determination.

In 1989-90, as City were relegated to Division Three for the first time in 63 years, Butler's performances marked him out amidst the dross. Occasionally he popped up with the odd goal, although his best seasonal total was three.

Following the appointment of Lou Macari in succession to Alan Ball, Butler wore the No 3 shirt, although he played at right-back. Butler's defensive partnership with the muscular Ian Cranson, Vince Overson and Lee Sandford, promised a brighter future for the club. Macari liked his teams to play quite 'narrow' and Butler tucked in, defending staunchly, although as the side's confidence improved he began to rove forward more frequently.

While solid and unshowy on the field, Butler was actually the arch prankster of the Stoke dressing room. He had a liking for practical jokes – and who better to be on the receiving end than new recruits. In 1993 Butler exploited Macari's reputation as a hard trainer at the expense of Kenny Lowe. After a pre-season friendly win over Real Sociedad, Lowe ripped off his sweaty shirt only to be told by the earnest Butler: 'Don't do that. The manager likes us to train for half an hour after every game.' It took Lowe several seconds to realise that the smirks all around were at his expense. Butler's star turn at the 1993 Players Christmas Dinner included a spot of conjuring and some sword swallowing.

In 1992, Butler flirted with signing for Coventry, although Macari convinced him to sign another two-year contract at Stoke. He missed only two of 57 fixtures as City won the (new) Second Division championship (the League had been reclassified due to the birth of the Premier League) and played a significant role as Stoke established themselves back in the First (the old Second) Division.

Handed a free transfer in June 1995, Butler returned to Wigan. He retired in 1997 having made 700 career appearances.

Magic Moment: *At Vale Park in March 1993, Butler jinked past three Vale defenders and crossed for Mark Stein to score the first goal of a 2-0 win which effectively sealed promotion to Division One.*

Worst Nightmare: *In February 1991 Butler was on the receiving end of an atrocious challenge from Bournemouth's Tony Pulis. He left the ground on crutches and did not play again until mid-April.*

STOKE RECORD	Appearances	Goals
Football League	258 (+4)	7
FA Cup	11	–
League Cup	19	–
Other	25	2

No 93. **IAN CRANSON**
Debut: v West Ham, 18 August 1989
Farewell: v Barnsley 10 September 1996

Throughout 1988-89 Mills failed to replace the commanding Steve Bould with a natural centre-half. Unsurprisingly, Stoke finished in mid-table. During the summer Mills chased Sheffield Wednesday's Larry May, Luton's Steve Foster, and Newcastle's Peter Jackson, but his collective failure left the board considering whether Mills' contract should be renewed. After protracted discussions Mills was handed a two-year deal along with £1 million to spend in order to launch a promotion challenge. His major signing, for a club record £450,000, was centre-half Ian Cranson.

Born in Easington, County Durham on 2 July 1964, Cranson began at Ipswich where he won five Under-21 caps before joining Sheffield Wednesday in March 1988 for £450,000. Unfortunately for Cranson the man who signed him, Howard Wilkinson, moved to Leeds and new manager Ron Atkinson dropped him.

Mills had known Cranson as an Ipswich apprentice and tempted him to Stoke with other new boys Derek Statham, Ian Scott and Wayne Biggins. Stoke seemed set fair for a promotion push, but despite Mills' splash-out City struggled. At least Cranson was not to blame. Known to have cruciate ligament problems in his left knee, his injury flared up within three months of his arrival. He had his knee completely reconstructed and missed the bulk of that dismal relegation season. Cranson fought back to fitness only for lightning to strike again, this time in his right knee, just twelve games into his comeback in March 1991.

Offered reduced terms that summer, which entitled him to a free transfer, Cranston attracted interest from Scottish Premier League Hearts and Dunfermline. But new manager Lou Macari persuaded him to stay. He played either as an orthodox centre-half or, occasionally, in a 3-5-2 formation, sweeping behind Lee Sandford and Vince Overson. Macari liked to use this system away from home to give Stoke extra solidity.

A solid, traditional stopper, Cranson's strength lay in his aerial ability. At 5ft 11in and 12st 4lbs, he put the whole of his upper body and muscular neck into timing the ball perfectly from a characteristic two-footed leap. He often sported a tight headband which kept his tightly curled black hair off his craggy face. Before a game he put his right boot on first and spent the minutes prior to running down the tunnel wishing each of his colleagues well, leaving his central defensive partner until last. A model professional, he took over as PFA representative after the departure of Peter Fox.

Cranson had a happy knack of scoring vital goals. In October 1992 his late header gave Stoke a 4-3 win against West Brom, sparking a club record unbeaten run of 23 games as Stoke cruised to the Second Division title in 1992-93. He missed only one game that season and two in 1993-94 to earn recognition from City fans as Player of the Year. Joe Jordan was now in charge, and City always seemed to miss Cranson's calming influence during his few absences. On one occasion, Stoke lost a 2-0 lead at Luton to capitulate 2-6. Such lapses, coupled with dreadfully boring displays, cost Jordan his job.

Although integral to the team that reached the promotion play-offs in 1995-96, Cranson suffered another injury to his left knee which necessitated the removal of a floating piece of bone. That kept him out of the run-in. In a desperate attempt to get fit for the play-offs, Cranson returned to the side too early. 'I had the fluid drained off the knee and played three reserve team games in four days in an attempt to get fit. My right knee could not take the strain as I was still carrying the left. It was becoming increasingly painful and taking increasingly long to recover'. He missed out on Stoke's 0-1 defeat over two legs by Leicester.

Appointed captain for 1996-97, Cranson crocked himself at Barnsley in September, but this time the damage was too severe. He retired on medical advice, receiving a testimonial at the Victoria Ground in which Everton beat Stoke 2-0.

After taking a year out to recover properly, Cranson was tempted back into the game to coach the Under-14 academy side on a temporary basis before new manager Brian Little appointed him as reserve-team coach. In three years Cranson oversaw the blossoming of new talent, with James O'Connor, Marc Goodfellow, Lewis Neale, Karl Henry and Clive Clarke making their first-team debuts. In the summer of 2001 Cranston returned to academy duties. The development of raw talent is surely the path along which lies the future of Stoke City FC, with Cranson, the perfect model for any young professional, at its heart.

Magic Moment: *In December 1992 against Huddersfield, Cranson set the seal on a 3-0 win by belting back a weak clearance from 25 yards with his left foot. 'I didn't know what to do when it went in.'*

Worst Nightmare: *At Vicarage Road in November 1993 Cranson's right boot split. Desperate for another he stole that of physio Richard Gray whilst he treated the injured John Butler. Gray was the only person on the bench to wear boots large enough for Cranny.*

STOKE RECORD	Appearances	Goals
Football League	220 (+3)	9
FA Cup	14	1
League Cup	16 (+1)	1
Other	25	1

No 94. **LEE SANDFORD**
Debut: v Newcastle, 26 December 1989
Farewell: v Leicester, 15 May 1996

To Ian Cranson's left in Stoke's promotion-winning defence of 1992-93 stood Lee Robert Sandford.

Born at the Elephant and Castle in London on 22 April 1968, Sandford's parents moved to Basingstoke where, aged thirteen, he trialed for the Hampshire team. Having won two England youth caps he joined Portsmouth, signing professional terms in December 1985. Portsmouth's youth-team coach was Alan Ball, who Sandford describes as his 'father in football'. Ball converted Sandford from midfield to left-back and he never looked back. When Ball succeeded Bobby Campbell as Pompey manager, Sandford was promoted straight into the first team.

In 1989 new boss John Gregory made it clear that Sandford did not feature in his plans, and Lee received an 11pm phone call from Ball, Stoke's new manager, inviting him to the Potteries to look around. 'I hired a car the next morning and drove up – although I didn't know where Stoke was so it took me longer than I thought. When I got there I realised what a big club Stoke was and I signed that day.' Sandford became one of Ball's first signings for £140,000.

Ball's downfall was in promising too much to the Stoke faithful who initially saw him as a man who shared their passion and could keep them afloat. But City won only five games before relegation was confirmed by a 0-3 defeat by Newcastle in April 1990, leaving the club with a £381,000 loss on the season. Ball compounded his error by bringing in his own players to try to help Stoke win instant promotion. Sandford's arrival was followed by Noel Blake, Vince Hilaire and Mick Kennedy. A spin-off was the high number of red and yellow cards, and therefore suspensions, earned by these players. Indeed, Sandford himself was no angel. In April 1990 he conducted a personal vendetta against Blackburn's Andy Kennedy, conceded a penalty and was sent off for lunging at the same player.

Sandford soon discovered the wrath of Stoke fans which accompanies a few bad games. 'I felt I was doing OK, but I was getting a lot of stick because I was seen as one of Bally's men.' Stoke fans eventually hounded Ball out of the club. By January 1991 he had resorted to sticking cotton wool in his ears to block out the language around the dugout. Ball should have fallen on his sword before he did, although the unedifying sight of a young fan spitting in his face after the 0-4 defeat at Wigan – which finally ended his reign – was rightly condemned. He left City in their lowest ever League position – fourteenth in Division Three. The situation was so bad that the Samaritans began to advertise in the Stoke programme – 'Would it help to talk to someone in confidence?'

Sandford proved to be Ball's only good signing. Nicknamed Sandy, his distinctive blond bowl haircut and gaping grin belied a winner's mentality. He benefited from new manager Lou Macari's renowned fitness regime. This included holding medicine balls above the head for prolonged periods and making players complete a one-minute lap around the Victoria Ground – with those who failed forced to run two more. 'I had always been a good trainer and never took that side of things lightly, so I enjoyed it. On the pitch we kept it simple. If you were a defender you defended. Macari did not trust any footballer. He banned alcohol on away journeys and ensured they worked hard daily to keep match fit.'

Playing at left-back, or on the left of three defenders, Sandford had a hand in Stoke's direct tactics. His trademark ball into the inside channel for the quicksilver Mark Stein to latch on to allowed Stoke an easy escape from pressure. 'We had a telepathic under-standing. We looked each other in the eyes and I would release the ball knowing he was on his way.' Sandford flicked on a free-kick for Stein to volley the winner in the 1992 Autoglass Trophy final.

As Stoke marched to the Second Division championship in 1992-93, Sandford became embroiled in the larking around that accom-panied Stoke's travels under Lou Macari. Light relief was provided by a former circus clown, turned club kitman, called Neil Baldwin – better known as 'Nello'. 'It was a 24-hour laugh,' recalls Sandford. 'Everyone mucked about play fighting. He dressed up as a clown on the coach to away games. I think Macari used him to take the edge off things.' On a trip to Africa, Macari tied Nello to a seat in the goal on the training ground and lined the team up for shooting practice.

But Sandford did not always see eye to eye with Macari, and in 1993-94 found himself dropped for 'disciplinary reasons', after handing in a transfer request. During 1995-96 his future attracted further speculation. Despite being ever present in Stoke's unsuc-cessful play-off campaign, rumours spread that a deal had been done with Howard Kendall, manager of Sheffield United. Sandford clears up matters: 'I didn't know anything about it. The club took £500,000, which was obviously very attractive, although I wanted to stay and get a testimonial.' He signed for the Blades in August 1996. The deal represented the first time any player bought by Alan Ball had been sold for a profit.

During his time at Stoke, Sandford studied for a Sports Science degree at Crewe and Alsager College, encouraged by Macari. He also holds a UEFA 'A' coaching badge. In April 2001, with a neck injury threatening to end his career, Sandford was offered a coach-ing job at Bramall Lane. Surgery was successful, however and, in the summer of 2001, 32-year-old Sandford signed a new contract.

Magic Moment: *Sandford headed in from an indirect free-kick inside the penalty area to earn a 1-1 draw against Port Vale which gave Stoke a fighting chance of achieving safety in 1994-95. The resulting chorus of 'Delilah' nearly lifted the roof off Vale Park.*

Worst Nightmare: *Trying to establish himself, Sandford fell vic-tim to the Stoke boo-boys after an own-goal against Shrewsbury in September 1990. He turned a cross past Peter Fox. Stoke lost 1-3.*

STOKE RECORD	Appearances	Goals
Football League	255 (+3)	8
FA Cup	16	2
League Cup	16	–
Other	27	4

No 95. **VINCE OVERSON**

Debut: v Peterborough, 31 August 1991
Farewell: v Sunderland, 22 November 1995

Lou Macari revisited Birmingham a number of times to bring players to Stoke. In terms of value for money, Vincent David Overson must rate as one of his best ever purchases.

Born in Kettering on 15 May 1962, Overson began playing for non-league Corby and followed his elder brother Richard in signing as an apprentice for Burnley, turning professional in November 1979 after representing England at youth level. After appearing in 249 games, Overson received a free transfer in June 1986. He joined Birmingham and played 213 games, captaining the Blues in 1988-89 when they plummeted into Division Three.

Shortly after his arrival in the summer of 1992, Lou Macari lambasted the existing City players for living the high life. His first signing, pointedly, was the out of contract Overson, who arrived with Macari's recommendation for being 'reliable on and off the field'. Overson captained the reserves that evening and the transfer tribunal set the fee at £55,000 – a steal.

A barrel-chested leviathan, Overson's presence and will to win supplied the vital ingredient missing from the Stoke team. At 6ft 2in and 13½st he was a man-mountain. His colossal thighs thundered into challenges but his muscular interventions got Overson into trouble with referees. He fitted neatly into a defence comprising Sandford, Cranson and Butler. This foursome provided a solid base upon which Stoke built their success of the next few seasons. Their collective weakness, however, was that, with each being tall and muscular, they were prone to being caught on the turn for pace.

Lee Sandford recalls: 'Vince loved his body. He was particularly fond of sunbeds. One day "Bertie" [Wayne Biggins] ran into the sauna and threw a bucket of cold water over him. He went berserk.' In October 1993 Overson was elected to represent the squad in the club shop's brochure modelling Stoke's new range of toiletries. He posed, lathered in a bath, gazing wantonly into the camera.

On the pitch, however, Overson's leadership and organisational skills meant the defence immediately tightened. City put together seven wins, their best run of victories since 1946-47, to head the table in February 1992. But suspensions told during the run in, and home defeats by Hull, Bury and Chester cost City automatic promotion. Despite deposing Noel Blake as captain, Overson proved to be a prime culprit, picking up two bans while Biggins, Cranson, Sandford, Ware and Blake all received one. Overson's suspensions arguably cost Stoke promotion as he missed four out of the final five games – none of which Stoke won. Significantly, he returned to subdue Stockport's gigantic striker Kevin Francis in the Autoglass Trophy final in May 1992.

Stoke's over-physical defenders cleaned up their act the following season and City, with their best defensive record for thirteen years, galloped to the Second Division title. Ironically Overson's one suspension that season arrived at a fortuitous moment. He had arranged to marry his fiancée Alison on the morning of 6 February 1993, believing he would play against Hull that afternoon. In the event he was suspended, which allowed him to celebrate his nuptials in traditional fashion. Overson became more responsible too, once his son, Dean, was born. He began cycling three miles from his home to the Victoria Ground to step up his personal fitness.

It didn't last long. Overson was sent off for elbowing Mansfield's Lee Wilson in the face in August 1993. That season he reached 41 disciplinary points, earning a fourth suspension in one season. New manager Joe Jordan lost patience and omitted him from the team to face Crystal Palace. Overson did not react well, demanding a transfer. A protracted battle of wills was won by Overson. Jordan was sacked a month into the new season. Overson won back his place, and the captaincy, following Macari's return.

In 1995-96 Overson sustained a calf injury against Sunderland. Achilles tendonitis flared up and Overson spent the summer recuperating at the FA's Sports Injuries Clinic at Lilleshall. On account of his condition he was only offered a one year deal, as were Nigel Gleghorn, Kevin Keen and Ian Cranson. Unlike the latter pair he decided to leave and joined Gleghorn in signing for Burnley on free transfers. In his second spell at Turf Moor, Overson played just nine times, plus two for Shrewsbury on loan, before retiring in October 1998 due to that recurring injury picked up at Stoke.

Magic Moment: *Overson lifted the Autoglass Trophy at Wembley in May 1992. Having done the same with Birmingham the previous season, he became the first man to collect the cup in consecutive years with different clubs.*

Worst Nightmare: *With the score goalless at Reading in August 1994, the ref awarded a free-kick to Reading. In trying to return the ball, Overson whacked it against an opponent and was sent off. This angered Wayne Biggins, who was also sent off. Stoke lost 0-4.*

STOKE RECORD	Appearances	Goals
Football League	167 (+3)	6
FA Cup	10	–
League Cup	10	1
Other	23	–

No 96. **NIGEL GLEGHORN**
Debut: v Port Vale, 24 October 1992
Farewell: v Leicester, 15 May 1996

Another player brought in by Macari from Birmingham City, Nigel William Gleghorn, was a classy midfielder whose prompting set up chances for Stoke's attackers.

Born in Seaham, near Sunderland on 12 August 1962, Gleghorn played for Seaham Red Star before joining Ipswich in August 1985. He was discovered by the same scouting network that unearthed fellow north-easterner Ian Cranson. Manchester City bought him in August 1988 for £47,500, followed by Birmingham in September 1989. During the summer of 1992 Gleghorn fell out with manager Terry Cooper. He wanted a three-year contract but was only offered two. Gleghorn put out the feelers and Macari swooped.

Gleghorn debuted in a Potteries derby at the Victoria Ground and acquitted himself well in the unfamiliar role of left wing-back. He replaced ageing former West Brom full-back Graham Harbey and was ever present until March 1994. He built a solid partnership down Stoke's left with Lee Sandford, who assesses Gleghorn's qualities. 'He made my game so easy. He never gave it away and his first touch was fantastic. He wasn't the quickest, but his brain was so sharp.' Gleghorn rarely failed to find his man and, when faced with an opponent, possessed a beguiling body swerve which would open up an opportunity for his left foot to play the ball down the flank. He also contributed half a dozen goals a season – none more important than that when Stoke won 2-0 at Vale Park in March 1993. That game effectively clinched promotion from Division Two.

The almost skeletal Gleghorn, 6ft tall but weighing under 12st, had sandy hair with a parting to the right which he kept neat and short, much like his passing. Nicknamed Gleggy by the players, but Foghorn by the fans – after the cartoon character Foghorn Leghorn – Gleghorn loved making presentations and personal appearances, which made him a popular figure around Stoke. After Macari's departure to Celtic, Gleghorn fared less well. Dropped to face Crystal Palace in March 1994, along with Overson, Gleghorn did not enjoy the deeper role demanded by the ultra-defensive Jordan.

That summer Jordan offered the 32-year-old, along with Toddy Orlygsson and Martin Carruthers, an unprecedented two-year pay-as-you-play deal. His contract encouraged Gleghorn to give of his best. But following Lou Macari's return in September 1994 he was moved inside, where his passing opened up countless opportunities for strikers Paul Peschisolido and Simon Sturridge, both short men. The arrival of Mike Sheron gave Gleghorn a focal point and the triangular passing of Sheron, Sturridge and Gleghorn ripped open defences as City finished fourth in the First Division in 1995-96. That summer, with Gleghorn having played 105 successive games (including some as substitute) and been handed the captain's armband, on account of another Overson suspension, he was only offered a further one-year contract. This he considered derisory.

The incensed Gleghorn signed for Adrian Heath's Burnley, along with Overson. The pair's departure meant that nearly half of the team which reached the play-offs had left the club. Stoke could not replace such experience and talent in one fell swoop. With hindsight it is probable that the board were simply clearing the decks of many of their highest wage earners in preparation for the upheaval of moving to the Britannia Stadium.

Gleghorn rounded off his career with loan spells at Brentford and Northampton. He retired from professional football in 1998.

Magic Moment: *Gleghorn scored the winner against Plymouth in April 1993 to clinch the Second Division championship. He coolly collected a right-wing cross and rounded a defender before ramming the ball past Plymouth player-manager Peter Shilton.*

Worst Nightmare: *Under Lou Macari the Stoke players contested a weekly skills contest in the gym, with the winner receiving a much coveted Mars Bar. In March 1996 Gleghorn lost the competition for the first time in 3½ years as Ray Wallace took the chocolate.*

STOKE RECORD	Appearances	Goals
Football League	162 (+4)	25
FA Cup	10	–
League Cup	10	2
Other	20	4

No 97. **MARK STEIN**
Debut: v Hartlepool, 17 September 1991
Final Farewell: v Norwich, 22 January 1997

Lou Macari plucked Mark Earl Sean Stein from the low point of his career and turned him into the most feared of strikers in England.

Stein was born in Cape Town, South Africa, on 28 January 1966. Both his elder brothers became professional footballers after the family moved to London in the 1970s. Brian, a natural finisher, scored 131 goals in 427 League appearances for Luton, and won one England cap, while Edwin became a stalwart at non-league Barnet, helping them attain League status in 1991.

Mark turned professional at Luton in January 1984 but never achieved the heights expected after his early promise won him three England Under-19 caps. After a loan spell at Aldershot, he moved to Queen's Park Rangers and then Oxford, but again disappointed and was dropped by a frustrated Brian Horton.

Seeking a goalscorer to play alongside Wayne Biggins, but hamstrung by a lack of cash, Stoke manager Lou Macari rescued Stein from Oxford's reserves – initially on loan – in September 1991. Stein's all round play improved Stoke's form to such an extent that Macari persuaded the board to part with £100,000 to buy him. The goals soon began to flow. Stein rattled in ten in fourteen games as City steamed to the head of Division Three. The League season ultimately ended in disappointment, although Stein gained revenge for Stoke's defeat in the play-offs by Stockport by lashing home a right-footed volley to win the Autoglass Trophy final.

Standing just 5ft 6in and weighing 11½st, the shaven headed Stein's speed off the mark and low centre of gravity made him a handful for opposing defenders as he ran onto the intelligent passes of Nigel Gleghorn and Steve Foley. Stein reached 50 goals in just 89 games, and top scored with 26 League goals to win Stoke the Division Two title and himself the Player of the Year accolade in 1992-93. Although a natural goalscorer Stein tended to score beauties rather then predatory goals inside the six-yard box – witness his stunning volley at Hartlepool in April 1992, although Stein admits 'I should have scored more tap-ins. I didn't get enough of those and I would criticise myself for it.' City fans, however, reverentially referred to him as the 'Golden One'.

Stein possessed the ability to keep his balance under heavy challenge, a trait that frustrated Macari: 'I'm not suggesting Mark should dive if he hasn't been touched,' he grumbled, 'but sometimes he's so determined not to go down we don't get the penalty we deserve.' Stein took the advice to heart and in the Potteries derby of October 1992 he hit the deck following a clumsy challenge by Vale keeper Paul Musselwhite. Stein picked himself up to net the match-winning penalty in front of the third highest gate of the day in England of 24,334. The controversy over his tumble raged for years in the Potteries.

Normally a quiet character, Stein erupted after he was racially abused at the end of the vital promotion clash with Stockport in March 1993. Stein struck the alleged offender, 6ft 5in Jim Gannon, in the left eye and both were hauled before the courts. Stein found himself the recipient of a £500 fine and a twelve-month conditional discharge. Judge Nortcote warned him: 'You have suffered the most extreme provocation ... but you have a responsibility to control your temper no matter what.' In the return match a month later a friend of the accused spat in Stein's face as he left the pitch. Stein conducted himself impeccably as the offender was escorted away.

But nothing could sway Stein from scoring goals. His form soon attracted interest from Premier League clubs. In 1992 Newcastle boss Kevin Keegan offered a laughable £300,000. Macari then had to fight off £1 million bids from Tottenham and West Ham.

Stein made it clear he wanted Premiership football, but his transfer request was rebuffed by Macari: 'He can't have it all ways just because he fancies an extra pound or two. The terms of Mark's contract say that he must stay with us until the end of the season and I aim to hold him to that.' Macari's words rang hollow when just a week later, after Liam Brady's sacking, he found himself in the spotlight as Celtic requested permission to approach the Stoke manager. The boot now on the other foot, Macari stated: 'If you are in any walk of life and *the* job comes up, wouldn't you want it?' Stein got his £1.5 million move to Chelsea in October 1993, a club record outgoing transfer fee. His wages rose from £400 per week to £4,000. The departure of Macari, who took his entire backroom staff to Parkhead, quickly followed.

At Chelsea, Stein set a Premiership record by scoring in seven consecutive games from 27 December 1993. But after manager Glenn Hoddle became England manager, Stein's opportunities tailed off. Ruud Gullit introduced seasoned internationals Mark Hughes, Gianfranco Zola and Gianluca Vialli. During 1996-97 Stein returned to Stoke on loan for two months and formed a promising partnership with Mike Sheron. However, with the impending move to the Britannia Stadium swallowing Stoke's resources, the £1 million asking price to re-sign Stein proved too high.

Stein played on loan at Ipswich, then signed for Bournemouth, then Luton. The Hatters, however, wound up relegated to Division Three for the first time in 33 years. Stein signed for Dagenham & Redbridge in 2001. By October his goals had propelled them to the top of the Conference and himself to the top of its scoring charts.

Magic Moment: *Stein rammed the winner past Peter Schmeichel as Stoke defeated Manchester United 2-1 in the League Cup second round first leg in September 1993.*

Worst Nightmare: *As he celebrated that goal by embracing the delirious crowd, Stein found himself booked by referee John Key, who, after the match, claimed he had done so on police advice.*

STOKE RECORD	Appearances	Goals
Football League	105	54
FA Cup	4	–
League Cup	8	8
Other	15	9

No 98. **LARUS SIGURDSSON**
Debut: v Portsmouth, 30 November 1994
Farewell: v Gillingham, 30 August 1999

The canny Larus Orri Sigurdsson's emergence brought a breath of fresh air after years of physical defenders at the Victoria Ground.

Born in Akureyri in Iceland on 4 July 1973, Sigurdsson's father, Sigurdur Larusson, played semi-professionally with Akranes, and proudly watched as his 16-year-old son debuted for Thor Akureyri at left-back in 1990. The following season Sigurdur became manager and made his son train harder than other players. Larus reaped the benefits, playing for Iceland Under-16 (7 caps), 18 (6) and 21 (16) before winning the first of his 33 full caps (to summer 2001) against the Faroe Islands.

Sigurdsson had not heard of Stoke until his cousin, midfielder Toddy Orlygsson, joined City from Nottingham Forest in August 1993. At the end of the Icelandic season, in October 1994, Orlygsson persuaded Macari to allow Sigurdsson to train with Stoke to retain his fitness for the coming Icelandic Under-21 internationals.

Sigurdsson impressed so much that, still on trial, he joined the first team on a trip to Portsmouth. He thought he was going along just for the experience but 45 minutes before kick-off Macari told Sigurdsson to get changed: 'I was marking Scottish Under-21 international Mark Green. He hit the bar early on after giving me the slip. Who knows what would have happened if he had scored.' But he didn't, and City paid Thor Akureyri £150,000 to buy Sigurdsson.

Sigurdsson's classic Nordic looks included blond floppy hair and steely blue eyes. His slim, athletic build contrasted markedly with that of the more solid Ian Cranson and Vince Overson. Sigurdsson utilised his speed and seemingly telescopic legs to reach balls which it appeared he did not deserve to, while his aerial ability was based on timing rather than power. This complemented the bigger men's physical presence. Despite making only 22 appearances, the fans voted 'Siggy' as Stoke's 1994-95 Player of the Year. His form was such that, against Arsenal in the Coca-Cola Cup in 1996, Siggy marked Ian Wright out of the game. The frustrated Wright tried to wind up Sigurdsson by continually untucking his shirt.

On the international stage Larus played in Iceland's most successful side, which almost qualified for the play-offs for Euro 2000.

Sigurdsson scored his first goal in the Ukraine in a 1-1 draw. 'There were 80,000 there and they all went quiet when I equalised. It was like someone turned off the noise. A great moment.'

During the run in to 1995-96, with Stoke going for the play-offs, Cranson injured a knee, leaving Sigurdsson, just 21, to cajole the inexperienced Justin Whittle through each game. City finished fourth. The duo then subdued Leicester's Claridge and Heskey during the play-off semi-finals. But Stoke's forwards could not capitalise and Garry Parker's volley at the Victoria Ground sent the Foxes to Wembley. That defeat proved to be the turning point of Sigurdsson's career at Stoke.

Following the retirement of Cranson early the following season Stoke struggled, and in his frustration Sigurdsson revealed his darker side. In January 1997 he fell, clutching his hands to his face, following a clash with Bolton's Nathan Blake. Blake was sent off, while TV replays suggested Sigurdsson had not been struck. In September 1997 he received his marching orders while playing for Iceland for a tackle on Ireland's Roy Keane.

Despite these lapses, Sigurdsson became Stoke captain, albeit under unusual circumstances. With Ray Wallace injured, Macari handed Siggy the job, knowing that he was just one yellow card short of a suspension. 'Macari said "Hopefully the ref will show you some mercy." 'It didn't help. I still got booked!' Siggy chuckles. Sigurdsson saw Stan Matthews ceremonially score at the Boothen End before the last match at the Victoria Ground, but miss at the new home end before the first game at the Britannia Stadium. This gave rise to a myth that the new ground was jinxed.

At the end of November 1997, after a 3-0 win over Wolves, Stoke stood ninth. 'We just fell apart. And the blackest day was the 0-7 defeat by Birmingham, the club's record home defeat [since surpassed by a 0-8 defeat by Liverpool in the Coca-Cola Cup in November 2000] and Chic Bates lost his job. I still think that was the wrong decision. If he had stayed until the end of the season we would not have gone down.' The shambles sparked chants of 'sack the board', a pitch invasion and even attempts by irate fans to climb into the directors box.

Relegation duly followed and Sigurdsson lost heart. In the summer of 1999 he refused to sign a new contract and surrendered the captaincy to Nicky Mohan, making it clear he wished to move on. Stoke declined a bid of £500,000 from Aberdeen, but accepted an offer of £350,000 from West Brom in September 1999, knowing that Sigurdsson would have been able to leave on a free transfer at the end of the season. He won the Player of the Year award in his first year at the Hawthorns, but ruptured cruciate knee ligaments in March 2000 which kept him sidelined for most of 2000-01.

For a modern footballer Sigurdsson is refreshingly honest in summing up his time in the Potteries: 'Stoke is a really special club for me and I still follow them closely, but you have to say that I left Stoke one division lower than I joined them in – and that hurts.'

Magic Moment: *Stoke hired a private plane to get Sigurdsson back from international duty in Iceland for the first Potteries derby at the new Britannia Stadium in October 1997. He kept Vale's Lee Mills so quiet that he was substituted with fifteen minutes to go.*

Worst Nightmare: *Having marked Arsenal striker Ian Wright out of a Coca-Cola Cup-tie in 1996, Sigurdsson lost him at the death. Wright netted, handling, which did not help Sigurdsson's humour.*

STOKE RECORD	Appearances	Goals
Football League	199 (+1)	7
FA Cup	6	–
League Cup	15	–
Other	4	–

No 99. **MIKE SHERON**
Debut: v Portsmouth, 18 November 1995
Farewell: v West Brom, 4 May 1997

While Sigurdsson marshalled the defence, Michael Nigel Sheron scored the goals which propelled Stoke to the 1995-96 play-offs.

Born in St Helen's, Lancashire on 11 January 1972, from the age of twelve Sheron was courted by numerous clubs in the north-west. He was enraptured by the sheer scale of Maine Road and – alongside the likes of Michael Hughes, Neil Lennon and Gerry Taggart – he starred as Manchester City won the FA Youth Cup in 1986.

After being loaned out to Bury by new manager Peter Reid, Sheron returned to play alongside Niall Quinn and David White in a prolific attack which saw City finish in the top six of the First Division for three consecutive seasons. He won sixteen England Under-21 caps, alongside future stars Andy Cole, Jamie Redknapp and Robbie Fowler. But Reid's sacking, just three games into 1993-94, led to Sheron being frozen out under Brian Horton.

Sheron was offloaded to Norwich for £800,000 in August 1994. A persistent lower back injury and four associated hamstring pulls left him languishing in Norwich's reserves when Lou Macari came calling. Offering the Canaries' manager Martin O'Neill misfit striker Keith Scott in part exchange, Macari pulled off one of his biggest coups. With Sheron valued at just £150,000, Stoke received cash as well as relieving themselves of the unwelcome burden of Scott.

Sheron began a superb scoring sequence which he attributes to Macari allowing him time in which to return to full fitness. 'He had me doing fitness work, gym, stamina and loads of press-ups. I loved it. He only played me as a substitute for the first month so I had plenty of time to get fit. It was the best thing that ever happened to me.' Macari simply wanted Sheron to concentrate on scoring goals, but it soon became apparent that his overall contribution was as important as his goalscoring ability.

Stoke set off on a run which carried them into the end of season play-offs, sustained by goals from Sheron and his strike partner Simon Sturridge, a £75,000 signing from Birmingham. Now a cult hero with a big grin stretching from one oversized ear to another, underneath his grade one haircut, Sheron revelled in the status which the Boothen End bestowed upon him. At 5ft 9in and a whisker over 11st, his wiry frame proved capable of spinning on a sixpence. Blessed with a cultured right foot with which he could score almost every type of goal, Sheron still needed to feed off chances and for those he had City's workaholic midfield to thank: 'Nigel Gleghorn was fantastic for me. The chances just kept coming and I always thought that I was going to score.'

Sheron notched seven goals in seven successive League games, breaking John Ritchie's 1963 club record, although Ritchie had scored further League Cup goals to extend his run to nine games. Two of Sheron's goals won games in the 90th minute as Stoke headed for the play-offs. There Stoke lost to Leicester, now managed by Martin O'Neill, the man who had sold him at Norwich. 'I was gutted', Sheron recalls. 'But when I stopped and thought how much progress I had made over the season I realised it wasn't all bad'.

Stoke stagnated during the final season at the Victoria Ground and struggled away from home. Sheron himself scored just three times in twenty games – his mind clearly wandering towards a much publicised move to Queen's Park Rangers, although both Sheron and Stoke denied any deal had already been made.

Stoke, desperate for income to fund the construction of the new Britannia Stadium – taking shape high on the hill overlooking the city – hardly stood in Sheron's way, although chief executive Jez Moxey tried to put a different spin on matters by proclaiming that if their leading scorer wanted to leave it was in the best interests of the club to get a good price for him. Sheron recalls: 'I wanted to play in the Premier League – I thought we'd do it at Stoke, but the financial situation meant it wasn't to be. The club were willing to sell. It was very disappointing. I got called Judas – all sorts of names, but I had to go.' It did not help Stoke fans' humour when manager Lou Macari announced that he, too, would be parting company with the club at the end of the season. A measure of the fans' disaffection

came with a 2001 poll by *The Oatcake* in which Sheron was voted
Stoke City's 'Most Hated Former Player'.

Sheron's £2.35 million move (a Stoke record outgoing transfer
fee) did not leave him any better off. QPR struggled and Sheron suffered a recurrence of his back injury. In January 1999 he moved on
to Barnsley for £700,000, playing in his old position, right midfield,
rather than the striking role in which he made his name. Following
the arrival of new manager Nigel Spackman in early 2001, Sheron
failed to make Barnsley's starting line-up and rumours abounded
that he would return to Stoke once Peter Thorne left the club.

Magic Moment: *At Portman Road in December 1996, Sheron, way
out wide, received the ball from Ray Wallace at waist height. He
swivelled and volleyed it into the far top corner of the net.*

Worst Moment: *In the Potteries derby at Vale Park in March 1996
Sheron unleashed a shot which rebounded off both posts before
nestling in the disbelieving arms of the keeper, Paul Musselwhite.*

STOKE RECORD	Appearances	Goals
Football League	64 (+5)	34
FA Cup	1	–
League Cup	4	5

No 100. **PETER THORNE**
Debut: v Birmingham, 9 August 1997
Farewell: v Huddersfield, 8 September 2001

Mike Sheron's replacement arrived within a month. Born in
Manchester on 21 June 1973, Peter Lee Thorne became a trainee at
Blackburn and signed professional terms in June 1991. He made
just one substitute appearance for Rovers before being loaned to
Wigan in March 1994. Unable to break the partnership of Shearer
and Sutton, which brought the Premiership title to Ewood Park,
Thorne moved on to Swindon in January 1995 for £225,000. He
became an instant hit when he scored twice in the Coca-Cola Cup
semi-final first leg against Bolton, and helped Swindon win the
Second Division championship in 1995-96.

In July 1997 new boss Chic Bates paid Swindon a Stoke record
£500,000 for Thorne, equalling the sum paid for Birmingham's Paul
Peschisolido. The expectancy heaped upon Sheron's replacement
did not sit well on Thorne's shoulders. He studiously avoided all
comparisons with his predecessor, insisting he was his own man.

It soon became obvious that Thorne's contribution to the team's
overall play would not match Sheron's. Possessing all the attributes

of a natural goalscorer, Thorne simply snaffled chances, generally with his stronger right foot and ability in the air. Consequently, if no goals were forthcoming his overall contribution seemed sparse. Despite this, Thorne averaged a goal every other game and, after each strike, as a staunch Catholic, he blessed himself. A wiry 6ft tall, Thorne soon earned the nickname of 'Pistol Pete' a reference to his resemblance to seven-time Wimbledon tennis champion Pete Sampras, also of that nickname.

In his first season Thorne suffered from the lack of a regular partner. First choice Simon Sturridge was sidelined with a long-term knee injury, replacement Paul Stewart proved too slow, Gerry McMahon lacked heart, while trialists Davide Xausa and Marco Gabbiadini proved unpalatable. New manager Chris Kamara's £500,000 signing from Coventry, Kyle Lightbourne, developed a blood disorder which restricted his appearances, even though he had passed a club medical. Thorne's sixteen goals were not enough to stave off relegation. The Britannia Stadium had sucked the life out of the team.

The takeover by an Icelandic consortium in November 1999 and subsequent installation as manager of former Icelandic national boss Gudjon Thordarson revived Thorne's fortunes. Back to full fitness after knee and back injuries, his confidence rocketed after a four-goal haul against lowly Chesterfield in March 2000 – the first Stoke player to notch four goals in a game since John Ritchie in 1966 – Thorne hit a hot streak which saw him strike fifteen times in the final thirteen games to propel Stoke into what had seemed an unlikely play-off place. He totalled 30 goals for the season.

Stoke's controversial defeat by Gillingham in those play-offs left City as hot favourites to win the Second Division championship the following year, but Stoke began 2000-01 without a recognised front-man. Thorne was sidelined by a knee injury and his partner to be, Rikhardur Dadason, an Icelandic international, had to complete his season in Norway with Viking FK before arriving in October 2000. The much-vaunted Dadason did not prove to be the cure which the Stoke management had promised. He and Thorne were too similar to play successfully together. Thorne's seventeen goals could not take Stoke any further than a second successive play-off semi-final.

From the start of 2001-02 Thorne wore a brand new badge on his Stoke shirt. Introduced to replace the intricate City crest which the club found prohibitively expensive in replicating for their merchandise, the badge features traditional red and white stripes on a blue crest, indicating the Icelandic ownership of the club.

As the season began, rumours abounded that Thorne would follow Graham Kavanagh to Cardiff, with concerns voiced by fans that the stated aim of the Icelandic owners of achieving promotion to

Division One within two season could not be realised. Could it be that the board had given up hope and were realising assets in order to make a quick getaway? Thorne joined the Bluebirds for £1.7 million in September 2001. His departure deprived Stoke of one of its few quality players.

Magic Moment: *Thorne prodded home Graham Kavanagh's cross at the far post in front of Stoke's massed support to clinch the 2-1 victory over Bristol City in the 2000 Auto Windscreens Shield final.*

Worst Nightmare: *On his debut in August 1997 at Birmingham, Thorne rounded keeper Kevin Poole but fired over an open goal.*

STOKE RECORD	Appearances	Goals
Football League	148(+11)	67
FA Cup	5 (+1)	–
League Cup	12 (+1)	6
Other	7 (+3)	6

No 101. **GRAHAM KAVANAGH**
Debut: v Birmingham, 14 September 1996
Farewell: v Walsall, 16 May 2001

As Stoke languished in the lower reaches of the Football League in the darkest days of their history, the major spark behind their promotion pushes was a midfielder, Graham Anthony Kavanagh.

Born in Dublin on 23 December 1973, Kavanagh's undoubted talent saw him win international recognition at schoolboy level. He played for Home Farm in Dublin before joining Middlesbrough in August 1991. Enticed to Stoke, initially on loan, in September 1996, Kavanagh soon signed permanently for £250,000.

Able to dictate a game in a Gascoigne-like manner, at 5ft 10in and nearly 13st Kavanagh looked like Gazza too. Clearly the most naturally talented player at Stoke, and capable of flashes of brilliance, the portly midfielder's form waxed and waned like the moon.

His twinkling Irish eyes matched the skills in his feet, particularly his right, which on a good day sought out colleagues with unerring accuracy. Universally known as 'Kav', his ability saw him regularly voted into the PFA divisional teams by his peers. But the strain of playing through one of the most turbulent periods in Stoke's history had an unexpected side-effect for Kavanagh – his short, curly hair had turned grey by the age of 25.

His booming right foot often brought spectacular goals. He scored the last by a Stoke player at the Victoria Ground, a flying lob, and also the first at the Britannia Stadium, an exocet from 30 yards. Such strikes encouraged Kavanagh to try his luck more often from long range, although those that flew in actually comprised a low percentage of his total goals scored. Stoke fans grew to tolerate his wilder attempts, revelling in his occasional bullseyes. In 1998-99 Kavanagh finished as leading scorer with twelve goals, although this was in part due to the lack of a settled forward line.

As good as his good days were, Kavanagh's off-days plumbed the depths. He was often guilty of inattentive or misplaced passes – the worst of which coming direct from the kick-off against Norwich at Carrow Road in April 1997, when a slack pass set up Norwich's Keith O'Neill to hammer a goal within ten seconds of Stoke's own kick-off.

His commitment occasionally landed him in hot water too. Kavanagh was no stranger to over-zealous two-footed challenges and was sent off at Bournemouth in the frustrating 1998-99 season for just such a tackle. During one Potteries derby, Kavanagh committed a lunging tackle on Neil Aspin, provoking the Vale defender to aim a punch at his assailant.

During the long years of strife at Stoke, Kavanagh, unfairly, often bore the brunt of the fans' frustration. As the perceived star of the team, if his performances dropped below the spectacular he would attract vociferous criticism, which hardly helped his confidence. Prepared to take on the responsibility of dead-ball specialist, Kavanagh's record from the penalty spot was patchy.

Having won nine Republic of Ireland Under-21 caps, he was rewarded in April 1999 with a late call up to the full squad and a substitute appearance. Kavanagh even scored as Ireland defeated Sweden 2-0 in a friendly. 'I just went mad,' he grins. 'I ran around like Forrest Gump! It's a good job the gates were locked or I'd be still running around now.'

The Mr Hyde side of Kavanagh's character reappeared in the play-off semi-final at Gillingham in May 2000 when he was sent off for allegedly striking Gills' midfielder Junior Lewis. His dismissal left Stoke with nine men, following Clive Clarke's first-half red card. City were 3-2 ahead at the time of Kavanagh's expulsion, but down to nine men they lost 3-5 on aggregate after extra-time.

Stoke began 2000-01 poorly. Discontent spread through the camp. Captain Nicky Mohan had a much publicised training ground bust-up with the manager, while Stoke's Irish trio – Kavanagh, Clarke and James O'Connor – also fell out with Thordarson, amidst rumours that factions had split the squad. For his part, Kavanagh had been told by Irish manager Mick McCarthy that he must be playing at a higher level to make the squad for the 2002 World Cup. In March 2001 Kavanagh was quoted in the *Irish Star* as saying he would leave if Stoke were not promoted.

Although arguably blessed with a squad as good as any in the division, Stoke just squeaked into the play-offs, when automatic promotion should have been theirs for the taking. Kavanagh was instrumental in the late-season perk in form. He put his all into a series of increasingly impressive performances, culminating in an imperious display at Oldham which inspired City to come from behind to win 2-1. But defeat in the play-off semi-final by Walsall, after Kavanagh had given Stoke the lead with another spectacular strike, left City facing a fourth season in Division Two – their longest period at that level in their proud history.

Kavanagh jumped ship on 29 June 2001, although his dream of playing at a higher level did not materialise. As he chose to sign for Second Division Cardiff (for £800,000), his choice of club came as something of a surprise. Could the newly promoted Bluebirds assist him achieve his dream of making the Republic of Ireland's World Cup squad?

His departure left Stoke the poorer. The 2001-02 season arrived with little expectancy of promotion. Thordarson, pressured to deliver after renegotiating his contract to a one year 'promotion or bust' deal, bolstered his defence, but did not replace Kavanagh.

Magic Moment: *Kavanagh wove past four members of the Bristol City defence to crash home a left-footed drive for the first goal in the 2000 Auto Windscreens Shield final at Wembley.*

Worst Nightmare: *Kavanagh celebrated wildly with Stoke mascot Pottermus after scoring against Charlton. Both ended up flat out on the ground and featured on the following weekend's edition of Channel 4's 'TFI Friday' hosted by Chris Evans.*

STOKE RECORD	Appearances	Goals
Football League	199 (+8)	27
FA Cup	8	–
League Cup	16 (+2)	7
Other	13	3

Mike Sheron departs for pastures new (May 1997)

Sheron's replacement, Peter Thorne, who left Stoke in September 2001

Subscriber	Favourite Player
Stephen Allen	Terry Conroy
Brian Andrews	Stanley Matthews
Frank Armitt	Alan Hudson
Luke & Matthew Armitt	Peter Thorne
Stephen & Angela Armitt	Peter Fox
Paul Atkins	Jimmy Greenhoff
Dennis John Ayling	Stanley Matthews
Rod Bailey	Alan Hudson
William Baker	Mark Stein
Daniel Bakk	Gordon Banks
Karl Bamford	Denis Smith
Gordon Barker	Alan Hudson
Stephen Barlow	Denis Smith
John (P G) Barnes	Gordon Banks
Brian Baxendale	Stanley Matthews
Peter Bebbington, (Wrenbury)	Johnny King
Alan Bennett	Alan Hudson
Paul Bestwick	Jimmy Greenhoff
Clive Bickley	Jimmy Greenhoff
Julian Boodell	Alan Hudson
David Bostock	John Ritchie
Ron Brackley	Gordon Banks
Robert E Bray	Neil Franklin
Robert Brookes	Alan Hudson
George Burgess	Jimmy Greenhoff
Brian Calvert	Frank Mountford
Phil Cartlidge	Gordon Banks
Paul Cashman	Stanley Matthews
Stephen Mark Chaldecot	Mark Stein
Jane Childs	Jimmy Greenhoff
Malcolm Clarke	Jimmy Greenhoff
Gordon Clowes	Jimmy Greenhoff
J G Corn	Denis Smith
Margaret Croucher	Stanley Matthews
Norman Croucher	Neil Franklin
Neil Cutcliffe	John Mahoney
Christopher Daplyn	Brynjar Gunnarsson
Neil Davies	Mark Stein
Rob Davies	Stanley Matthews
Pete Divall	Stanley Matthews
David B J Dooley	Gordon Banks
Stephen Dray	Gordon Banks
Stephen Dunn	Alan Hudson
Dr Alan Eardley	Terry Conroy
Daniel Edgar	Peter Fox
Ole Egeriis	Gordon Banks
Malcolm Ellerton	John Ritchie
Steve Ellis	Denis Smith
Stein Erik Finne	Denis Smith
Adam D Fishwick	Mark Stein
Neil A Fishwick	Denis Smith
Paul D Fishwick	Stanley Matthews
Paul H Fishwick	Mark Stein
Steve Fowler	Gordon Banks
Duncan Gilchrist	Vince Overson
William Gilchrist	Alan Hudson
Darren Goodall	Mike Sheron
James Goodman	Gordon Banks
Michael Grayson	Mark Stein
Adam Greasley	Mickey Thomas
Dave Greenfield	Jimmy Greenhoff
Kevin Hall	Jimmy Greenhoff
Tony Hancock	John Ritchie
Edd Hankey	Neil Franklin
Austin Hannaby	John Ritchie
Robert Hannaby	Mickey Thomas
Gunnar Hansen	Alan Hudson
Nigel Haynes	Jimmy Greenhoff
Philip W J Healey	Peter Dobing
Les Holdway	Neil Franklin
Neil L Holdway	Jimmy Greenhoff
Ian Howe	Alan Hudson
Joyce, Kevin & Janette James	Jimmy Greenhoff
Terry Jinks	Ken Thomson
Robert James Keeling	Mark Stein
Neil Kirkham	Jimmy Greenhoff
Peter J Kirkham	Neil Franklin
Stephen Knowles	Alan Hudson
Roger Lamb	Gordon Banks
Mr K Lawson	Jimmy Greenhoff
Miranda Lawton	Gordon Banks
Pete Lees	Gordon Banks
Barry Leigh	Jimmy Greenhoff
Chris Lowe	'Nobby' Steele

Paul Andrew Lunt	Denis Smith
Keith & Ellis MacKenzie-Ingle	Gordon Banks
Kevin Maidlow	Gordon Banks
Matthew Male	Peter Fox
Roger Malkin	Alan Hudson
Paul Marriott	Denis Smith
Duncan & Pat Mason	Stanley Matthews
Robert Alfred Matthews	Brynjar Gunnarsson
Ted & Danny McCoy (South London)	Alan Hudson
Cedric McMillan	Jimmy Greenhoff
Douglas Mellor	Denis Smith
Keith & Marilyn Mellor	Wayne Biggins
Chris Mills	Jimmy Greenhoff
Lawrence Milrose	Mark Chamberlain
Christopher John Moreton	Denis Smith
Alan Morse	Denis Smith
Gordon Morse	Jimmy Greenhoff
Ian Murray	Gordon Banks
Richard Myatt	Jimmy Greenhoff
Bob Nicholls	Gordon Banks
Svein Nilsen	
Sam Norcop	Denis Smith
Lars Normann	Jimmy Greenhoff
Mick O'Rourke	Alan Hudson
John Oakden	Jimmy Greenhoff
Thor-Egil Okern	Gordon Banks
Dougie (Bristol) Old	Neil Franklin
Mark Oliver	Terry Conroy
Craig Jason Ottolini	Stanley Matthews
Mark Pearce	Jimmy Greenhoff
Jim Poole	Denis Smith
John & Kath Rhodes	Jimmy Greenhoff
Gareth Richardson	Brynjar Gunnarsson
Michael W Richardson	Alan Hudson
Mark Rogers	Jimmy Greenhoff
Gary Rowland	Peter Fox
Stuart Rowland	Wayne Biggins
Carolyn & Paul Ruane	Denis Smith
Nigel John Rushton	Alan Hudson

Gerald Sabin	Stanley Matthews
Nic Sabin	Mark Stein
David Salmon	Neil Franklin
Les Scott	Stanley Matthews
Col Shaw	George Berry
Lee Shaw	Mark Stein
Andy Slee	Denis Smith
Dan Slee	Mark Stein
George W E Smith	Jimmy Greenhoff
Simon Smith	James O'Connor
Keith Southall	Stanley Matthews
Mark Stanley	Stanley Matthews
Richard Stocken	
Paul 'Charlie' Stokes	Alan Hudson
Neil & Sue Surman	Nigel Gleghorn
Tates	Alan Hudson
Graham Thwaites	Gordon Banks
Kirsty Tideswell	Jimmy Greenhoff
Alex Tindall	Mark Stein
Jo Ragnar Tremoen	Jimmy Greenhoff
Craig Turner	Jimmy Greenhoff
Philip John Unwin	Jimmy Greenhoff
Mr Peter Vaughan	Jimmy Greenhoff
Graham Walker	Gordon Banks
Geoff Ward	Gordon Banks
Gary P Wilcox	Stanley Matthews
Craig Williams	Vince Overson
Robert E Wills	Stanley Matthews
Kerry Wilshaw	Graham Kavanagh
Bernard Wood	Gordon Banks
Peter J Wyatt	Alan Hudson

Most Popular Stoke City players
(27 different players received votes)

1 Jimmy Greenhoff
2 Gordon Banks
3 Alan Hudson
4 Stanley Matthews
5 Denis Smith
6 Mark Stein
7 Neil Franklin